Faulkner and Popular Culture

FAULKNER AND YOKNAPATAWPHA
1988

Faulkner and Popular Culture

FAULKNER AND YOKNAPATAWPHA, 1988

EDITED BY
DOREEN FOWLER
AND
ANN J. ABADIE

UNIVERSITY PRESS OF MISSISSIPPI
Jackson and London

Library of Congress Cataloging-in-Publication Data
Faulkner and popular culture : Faulkner and Yoknapatawpha, 1988 /
edited by Doreen Fowler and Ann J. Abadie.
    p. cm.
    Essays which were originally presented at the University of
Mississippi's 15th Faulkner and Yoknapatawpha Conference held in
1988.
    ISBN 0-87805-433-2 (alk. paper). — ISBN 0-87805-434-0 (pbk. :
alk. paper)
    1. Faulkner, William, 1897-1962—Criticism and interpretation—
Congresses. 2. United States—Popular culture—History—20th
century—Congresses. 3. Popular culture in literature—Congresses.
I. Fowler, Doreen. II. Abadie, Ann J. III. Faulkner and
Yoknapatawpha Conference (15th : 1988 : University of Mississippi)
PS3511.A86Z78321124 1990
813'.52—dc20   89-29587
                                                          CIP

British Library Cataloging-in-Publication data available

IN MEMORIAM,
Malcolm Cowley
1898-1989

Contents

Introduction

William Faulkner, author of dense, riddling novels like *The Sound and the Fury* and *Absalom, Absalom!*—his very name seems almost to connote high modernist art. What possible connection could there be between this towering genius and the masses? Of course, in Hollywood Faulkner worked on film scripts, like *The Big Sleep* and *To Have and Have Not*, for mass consumption; and he did write at least one novel, *Sanctuary,* which appealed to a wide popular audience; but Faulkner repeatedly denounced Hollywood's commercialism and even parodied the film industry in the short story "Golden Land." As for *Sanctuary,* in his introduction to the Modern Library edition of the novel, Faulkner seemed to disown his creation, calling it "a cheap idea . . . deliberately conceived to make money."

The relationship between Faulkner, a novelist who has never been known for his accessibility, and the culture of the masses is the subject of this volume's essays, which were originally presented at the University of Mississippi's 1988 Faulkner and Yoknapatawpha Conference.

In the opening essay Joseph Blotner, Faulkner's friend and biographer, explores the author's deep personal ambivalence toward popular culture. On the one hand, Faulkner delighted in *Car 54, Where Are You?* and praised Anita Loos's *Gentlemen Prefer Blondes*. On the other, his letters to his editors reveal a man scrambling to write enough "trash,"[1] which would appeal to a general audience, to subsidize the composition of masterpieces like *Absalom, Absalom!*, which would not.

If Faulkner's responses to mass culture were ambivalent, he nonetheless contributed to its cluttered content by promoting his own popular image, or at least so argue two essayists, Thomas

Inge and Louis Budd. According to Inge, Faulkner—like Whitman, Twain, Fitzgerald, Hemingway, and countless other literary figures—took pains to construct a public persona; more specifically, for his public, Faulkner masqueraded as an unlettered, simple country man who happened in his spare time to write works of genius. Analyzing further Faulkner's image-consciousness, Budd observes that the Mississippi writer's celebrated hatred of publicity simply does not correspond with the quantity and the intimacy of the interviews he granted: "Among the major writers of our time Faulkner was altogether exceptional for the frequency and frankness with which he talked about himself as an artist-writer." Faulkner, Budd concludes, hungered for public recognition and disguised this hunger by pretending to be publicity-shy.

Faulkner's concern with his public face might seem to imply that he conceived of himself as a writer with a large popular following. Does Faulkner's art have wide popular appeal? According to George Garrett, Faulkner—at least before he wrote *Sanctuary*—attempted to be both a serious artist and a commercially successful novelist, but with the publication of *Sanctuary* he despaired of ever combining high and popular art: "In the heart, the dead center of the Great Depression, in (of all places!) America, William Faulkner begins [the introduction to the Modern Library edition of *Sanctuary*] with an apology for even entertaining the vague idea that he might possibly earn some money from this book, any book." Taking a somewhat different view, Leslie Fiedler contends that Faulkner, like Dickens and Twain, is a popular entertainer who both reflects and creates the culture of the folk. Like all truly popular writers, Faulkner exploits the erotic myths embedded deep in the unconscious; and *Sanctuary*, Fiedler claims, is Faulkner's quintessential pop novel.

Sanctuary, which seems to represent Faulkner's deliberate attempt to write a novel with wide popular appeal, is also the subject of David Madden's essay. Focusing on Faulkner's use of an artifact of popular culture—photographs—Madden argues that the photographs included in the original (1929) text of *Sanctuary* emblemize the meaning of the novel: four characters—Little Belle-Temple and Horace-Popeye—are all facets of Horace Benbow's psyche. Like Madden, Judith Sensibar also considers the function of photographs in Faulkner's novels. According to Sensibar, Faulkner uses photographs "to critique phallocentric ways of seeing, speaking, and acting out desire." Contrasting Horace Benbow's and Rosa Coldfield's appropriation of photographs, Sensibar finds that while Charles Bon's photo in *Absalom, Absalom!* causes Rosa to become "all polymath love's androgynous advocate," Little Belle's photograph in *Sanctuary* triggers Horace's identification with the rapist, Popeye.

In Judith Sensibar's essay, popular culture and issues of gender converge. In a related essay, Anne Goodwyn Jones argues that Faulkner associates women with lowbrow culture. As evidence, Jones cites a 1936 letter in which Faulkner's words seem to equate formula writing for popular magazines with a woman's menstrual cycle: "Since last summer I seem to have got out of the habit of writing trash, but I will still try to cook up something for Cosmopolitan. . . . I seem to be so out of touch with the Kotex Age here that I cant seem to think of anything myself." Expanding her argument and making reference both to Janet Radway's *Reading the Romance: Women, Patriarchy, and Popular Literature* and Nancy Chodorow's *The Reproduction of Mothering*, Jones argues that *The Wild Palms* is a masculine romance plot, "written by men for men," which articulates a male fear of feminine engulfment: in "Old Man" the tall convict desperately battles the raging river, a feminine symbol, with his tiny phallic oar.

No account of Faulkner and popular culture would be complete without an investigation of the author's relationship to his publishers, the medium through which his work was made available to the public. Two essayists, Tom Dardis and Susan Donaldson, discuss the influence on Faulkner's career of, respectively, Harrison Smith, Faulkner's chief editor and publisher from 1928 to 1936, and the *Saturday Evening Post*, the most popular and influential American magazine in the 1930s. According to Dardis, the crucial role Hal Smith played in supporting Faulkner's literary career has yet to be widely appreciated. Not only did Smith publish *Sartoris* when no one else would, but he had the good sense to recognize the genius of *The Sound and the Fury,* to publish Faulkner's manuscripts with only minor alterations for house-styling, and, over the years, to supply Faulkner with much-needed advances. During the early years of the Great Depression when Faulkner's books were commercially unsuccessful, Smith's commitment to Faulkner never faltered, causing Faulkner to call Smith "my friend in the North, one man I like." Like Hal Smith, the *Saturday Evening Post* exerted an important influence on Faulkner's literary career. But whereas Smith offered Faulkner almost unqualified support, the *Post* rejected more Faulkner stories than it published and made Faulkner revise his stories to "increase the number of appreciative readers." In other words, to publish his stories in the *Post* Faulkner had to accommodate what Roland Barthes calls "a comfortable practice of reading" elicited from a text "that comes from culture and does not break with it." Susan Donaldson proposes, however, that Faulkner had his revenge on the *Post,* and this revenge took the form of the passages Faulkner added and changed when revising the original *Post* tales for book publication. Taken altogether, Faulkner's final revisions and particularly "An Odor of Verbena," the story which Faulkner added to complete the book, expose the circumscribed nature of the expectations of the *Post*'s readership.

Like the *Saturday Evening Post,* the film industry also sought to impose popular standards on Faulkner's art. In an essay that details the indignities of screenwriting, Bruce Kawin proposes that what appears to have bothered Faulkner most about scriptwriting was Hollywood's "dumbfounding alienation from what Faulkner, both as an artist and as a moral being, considered universal truths and values." How, then, did Faulkner cope with Hollywood's disinterest in any values except commercially profitable ones? How did he "reconcile modernist and commercial values as well as Southern and Southern California values"? For answar, Kawin offers the image of sharecropping: "Since he never took the easy out of writing as less than himself, the only way I can see that he could . . . write well for the studios, live up to his own sense of values, and care enough about the popular culture he was affecting to structure his best scripts around the truths he respected—was to have reminded himself, as often as necessary, that he worked as a sharecropper in the golden land."

In a sense, then, Faulkner "reinvented" the Hollywood filmscript and the *Post* yarn. In an essay that considers a constant of Afro-American folk culture, the reinvention of life, Leon Forrest contends that Faulkner admires and adopted this survival tactic of black Americans. Forrest defines reinvention as "the cultural attribute of black Americans to take what is left over or, conversely, given to them and make it work for them, as a source of personal or group survival, and then to place a stamp of elegance and élan upon the reinvented mode." Reinvention is the art of improvisation; it is exemplified in jazz or in characters like Faulkner's Deacon, who in *The Sound and the Fury* reinvents the imposed role of black servant by parodying it.

In closing, the volume returns to its starting point: Faulkner's deep ambivalence toward popular culture. On the one hand, Faulkner distrusted and even despised the vulgar meretriciousness of some formulations of popular culture; on the other, his art was rooted in the culture of the folk. What Faulkner liked least about popular culture is epitomized in the glowing neon sign. In an essay that focuses on Faulkner's representation of neon, William Brevda argues that "like a latter-day Roland Barthes, Faulkner exposes the mythologies or ideologies latent in cultural signs." For most Americans in the 1930s, the neon sign was the signifier of modernity and material gain; but, for Faulkner, the tubes of burning gas denoted only the cheapening of human life in the name of progress. While Brevda focuses on Faulkner's distrust of widely held cultural values, Louis Rubin identifies Faulkner's debt to his culture. The volume's concluding essay argues that, to a large extent, Faulkner's art is culturally driven. Examining Faulkner's own pronouncements on the nature of his talent, Rubin finds that Faulkner repeatedly cites his conflict with his community as the force that propels his genius. For example, in the 1933 introduction to *The Sound and the Fury*, Faulkner provides a concrete image for the uneasy collaboration of artist and culture which alone produces art. According to Faulkner, the Southern artist "has, figuratively speaking, taken the artist in him with one hand and his milieu in the other and thrust the one into the other like a clawing and spitting cat into a croker sack. And he writes." What, then, is Faulkner's attitude toward popular culture? Perhaps Faulkner expressed his own ambivalence toward popular culture when he penned Quentin Compson's deeply conflicted cry, *"I dont hate it! I dont hate it!"*

Doreen Fowler
The University of Mississippi
Oxford, Mississippi

NOTES

1. Joseph Blotner, ed., *Selected Letters of William Faulkner* (New York: Vintage, 1978), 85.

A Note on the Conference

The Faulkner and Yoknapatawpha Conference, a week-long event held at the University of Mississippi every summer since 1974, has attracted literary enthusiasts from all parts of the world for programs that feature lectures and discussions by the leading authorities in Faulkner scholarship. Sample titles of the published proceedings—*Fifty Years of Yoknapatawpha, Faulkner and the Southern Renaissance, New Directions in Faulkner Studies, Faulkner and Women, Faulkner and Race*—illustrate the wide range of topics these conferences explore. In addition to scholarly discourse, the programs include readings, dramatizations, musical performances, films, slide presentations, exhibitions, and guided tours. Papers from the 1988 conference on "Faulkner and Popular Culture" are collected in this volume. Brief mention is made here of some of the other events that occurred throughout the week.

The conference began on Sunday, July 31, with a reception at the University Museums for the opening of the exhibition "Boys of Mississippi: Paintings by Glennray Tutor and Bill Dunlap." Later that day, in a session entitled "Deep Pop," the artists discussed Faulkner's influence on their work. Dunlap, a Mississippian who now lives in McLean, Virginia, has gained a national reputation for his paintings, which exhibit a strong narrative tradition rooted in his native state. Tutor came to Oxford to study painting and printmaking in 1973 and remained here, working in a studio that overlooks the courthouse square. His paintings have been widely exhibited, and his drawings have appeared in several books and magazines. Although primarily a visual artist, he has published many stories and poems.

Barry Hannah, author of the exhibition catalog, joined Dunlap and Tutor in the panel discussion and assisted with the presentation of the second annual Eudora Welty Awards to young Mississippi writers. John Howell, Jr., of Batesville won first place in the 1988 competition and Kevin Spears of Tupelo, second. Hannah, who lives in Oxford and teaches creative writing at the University, received the William Faulkner Prize for his first novel, *Geronimo Rex*, and the Arnold Gingrich Short Fiction Award for *Airships*, a collection of stories. His sixth novel, *Hey, Jack!*, is set in a small town in rural Mississippi.

On Sunday evening, in a repeat conference appearance, John Maxwell presented his one-man show *"Oh, Mr. Faulkner, Do You Write?"* The play, based on a variety of biographies, recordings, films, and speeches, had its world premiere at New Stage Theatre in Jackson on April 1, 1981, and was presented a few months later at the Eighth Annual Faulkner and Yoknapatawpha Conference. Since then, Maxwell has performed *"Oh, Mr. Faulkner"* in more than two hundred places throughout the continental United States and in nine countries.

Larry Brown, a new writer from Faulkner's county, read from *Facing the Music*, a collection of stories published in 1988 by Algonquin Books of Chapel Hill. A sharecropper's son raised in Potlockney and now a resident of Yocona, he served in the Marines for two years after graduation from high school and has worked as a captain in the Oxford Fire Department since 1973. He began writing in 1981 and was repeatedly rejected by magazine and book editors before finally breaking into print in 1982 with a story published in *Easyriders*, a bikers' magazine. His stories have subsequently appeared in *Fiction International, Mississippi Review, St. Andrews Review, The Greensboro Review*, and other literary magazines. In addition to reading from *Facing the Music*, his first collection, Brown told conference participants about his reactions to the "other writer" from Lafayette County.

Oxford residents who knew Faulkner served as panelists during sessions moderated by M. C. Falkner and Chester McLarty, J. M. Faulkner and Jo Marshall presented their slide lecture

"Knowing William Faulkner," and Sister Thea Bowman of the Catholic Diocese of Jackson combined commentary and performance in her presentation "Mr. Faulkner, Blacks, and Popular Culture in *Requiem for a Nun.*" The program also included small-group discussions led by conference lecturers, tours of North Mississippi, and a picnic at Faulkner's home, Rowan Oak. Faulkner books, manuscripts, photographs, and memorabilia were on display at the John Davis Williams Library, and Faulkner films were shown throughout the week. Also, the University Press of Mississippi hosted an exhibit of Faulkner books published by various university presses throughout the United States.

The conference organizers are grateful to all the individuals and organizations that support Faulkner and Yoknapatawpha annually and offer special thanks to Dr. and Mrs. M. B. Howorth, Jr., Dr. and Mrs. C. E. Noyes, Mr. Richard Howorth of Square Books, the Yoknapatawpha Arts Council, and the Mississippi Arts Commission.

Faulkner and Popular Culture

FAULKNER AND YOKNAPATAWPHA
1988

Faulkner and Popular Culture

Joseph Blotner

I am happy to be here at Ole Miss again and to take part in this conference. On two previous occasions I have been the last speaker of the week. On the first occasion the topic was "The Sources of Faulkner's Genius," and it seemed to me that by the time my turn came the previous speakers had used all my best observations. On the second of these occasions, when the topic was "Faulkner: International Perspectives," I had agreed to try to do a kind of summation, and as a result it seemed to me that I spent most of my time taking notes on everybody else's lectures before trying frantically, virtually up to the last minute, to write my own. On another occasion, like today's, I was the first speaker. The topic was "Faulkner and Women," and I was able to prepare my part at home. The only problems then were unintentionally preempting something somebody else might want to treat or treating something so briefly that subsequent lectures might make mine seem superficial. But on the whole I prefer this spot in the lineup in spite of the fact that, given this year's topic, it presents a special problem. It is one which, I daresay, every one of our speakers has wrestled with at some point.

In the Winter 1988 issue of the *Southern Register* Ann Abadie wrote, "Lectures on the impact of popular culture on the author and questions about his impact on the public and on cultural forms—from literature and the movies to art and music, including the Sound and the Fury rock band formed by Ole Miss English major Scott Coopwood—point to a rich but largely uncharted territory of Faulkner studies, one that will be explored in detail during the 15th Faulkner and Yoknapatawpha Conference." She

3

also wrote, "Joseph Blotner will give the keynote lecture, setting the stage for other lectures and programs to follow."[1] I am as willing as the next one to set a stage, but perhaps you will understand my being a bit apprehensive at the idea of setting such a large one. Ann Abadie noted previous conference lectures exploring some of this territory: Bruce Kawin and Horton Foote in 1978 on Faulkner as a scriptwriter, Lothar Hönnighausen in 1982 on Faulkner's graphic art, and Thomas Inge in 1984 on the influence of popular comic art on Faulkner. Looming up before me, obviously, was the problem of definition: what is popular culture? And it made me more apprehensive to know that among those speaking after me would be a past president of the Popular Culture Association, a past vice president of the Popular Culture Association, and the editor of the three-volume *Handbook of American Popular Culture*. So I would be setting the stage for David Madden, Leslie Fiedler, and Thomas Inge, among the other speakers.

Like most people, I have been reading about definitions—for example, Jane Tompkins on what should be in the literary canon, Frederick Barthelme on what is minimalism, and Joseph Brodsky on how to read a book. At times I have felt like the grandfather in one of the final scenes of *Moonstruck*—a film I found a deeply satisfying example of popular culture. You may remember how, even as the problems of Loretta and Ronnie seem marvelously to be working out around that crowded kitchen table, the old man bursts into tears. When they ask him why, he replies, "I'm confused." In an attempt to dispel my confusion I turned to the Popular Culture Association. It was founded in 1971, I learned, "to study thoroughly and seriously those productions, both artistic and commercial, designed for mass consumption. . . . This vast body of material encompassed in print, film, television, comics, advertising, graphics, folk culture and outdoor entertainment, as well as many other media, reflects the values, convictions and patterns of thought and feeling generally dispersed through and approved by American and world society." One of the officers of the association and one of its most energetic researchers, Ray Browne, supplied me with an additional definition: "Popular Culture is the everyday lifeblood of the experiences and thinking of all of us: the daily, vernacular, common cultural environment around us all, the culture we inherit from our forebears, use throughout our lives and then pass on to our descendants. Popular culture is the television we watch, the movies we see, the fast food, or slow food, we eat, the clothes we wear, the music we sing and hear, the things we spend our money for, our attitude toward life. It is the whole society we live in, that which may or may not be distributed by the mass media. It is virtually our whole world."2

For a moment I thought of the response of a painter, a non-representational painter, to a well-meaning questioner standing before one of his canvases who asked: "What does it mean?" The curt reply was, "It means whatever you want it to mean." I wondered, can we narrow the definition down then? Can we emphasize the word "popular"? Can we agree that popular culture is likely to exclude, for example, *The Waste Land, Finnegans Wake*, and *A Draft of XXX Cantos?* Probably. But popular culture can be seen to feed into—and perhaps in a few cases emerge out of—high culture, if that is the right term. Consider, for example, Eliot's use of "The Indiana Rag," Joyce's use of "The Ballad of Tim Finnegan," and Pound's use of John Quinn's joke about the drunken sailor. (When one of my daughters read this, she told me that Bob Dylan is said to have written "Ballad of a Thin Man" in response to Dylan Thomas's "Ballad of the Long-Legged Bait." Other members of the Woodstock generation can doubtless supply similar examples.) But if one were to make a count of borrowings from high culture and popular culture, it would certainly be a lopsided one. Perhaps the best we can do is to let some definition emerge, if it will, from this week's efforts.

The most practical approach for me, I think, is simply to go ahead and to take advantage of my place in the batting order. When I started making notes I kept thinking of all the borrowings and echoes in Faulkner's work from writings one would not classify as high art and from media other than print. Of elements of his work that have passed into popular culture, I said to myself, like Scarlett, I'll think about that tomorrow. When the preliminary program came in the mail, I was struck by George Garrett's subtitle: "What William Faulkner Got and Gave Us from Pop Culture." To change the metaphor, I decided to go ahead and to poach a bit along his side of the net, hoping that, as an old friend and colleague, he will forgive me, and knowing that, if he doesn't reject observations I make, he is certainly likely to improve on them.

William Faulkner had a head start. Schoolmates remembered that when he was asked what he wanted to be when he grew up, he responded, "I want to be a writer like my great-grandaddy." To help a newspaper publisher friend, Colonel William C. Falkner began writing a serial. *The White Rose of Memphis* combined action, suspense, romance, and mystery. A frame story set aboard a Mississippi riverboat, it was published in book form in June 1881 and sold ten thousand copies before the year was out. In 1909 the publisher's preface to a thirty-fifth edition from new plates recorded sales to that time of 160,000 copies.[3] Not bad for a man with several other careers for whom writing was a sometime avocation. As a grown man William Faulkner would not express a very high opinion of the novel, but it was one kind of popular culture there in his background or gene pool, and there must have been many times when he wished he could duplicate his great-grandfather's popular appeal.

Very early he was aware of the visual arts in several forms. His grandfather owned the Oxford Opera House and his uncle managed it. There young William Faulkner could have seen comedies as diverting as *Buster Brown* and *Peck's Bad Boy* and melodramas as harrowing at *Ten Nights in a Barroom* and *East Lynne*. His maternal grandmother was a talented artist, and apparently he showed a similar skill quite early. She encouraged him and so did his mother. Early in his teens he entered a drawing contest in *St.*

Nicholas magazine requiring "India ink, very black writing ink or wash." He didn't win, but his name was listed among those who "because of the merit of their entry, did deserve the encouragement of seeing their name in print."[4] He had sketched before that, as he would continue to do to the end of his life. His great-grandfather's railroad was part of his inherited lore, and his brother Jack recalled their delight in watching the fruit trains steam through the countryside on summer mornings. Billy Falkner drew pictures of them—in church in the Baptist hymnal and in school in his first-grade reader. He drew cartoons and caricatures for a high-school year book. He made sketches of aircraft and airmen as an RAF cadet. He made varied drawings for the *Ole Miss* annual and then a whole series of gift books such as *Mayday*. He drew cartoonlike sketches for his daughter when he was working in Hollywood—one of his best depicting his winged self flying home from Hollywood grasping a bag of money he had earned with his screenwriting.

Other cartoonlike drawings were of a different nature. In 1936 he gave Meta Carpenter twenty-six drawings evoked by their longterm relationship. Carvel Collins has described them this way: "The basic concept of Faulkner's drawings was witty: Working at a film studio, Faulkner on a slack day, thinking of Meta while being paid to be there to make films, made drawings which suggest they are animation stills and would give the illusion of movement if seen in rapid sequence. . . . His humorous perspective continued . . . in the detumescence of the final picture, which Meta describes in *A Loving Gentleman*. Faulkner strengthened his suggestion that the drawings are a sequence of animation stills," Collins continues, "when he wrote at their conclusion all but the last word of the brief sentence with which a long-running series ends each of its animated cartoons: 'That's all folks.'"[5] (One would like to see these drawings to test out that thesis. To some of us they may suggest instead a species of underground cartoon book one knew in youth and encountered again on the magazine stands in the wilder 1950s and thereafter.)

Much later, in New York, Faulkner bought expensive Windsor Newton watercolors and sable brushes and used them at home in Oxford on grocery bags from Kroger's. Many of us have seen Lothar Hönnighausen's fascinating treatment of his borrowings from popular illustrators of his youth and from artists such as Beardsley in *William Faulkner: The Art of Stylization in His Early Graphic and Literary Work.*[6] And some of us were here ten years ago when Ilse Dusoir Lind spoke on "The Effect of Painting on Faulkner's Poetic Form."[7] As a grandfather he drew pictures of animals for his grandsons. As for movement in the opposite direction—from the printed word to the sketch—the earliest instance that comes to mind of Faulkner in popular graphic art is the caricature of him accompanying the friendly burlesque which Corey Ford published in *Vanity Fair* in 1932 entitled "Popeye the Pooh." Since then, of course, there have been many such, including the familiar one by Levine which first appeared, I think, in the *New York Review of Books.* Tom Inge has dealt with Popeye the Sailorman and *Sanctuary.* I am tempted to say too bad the order of appearance wasn't reversed.

Faulkner was an avid reader all his life though he would say, from his fifties on, that what he read most then were the books, classics all, that he had first loved as a young man, and for the most part that seems to have been true. As a boy he read and enjoyed the *Youth's Companion* and the *American Boy,* to which he subscribed. John Faulkner recalled that the *American Boy* provided the plans from which his brother built an airplane of sticks and string and paper, which did not survive its first and only test flight. What he might have gained from the fiction in those publications awaits further research. When he was a cadet in Canada he wrote his mother how much he enjoyed the copies of the Memphis *Commercial Appeal* she had sent to him. At home he had read it faithfully, as in all likelihood he read the *Oxford Eagle* as well. Years later his reading in the *Commercial Appeal* provided the stimulus for the several letters he sent to that same paper on the civil rights crisis. And later in Virginia the same process was true with respect to the *New York Times*, though the range of topics he wrote on was broader.

We know that he read widely in another area that would profit him as a professional writer of fiction: the popular mass magazines of his youth. Early in his tenure as acting postmaster of the University of Mississippi post office he became notorious for his grudging service and his clear interest in reading periodicals rather than processing them. One patron had to tap a quarter on the stamp window insistently before he could get Faulkner's attention, and when he came to the window he was holding the copy of *Liberty* he had been reading on government time. (Incidents such as this doubtless provided the stimulus for his celebrated valedictory remark on his last day as postmaster.) Years later he would acknowledge specific indebtedness to a writer named Thomas Beer who published many short stories in the *Saturday Evening Post* and other popular magazines in the years between 1918 and 1925. "I got quite a lot from him," Faulkner said, "a good tool, a good method, a good usage of words, approach to incident."[8]

Many kinds of popular writing seem to have provided grist for his mill. On April 4, 1925, the New Orleans *Item-Tribune* ran a piece answering the question "What Is the Matter with Marriage?" The trouble was not the institution but the people, wrote the author. Too many were unprepared to give and to understand. "The first frenzy of passion, of intimacy of mind and body, is never love. That is only the surf through which one must go to reach the calm sea of real love and peace and contentedness. Breakers may be fun, but you cannot sail safely through breakers into port." The famous Dorothy Dix? John J. Anthony? Some other precursor of Ann Landers? No. Twenty-six-year-old bachelor William Faulkner, who has just won himself $10 in 250 words or less.[9] One suspects that the florid style of the essay was not so much Faulkner as what Faulkner thought would win the contest.

Perhaps this is the place to mention another popular form with which Faulkner showed his familiarity years later. It is the "As told

to" school of writing. Many of you will recall the efforts of Ernest
V. Trueblood in "Afternoon of a Cow," who begins his account of a
disastrous day at Rowan Oak with the explanation "my position in
the household is in no sense menial, since I have been writing Mr.
Faulkner's novels and short stories for years."[10]

There was much that would be useful to him that he simply
absorbed. Some years ago James Mellard wrote about Faulkner
and the tradition of oral narrative. As we know, this tradition has
been particularly strong in the American South. And the Falkners
were a family of storytellers. Mellard observed that "perhaps
William Faulkner, of the moderns, offers the best evidence of the
enduring strength of oral narrative."[11] He enjoyed not just the
storytelling of lawyers such as his grandfather and his friend, Phil
Stone, but particularly that of the country people. He employed it
early in his career. In "The Liar," which appeared in the New
Orleans *Times-Picayune* in July of 1925, he made skillful use of the
title character, a countryman named Ek (who appears to be a first
study of V. K. Suratt, later Ratliff). But the usage is somewhat
patronizing. Faulkner wrote, "His fabling was well known. And
though like all peoples who live close to the soil, they were by
nature veracious, they condoned his unlimited imagination for
the sake of the humor he achieved and which they understood."[12]
Faulkner would later say that he fell in love with his character
Ratliff, and his use of him is anything but patronizing. He knew
written forms of this sort of narrative well, as in George Washington Harris's tales of Sut Lovingood. And he used what he read
as well as what he heard, drawing on folklore, tall tales, frontier
humor, for his richly varied purposes. Apropos his use of living
speech from popular culture, I recall four lines in *Light in August*
chanted by an overalled boy as he goes on his way after answering
Joe Christmas's question about Joanna Burden. It is "tuneless,
rhythmical, musical":

Say dont didn't.
Didn't dont who.

Want dat yaller gal's
Pudden dont hide.[13]

Meaningless? Perhaps not if one thinks of the way Jelly Roll
Morton used some of his material.

One thinks of writers Faulkner knew personally (some from
backgrounds very different from his own) who also went to school
to popular writers. Thinking of his newspaper essay on marriage,
one recalls his sometime hunting companion on Santa Cruz Island, Nathanael West, the author of *Miss Lonelyhearts*. For a time
Faulkner worked on a script with Frederick Faust, who wrote
Western stories under the name of Max Brand and was called "the
King of the Pulps." He also wrote under other names and sold to
the slick magazines too. He was a great admirer of Faulkner's, and
one day when they went to lunch together, their producer, Robert
Buckner, went along just to hear the conversation. To Buckner's
great disappointment, however, they talked not about writing but
about the best vehicle for a two-day drunk, Faust espousing rum
and Faulkner advocating bourbon.

If Faulkner had cared to talk with Faust that day about successful formulas for selling to the pulps, a number of passages in
his work suggest that he could have done so. Five years before, he
had written a novel in which pulp fiction played a crucial part in
the life of one of the protagonists and an important part in the life
of the other. Faulkner wrote of the tall convict, who "had saved the
paper-backs for two years, reading and re-reading them, memo-
rising them, comparing and weighing story and method against
story and method. . . . And then when the day came, he did not
even have a chance to go through the coaches and collect the
watches and the rings, the brooches and the hidden money-belts,
because he had been captured as soon as he entered the express
car where the safe and the gold would be. He had shot no one
because the pistol which they took away from him was not that
kind of a pistol although it was loaded; later he admitted to the
District Attorney that he had got it, as well as the dark lantern in

which a candle burned and the black handkerchief to wear over
the face, by peddling among his pine-hill neighbors subscriptions
to the *Detectives' Gazette*."[14] Faulkner said of Harry Wilbourne,
"he wrote and sold to the confession magazines the stories beginning 'I had the body and desires of a woman yet in knowledge and
experience of the world I was but a child' or 'If I had only had a
mother's love to guard me on that fatal day'—." Harry continues,
working each day on "his latest primer-bald moronic fable, his
sexual gumdrop," until at last he realizes how far he has come from
the romantic passion which has driven Charlotte Rittenmeyer and
himself when he tells a friend, "I had even stopped being
ashamed of the way I earned the money, apologising even to
myself for the stories I wrote. . . . In fact, I had come to really like
to write them, even apart from the money."[15] As we know, an
excess of romantic love combined with bad judgment has undone
both the tall convict and Harry Wilbourne. Through *The Wild
Palms* there blows a black, bitter, and derisive wind that works like
a leitmotif or the sound track of a film. I think there is something
of that same tone in these passages about pulp fiction.

Here is one more passage in which pulp fiction is linked with
disaster. "He took a cloth cap from another nail, and from the floor
beneath his cot a magazine of that type whose covers bear either
pictures of young women in underclothes or pictures of men in the
act of shooting one another with pistols." Then later, "He had
previously read but one story; he now began upon the second one,
reading the magazine straight through as though it were a novel."
Finishing it, he "struck a match to the magazine and prodded it
patiently until it was consumed."[16] You have all recognized the
man as Joe Christmas, and we know what is going to happen
before very long to Joanna Burden, and later to him. One would
hardly argue a causal relationship in *Light in August* involving
pulp fiction, but this passage somehow fits into the total context of
Joe Christmas's life. As a footnote to Christmas's reading, let me
interpolate here part of a letter Faulkner wrote to his publisher in
April of 1929. "I would like to see the duplicate reviews of Sartoris

very much, if you will send them to me. I have not seen but one review here. I live in a complete dearth of print save in its most innocent form. The magazine store here carries nothing that has not either a woman in her underclothes or someone shooting someone else with a pistol on the cover; that includes newspapers too."[17]

Perhaps this is the place to raise the question, how did Faulkner feel about writing fiction for a mass market himself? The short answer is that, like Fitzgerald, Hemingway, and most of their contemporaries, he was happy to sell to the *Post* or *Collier's* whenever he could and often took deliberate aim at them. But sometimes he called such stories potboilers or even "trash stories." He once complained that he had to write them because good stories "fetch no money" in the United States, and obviously his novels were not going to provide a steady living. He certainly needed the money from such sales, but when he couldn't make them, he often settled for much less. That usually meant monthly or quarterly magazines and sometimes little magazines. As late as 1943 he sold one story, "Shall Not Perish," to *Story* for $25. Over the years he gained a justified reputation, especially among fellow writers, for artistic integrity, but he had to make compromises. He had to deal with the conventions of magazine writing. He reluctantly agreed to a change that H. L. Mencken requested before he would publish "That Evening Sun Go Down" in the *American Mercury*. He deleted the charge by the murderer-to-be, Nancy's husband, Jesus, that she is carrying a watermelon that came off somebody else's vine. When Faulkner returned the story, he wrote Mencken, "I did remove the 'vine' business. I reckon that's what would outrage Boston."[18]

Sometimes he wrote stories he must have known would run counter to taboos. "My Grandmother Millard and General Bedford Forrest and the Battle of Harrykin Creek" turned on a stratagem devised by Mrs. Compson to save her silverware: she sat on it in an outhouse, for not even the Yankees would invade her privacy. Even as he sent the story to his agent, Harold Ober,

Faulkner foresaw problems. "They may throw it out because of the can motif," he wrote. He was right. After a number of rejections it was finally purchased by *Story* for $50.

I can think of only one story of his appearing in a pulp magazine or something close to it. After trying unsuccessfully to sell one called "Christmas Tree" he rewrote this story of a bizarre courtship involving dancing, drinking, and gambling. Labeled by the editor "a pungent panorama of reckless youth" ending in "madcap matrimony," it appeared in January of 1936 in *College Life,* to remain there in almost total obscurity for thirty-five years.

These problems left scars. Even after the Nobel Prize and belated financial security, they rankled and contributed to an attitude that went beyond the matter of what was involved in selling one's work. "The artist is still a little like the old court jester," he told one friend. "He's supposed to speak his vicious paradoxes with some sense in them, but he isn't part of whatever the fabric is that makes a nation. It is assumed that anyone who makes a million dollars has a unique gift, though he might have made it off some useless gadget."[19]

Having talked about what outraged him, perhaps we should say something about what pleased him in popular culture. Let's start with what might be called a multimedia example. In February of 1926 he wrote Anita Loos, "I have just read the Blonde book. . . . Please accept my envious congratulations on Dorothy—the way you did her through the intelligence of that elegant moron of a cornflower. . . . My God, it's charming—the best hoax since Witter Bynner's Spectral School in verse."[20] This passage also suggests the breadth of Faulkner's reading, from poetry magazines to a best seller, *Gentlemen Prefer Blondes.* Like Mark Twain and many other writers, Faulkner enjoyed hoaxes, having perpetrated one himself on the Ole Miss campus in the *Mississippian* with an offer from "The Blue Bird Insurance Co." to insure students "Against Professors and Other Failures."[21] Miss Loos's book also provided him with a maxim he quoted often: "the only rule for writing I have is to leave it while I'm still hot—while I'm still looking good, as *Gentlemen Prefer Blondes* put it."[22]

There was something else from popular culture that understandably got into his work. (I'll mention this area briefly though I'll also offer it as an unsolicited suggestion for a future conference topic, given that it must be a bit more difficult each year—even for talented people such as our colleagues—to devise a new topic. What occurs to me is something like "William Faulkner and Sports," or, if it should be a bit more highbrow, say, "Faulkner and the Esthetic of Sport.") One finds no bullfighting in Faulkner so far as I am aware, nor prizefighting, nor professional big game hunting, nor deep sea fishing. But he was an American boy who played baseball and football. He did some fishing; he became a yachtsman of sorts; he rode; and he engaged in hunting of various kinds: of rabbits and raccoons as a boy, of deer and bear as a young man, and of foxes from horseback as an old man. The references to baseball in his writing are few, but who other than Faulkner could create a character who hates Babe Ruth? Perhaps the paucity of references comes from his not being reverential enough, from his preferring Little League games to those on television. He once told me a story about Abner Doubleday. The background is the finding of the A. G. Mills commission in 1908 that Doubleday had invented the game at Cooperstown in 1839. Faulkner told me how General Doubleday had fired the first shot in defense of Fort Sumpter. Then, he said, as Doubleday stepped back to watch the continuing cannonade, an artilleryman spoke to him. He said, "This is more fun than baseball, ain't it, General?" And Doubleday replied, "What's baseball, son?" As for football, the only extended reference that comes to mind is in *The Hamlet* and there for comic purposes. One remembers the brief glimpse of the great-grandmother of Labove, the student who works his way through Ole Miss on what amounts to a football scholarship, with certain perquisites for his large family. "The Old lady . . . had fastened upon the first pair to emerge from the box and would let no one else wear them at all. She seemed to like the sound the cleats made on the floor when she sat in a chair and rocked." Talking to Labove about football, Will Varner says, "I hear it aint much different from actual fighting."[23] And Faulkner's description of the games suggests to me nothing so much as Andy Griffith's comic recording called, I think, "What It Was Was Football."

It is possible that the only acquaintance some Americans have had with the works of William Faulkner came through the pages of *Sports Illustrated*. The first, "An Innocent at Rinkside," (published a third of a century ago) must have disappointed, perhaps even outraged, innocent hockey fans when they read, "perhaps something is happening to sport in America (assuming that by definition sport is something you do yourself, in solitude or not, because it is fun), and that something is the roof we are putting over it and them. Skating, basketball, tennis, track meets, and even steeple-chasing have moved indoors; football and baseball function beneath covers of arc lights and in time will be rain- and cold-proofed too. There still remain the proper working of a fly over trout water or the right placing of a bullet in a deer or even a bigger animal which will hurt you if you dont. But not for long: in time that will be indoors too beneath lights and the trapped pall of spectator tobacco."[24] The kind of hunting that moved him was the kind he depicted in *Big Woods* and *Go Down, Moses*, the kind that verged on the mythic, that required metaphors from history and legend for the mighty bear and the huge dog. It was a contest that evoked images of racing locomotives, and epic contests: "the boy slept again while Boon and the conductor and brakeman talked about Lion and Old Ben as people later would talk about Sullivan and Kilrain and, later still, about Dempsey and Tunney."[25]

The subject of the second piece for *Sports Illustrated* was much more to his liking and elicited a paean rather than a polemic. The very beginning of "Kentucky: May: Saturday," the first lines of the fine Faulknerian one-sentence paragraph set the tones: "This saw Boone: the bluegrass, the virgin land rolling westward wave by dense wave from the Allegheny gaps, unmarked then, teeming with deer and buffalo about the salt licks and the limestone springs whose water would make the fine bourbon whiskey."26 Horses were in his blood. He once called himself "the cat who walks by himself," but I think if he had a totem animal it was the horse. When he got into trouble with *A Fable* he interpolated the long sequence about the crippled champion racehorse who lived to run again. When he turned nostalgically to the past in what would be his last novel, an epic horse race would provide the climax, and much of the setting of *The Reivers* was taken from memories of Murry Falkner's livery stable in Oxford. When Malcolm Cowley asked him about his style, he responded, "You might say, studbook style: 'by Southern Rhetoric out of Solitude.'"27 When he was asked about the same characters appearing in different books he would say they were all horses in his stable and he could run them whenever he wanted to. When he said his new editor was doing a good job and his questioner asked why, then, didn't Faulkner take the time to tell him so, Faulkner said that when a horse was running well you didn't bother him with lumps of sugar. From early until late, from "Carcassonne" to *The Reivers*, the image of horse and rider was a constant motif in his work. And up to the last months of his life he was foxhunting, living out the kind of action he had described more than thirty years before in a story called "A Fox Hunt."

There are many areas of his life experience and his fiction I haven't even mentioned. He used to say that the writer got his material from observation, imagination, and experience. They fused and interpenetrated for him. Some of us were at West Point a few years ago for the conference at the Academy on "Faulkner and the Military." There was much that we didn't get around to mentioning. In *Soldiers' Pay* he used for chapter epigraphs phrases and formulas he had heard as an RAF cadet. In *Sartoris* he probably drew on *War Birds: The Diary of an Unknown Aviator*, which had been serialized in *Liberty* before book publication in 1926. Much of this lore had been in the public consciousness for a decade. I am thinking of films such as *Hell's Angels* and *Dawn Patrol*, which appeared a year after *Sartoris*. A dozen years earlier he had doubtless read a series in the *Eagle* called "The Training of an Air Man," which romantically described the making of a pursuit pilot and probably contributed to his own experience. It is a familiar phenomenon that I know from hours spent a long time ago in the pages of *Daredevil Aces* and *G-8 and His Battle Aces*. Since we are attending a conference featuring popular culture, perhaps I should put in a plug here for the meeting of the Popular Culture Association in St. Louis, particularly for a friend, who will be speaking about the influence of pulp fiction and movies about World War I on the mental attitudes of fighter pilots of World War II.

I am not going to say much about crime stories and mystery stories. Faulkner's fondness for mystery stories is well known, as is André Malraux's comment that *Sanctuary* demonstrates the intrusion of Greek tragedy into the detective story. Some years ago in a lengthy study entitled "Elements of the Detective Story in William Faulkner's Fiction," Mick Gidley called *Intruder in the Dust* and some of the stories in *Knight's Gambit* "works of a lower imaginative order," praising, however, detective story techniques in *Absalom, Absalom!*[28] As a young man Faulkner was an avid reader of mystery and detective fiction. Clearly he learned things there, but also he obviously derived material from friends in the Memphis demimonde and from newspaper friends in New Orleans. One short story about bootleggers, "Once Aboard the Lugger," is quite possibly a part of a discarded novel on that subject, with characters conceivably modeled after people he and his newspaper friends knew. The mass media culture of the newspaper world got into his form as well as his content in *Pylon*. Once when I asked John Dos Passos if he didn't think Faulkner's use of newspaper headlines and sketches didn't owe something to his own *USA*, Dos Passos answered with characteristic modesty that he thought not, that those things were in the air at that time. Faulkner did not, of course, need to read much about the world of barnstorming aviators, having lived it with his friends and brothers, but he cared enough about that world to review Jimmy Collins's posthumous *Test Pilot* for the *American Mercury*.[29] (Parenthetically, does anyone here remember a film starring James Cagney called *Ceiling Zero?* It came out in 1935, the same year as *Pylon.*)

In talking about fiction and popular culture, where does one put Juveniles? I realize that this is tricky ground. For instance, where do we put *Winnie the Pooh* or *Alice in Wonderland* or *The Adventures of Tom Sawyer?* Faulkner hand-lettered copies of *The Wishing Tree* for little Margaret Brown and for Estelle Franklin's daughter, Victoria. He read stories to his daughter, Jill (he also read *Moby-Dick* to her), and he made up stories for her. They involved fairies and forest creatures. One of the latter, who appeared in several of the stories, was a squirrel named Virgil Jones who played the guitar. When Faulkner was in Hollywood, Jill wondered what Virgil was doing, and so her father made up some new stories of his adventures and sent them to her on a phonograph record.

Faulkner earned money in the 1950s and '60s from that most powerful medium of popular culture, television, most from sales for dramatizations though he adapted a few works himself. But he cared little for watching television, even less than for watching movies. He did enjoy the series *Car 54, Where Are You?*, and he also enjoyed the program featuring the cartoon character Huckleberry Hound. This seemingly strange preference for the creator of Lion was finally understood by Faulkner's nephew, Jimmy. "You enjoy watching the children watching the program don't you," he said, and Faulkner smilingly agreed.

It is time to return to one of the questions with which we began. What of Faulkner's work has passed into popular culture? Little, I fear, that would please him. When he gained increasing attention in the decade of the thirties, many critics, especially Northern ones, lumped him with Erskine Caldwell and thought of his work largely in terms of the deprived, depraved, and violent. He knew this. At a Columbia football game, after Faulkner had accurately predicted the next play, his editor, Saxe Commins, told him, "From now on you'll always be known as the grandstand quarterback." Faulkner replied, "No. I'll always be known as the corncob man." Have any words and phrases of his passed into popular culture? Perhaps some of the affirmations in his Nobel Prize Acceptance speech? Perhaps Harry Wilbourne's "Between grief and nothing, I'll take grief"? (Not averse to self-parody, bourbon drinker Faulkner was said to have remarked, "Between scotch and nothing I'll take scotch.") Can *Bartlett's Familiar Quotations* give us any sense of what has passed even beyond a common cultural heritage into popular culture? If so, it is interesting to see seventeen items there from Faulkner, including four from the Stockholm speech and four from *Light in August*. (There are twenty-one there from Hemingway.)

I suppose that one generalization we can make is that the master artist has a great capacity to absorb, as well as to create, though we tend naturally to think first of the latter quality. James Joyce is as good an example as I can think of. I recall his being quoted somewhere as saying, "I can do anything with language." In 1946, when Random House was planning to publish two of Faulkner's novels in one volume in The Modern Library, Faulkner wrote Robert Linscott "I dont agree with you about printing TSAF and AS I LAY DYING together. It's as though we were saying, 'This is a versatile guy; he can write in the same stream of consciousness style about princes and then peasants,' or 'This is a universal writer.'"[30] In spite of his modest response, I think Faulkner, in a moment of euphoria (as when he added a P.S. to a letter to Robert Haas that said, "I am the best in America, by God."[31]), might have at least thought the same thing Joyce said, about himself.

The topic of this conference is enormous, and perhaps it requires large statements about large writers. To deal with artists such as Joyce and Faulkner, perhaps we should hearken back to Walt Whitman, the one who said, "I am large, I contain multitudes."

NOTES

1. Ann J. Abadie, "1988 Faulkner and Yoknapatawpha Conference," *Southern Register* (Winter 1988), 3–5.
2. Ray Browne to Joseph Blotner, 4 December 1987.
3. Joseph Blotner, *Faulkner: A Biography*, 2 vols. (New York: Random House, 1974), 1:39, *24*.
4. Joseph Blotner, *Faulkner: A Biography*, 1 vol. (New York: Random House, 1984), 39.
5. *Helen: A Courtship and Mississippi Poems: by William Faulkner*, Intro. essays by Carvel Collins and Joseph Blotner (Oxford and New Orleans: Tulane University and Yoknapatawpha Press, 1981), 60–61.
6. Cambridge: Cambridge University Press, 1987.
7. *Faulkner, Modernism, and Film: Faulkner and Yoknapatawpha, 1987*, ed. Evans Harrington and Ann J. Abadie (Jackson: University Press of Mississippi), 127–48.
8. *Faulkner in the University*, ed. Frederick L. Gwynn and Joseph L. Blotner (Charlottesville: University Press of Virginia, 1959), 20.
9. *Faulkner: A Biography* (1974), 1:411.
10. *Uncollected Stories of William Faulkner*, ed. Joseph Blotner (New York: Random House, 1979), 424.
11. James M. Mellard, "Faulkner's Jason and the Tradition of Oral Narrative," *Journal of Popular Culture*, 2 (1968), 195.
12. *William Faulkner: New Orleans Sketches*, ed. Carvel Collins (New York: Random House, 1958), 93.
13. William Faulkner, *Light in August* (New York: Random House, 1932), 214–15.
14. William Faulkner, *The Wild Palms* (New York: Random House, 1939), 24–25.
15. Ibid., 121, 123, 132.
16. *Light in August*, 102–3, 105.
17. *Selected Letters of William Faulkner*, ed. Joseph Blotner (New York: Random House, 1977), 43.
18. Ibid., 49.
19. *Lion in the Garden: Interviews with William Faulkner, 1926–1962*, ed. James B. Meriwether and Michael Millgate (New York: Random House, 1968), 82.
20. *Selected Letters*, 32.
21. *Faulkner: A Biography* (1974), 1:350.
22. *Faulkner in the University*, 193.
23. William Faulkner, *The Hamlet* (New York: Random House, 1940), 104, 107.
24. *Essays, Speeches, and Public Letters by William Faulkner*, ed. James B. Meriwether (New York: Random House, 1965), 50.
25. William Faulkner, *Go Down, Moses* (New York: Random House, 1942), 230.
26. *Essays, Speeches, and Public Letters*, 52.
27. Malcolm Cowley, *The Faulkner-Cowley File: Letters and Memories, 1944–1962* (New York: The Viking Press, 1966), 78.
28. *Journal of Popular Culture*, 7 (1973), 97–123.
29. *Essays, Speeches, and Public Letters*, 188–92.
30. *Selected Letters*, 228.
31. Ibid., 113.

Faulknerian Folklore: Public Fictions, Private Jokes, and Outright Lies

M. Thomas Inge

While William Faulkner seldom addressed himself directly to the subject of popular culture—aside from his own efforts in writing film and television scripts and detective fiction—he was fully aware of its all-pervasive presence in the social and cultural milieu of the twentieth-century world in which he lived and worked. Although the development of a modern mass culture began with the invention of the printing press and the technology necessary to wide dissemination of multiple reproductions of pictures and texts, it was not until the twentieth century that the means became available for reaching millions of people through improvements in linotype machines, photography, film, color printing, and airwave communications—so much so that no small corner of the continent was left untouched, even the remote, rural areas of the South, or a place like Oxford, Mississippi. Thus Faulkner's fictional world is filled with the various forms and ways we have entertained and informed ourselves in this century.

As we move through his fiction, Faulkner unobtrusively mentions and displays the popular culture of the time in which the novel is set. In *Sartoris* Dr. Peabody is always reading what Faulkner calls "lurid, paper-covered nickel novels";[1] the women are frequently found leafing through the pages of magazines, while Miss Jenny prefers the salacious tabloid newspapers filled with "accounts of arson and murder and violent dissolutions and adultery."[2] In addition to mentions of the circus, Coca-Cola, Babe Ruth, and baseball, *The Sound and the Fury* includes among its minor characters the Yoknapatawpha County librarian who attempts to "keep out of the hands of highschool juniors and seniors" copies of *Forever Amber* by Kathleen Winsor, *Jurgen* by James Branch Cabell, and the *Topper* novels of Thorne Smith—some of the most titillating and sexually suggestive popular fiction of the period.[3] A member of the same high school class as Caddy, she is the one who confronts Jason and Dilsey with the photograph clipped from a magazine of Caddy with a German officer in a European setting; thus it is a medium of popular culture that gives us our last glimpse of the fate of Caddy Compson.

Light in August contains that haunting scene in which Joe Christmas compulsively reads a men's magazine from cover to cover before heading for town to wander the streets and end up in Joanna Burden's bedroom with a razor in his hand. The magazine, Faulkner says, "was of that type whose covers bear either pictures of young women in underclothes or pictures of men in the act of shooting one another with pistols,"[4] in other words, of the police detective or murder variety, with an emphasis on masochism and bondage. In any case, Christmas was receiving suitable visual and emotional reinforcement for the horrible mutilation he was about to enact.

The boxer John L. Sullivan, motion pictures, and the stage version of *Ben Hur* are sources of comparison and metaphor in *Absalom, Absalom!;* college football is central to the plot of *The Hamlet;* and one of the themes of *The Reivers* has to do with the impact of the automobile on Southern life—after the first one arrives, the manners, mores, and morals of the isolated rural community are never to be the same again. The automobile becomes the instrument of man's final fall in the Garden of Eden—once Memphis is put within easy distance of Jefferson. The automobile was also the conveyance by which Temple Drake was delivered to her disgrace and corruption in *Sanctuary*, a novel that refers to the fashions of the 1920s, popular slick magazines, the mail-order catalog (used as it was in the outhouse), and the film actor John Gilbert (compared in ironic counterpoint with the

unromantic, ungentlemanly, debased Popeye). *Sanctuary* also
draws on the comic strips when the author gives the villain the
name Popeye, and as I have pointed out elsewhere, Faulkner used
names from and allusions to comic strip characters in much of his
fiction.[5] What is clear from these selected references is that
Faulkner used elements of popular culture as ways to reflect on
the characters of the people who populate his fiction and to reveal
indirectly important things about their symbolic functions.

Since he was a man who professed to scorn public attention, it is
interesting to note that Faulkner has also entered popular culture,
whatever his own wishes might have been. His presence is not as
extensive as that of Fitzgerald or Hemingway perhaps, the first
the inevitable figure included in all illustrations and commercial
paintings of the jazz age on book covers, in magazines, and in
advertisements, and the second so popular among clothing, food,
fishing rod, and gun vendors that the Hemingway family has
registered the name as a trademark for all commercial uses. For
example, I have seen only one greeting card using Faulkner. The
outside reads, "I know what you are thinking. . . . If William
Faulkner could write 23 novels, 72 short stories, 109 essays, and 6
plays [those figures, of course, are purely fictional] . . . the least I
could do is write one lousy letter—Well, I just want you to know
. . . ," and the inside concludes, " . . . I ain't no Faulkner!"[6]
Faulkner does appear in advertisements from time to time—a
want-ad promotion notes that "William Faulkner Wrote Want Ads,
Too!" and quotes one he published in the *Oxford Eagle*,[7] and the
Davey Company promoted its book binding service through a full
page ad with the words in bold red letters, "Bound to Last."
Beside a photograph of Faulkner in his hunting outfit, the text
describes him as "Literature's glib escort into modern Southern
Lifestyles," and like the Davey product we assume, "His views of
Southern America were uncompromising, reliable, tough and
true."[8] The U.S. Post Office once used Faulkner on a poster to
promote careers in the postal service, apparently overlooking his
having been officially reprimanded for his own poor performance

as postmaster in Oxford and hardly, therefore, a proper model for beginners. Perhaps all has been forgiven, though, as witnessed by the special stamp issued with his portrait in August of 1987. Faulkner, who didn't want to be at the beck and call of every son of a bitch with the price of a two-cent stamp, can now be licked by anyone with the price of a twenty-two cent stamp, thanks to inflation.

One book reviewer has created a scheme for rating books according to how many little old ladies they are worth, with reference to Faulkner's famous statement that Keats's "Ode on a Grecian Urn" is, in the larger scheme of things, worth any number of old ladies, including his own mother, whom he would rob for the sake of art. The maximum rating on the Old Lady Scale is four, I might note.[9] Three seasons ago, off-Broadway theatre was treated to a play by Heather McDonald called *Faulkner's Bicycle* in which Faulkner, played by Addison Powell, whizzes through Oxford at midnight on a bicycle whistling "Toot, Toot, Tootsie, Goodbye," and having had too much bourbon, repeatedly crashes into a pond.[10] There is nothing biographical or factual in the play, but Faulkner's eccentricity is used as a symbolic touchstone for the three eccentric women on which the play centers. One of the most mysterious and engaging presences of Faulkner in popular culture, or rather his creation Quentin Compson, is found in a brass plaque on the Anderson Bridge over the Charles River at Harvard University which originally read "Quentin Compson III. June 10, 1910. Drowned in the fading of honeysuckle." It was placed there secretly in 1965 by students who admired Faulkner and identified with Quentin's sense of displacement and tragic idealism. Although accidentally destroyed in 1983, and replaced by another plaque, it has been for over two decades secretly visited by ardent readers on the anniversary of Quentin's suicide from the bridge. Few literary characters are paid such a tribute in the minds and imaginations of his admirers.[11]

The main intention of this essay is not to explore Faulkner's use of popular culture in his fiction or his continued presence in popular culture since his death, either of which merits examination. Rather, I want to address the way he consciously used the media of his time to create an image carefully calculated, I believe, to achieve a predetermined effect. Faulkner was given to creating, encouraging, or simply refusing to deny all sorts of outrageous stories about himself. While many of these public fictions, private jokes, and outright lies may seem to be a result of his reluctance to share his private life with the world, they have also been intended to create a persona that in its own way competed with those of Hemingway, Fitzgerald, and other authors who used the media to promote their personalities and books.

The tradition of the self-promoting author who creates an image of himself in the public eye to attract media attention and sell books has been well established in America, at least since Walt Whitman. At the start of his career, he set the type for and printed his first book of poetry, *Leaves of Grass,* anonymously reviewed it for the press, and shocked the public by portraying himself in the poetry as a sensualist and freethinker. He even had little enough scruple to extract a comment from a private letter by Ralph Waldo Emerson and emblazon it as an endorsement on the cover of another edition of *Leaves of Grass.* The Walt Whitman that attracted public attention in *Leaves of Grass* was, of course, simply a fictional creation of the Walter Whitman who masterminded the entire promotion scheme, and it was so successful that to this day we have difficulty in separating the character from the author. Another writer who understood the dollar value of publicity was Mark Twain. As Louis Budd has reminded us in his excellent work on Clemens, the figure and image of Mark Twain, the man in the white suit who became spokesman for the American conscience, was one of Samuel Clemens's most successfully promoted fictional creations. The only modern writer to match the genius of Whitman and Twain on this score was Truman Capote, who also made of himself a shocking figure for the world stage, sexually ambiguous like Whitman and willing to use his notoriety as a way to hustle his books (very well written books, I might add). Capote had learned from other master publicity stunts of the literary world—Fitzgerald's outlandish parties and his tragic posing in Hollywood, Hemingway's big game hunts and macho activities as a war correspondent, or Norman Mailer's public pugilism and boasting as the best writer in the room. Some would consider Faulkner closer to J. D. Salinger in his shyness and reticence than these writers, yet Salinger truly seems to be an individual unable to adjust to normal social relationships. Faulkner was a social and sociable being when he chose to be; thus his need for privacy seemed to be something he could control to his own advantage—both by asserting it and thereby attracting even more attention to himself than he would otherwise. Nothing makes information more attractive to the journalist and publicist than the inability to obtain it.

Even as a child, young Billy Faulkner was engaged in the craft of manipulating the truth to serve his own ends. One cousin reported, "It got so that when Billy told you something, you never knew if it was the truth or just something he'd made up."[12] And in his maturity, when fame came knocking at his door in intrusive ways in the form of journalists and students seeking interviews, he persuaded his brother John to make a peculiar promise. As John tells it:

> It was about this time that Bill made a rule. He said it would be best to reach an agreement right then that neither of us would ever have anything to do with the other's work, that we wouldn't even talk about it to anybody else. . . .
>
> We both held to that agreement as long as he lived. I have been offered extra inducements to review his books but I never would. I'm sure he has been offered like propositions, and turned them down. All of us have had any number of people try to talk to us about Bill, Mother and I in particular. I kept my agreement in that and Mother, knowing Bill did not want any of us to talk about him, would not either.
>
> She was inordinately proud of him, as she might well be, but she respected his wishes too. The only times we ever talked about him to others was to foster some of the stories he got up on himself. The three

of us foisted many of them off on the public and I have seen them
incorporated in what they call critical analyses.[13]

When I read this passage, I am always struck by the gullibility of
John and the cleverness of William Faulkner. Who was likely to
ask William to write about John or his novels? I'm afraid that John
got the worst end of this rue bargain and gave up more than he
would ever know by such an agreement. The passage also reveals
William the manipulator at work, not only in controlling what
John could say or write but in encouraging him to support the
false stories he had already generated about himself, such as the
one that he had been shot down over France during World War I
and as a result had a steel plate in his head.

Speaking of the entire Falkner family and its penchant for grand
tragedy and romantic gesture, from the time of Colonel William
Clark Falkner's duels and violent death down to the early death of
Dean Faulkner in an airplane crash, an Oxford neighbor noted,
"The Falkner men are always heroes and the Falkner women
heroines of their own stories."[14] In creating his own story,
Faulkner once expressed the desire simply to become someone
else in a conversation with Lenore Marshall, the woman who
claimed to have discovered and edited *The Sound and the Fury* for
Jonathan Cape and Harrison Smith. As she reports it:

> That . . . morning in my living room he speculated, gentle and
> remote, upon the idea of changing his identity, disappearing, settling
> somewhere in a desert. . . . The desert would be the best place in
> which to lose oneself, he ruminated in his low voice, out of some
> subterranean cosmos—could one change one's appearance, become
> a different person?[15]

Robert Coughlan, who pushed beyond Faulkner's insistence that
no one was to write about his private life for *Life* magazine by
gathering material from his family and friends, wrote after meeting him, "He prefers to be an enigma and one can believe that he
will always remain one, even to himself, for his inconsistencies
pass artistic license. He is not a split personality but rather a

fragmented one."[16] There is a possibility, in other words, that many of the attitudes struck by Faulkner in his lifetime were calculated to create the image of an eccentric, rude, and extremely shy individual, who was uncomfortable with the fame that had suddenly come—not that reticence was indeed not a part of his character but rather that he used this tendency as a way of attracting attention. His hunting companion, John B. Cullen, felt this way about him:

> When Faulkner wears his old ragged clothes, digs holes in his driveway, and walks on the streets with a vacant stare in his eyes, he may be using the same psychology that Diogenes used when he pretended to be looking for an honest man and carried a lantern in the daylight to find him. This was one of the greatest publicity stunts in history. Faulkner knows when not to comment, and when to give an interview or write a letter to an editor about a subject of public interest. He always differs with the general public opinion. He is an individualist, an excellent publicity agent for himself, and a genius.[17]

As that neighbor suggested of all the Faulkners, perhaps William too was creating a persona as a hero for his own story.

If we are to believe many of the apocryphal stories about him, those that abound in the popular articles and press agentry that surround his legend and often based on imperfect memories, Faulkner was always ready with the quotable quip that would make a good story or filler copy. Robert N. Linscott, an editor at Random House, recalled two such occasions in his memoirs of Faulkner for *Esquire:*

> Bill was window-shopping with me on Fifth Avenue when a woman rushed up to him and cried: "Oh, I know who you are. You're William Faulkner. You look just like your pictures." Bill said coolly but courteously, "Madam, you're mistaken. I am *not* William Faulkner. But I have been told before that I look like him."
>
> This was typical of the man; he had a deep aversion to public recognition. When he was presented with the annual booksellers' award, the crowd closed in to shake his hand, and he beckoned me to escape with him. At the hatcheck counter, he laid down the big plaque that had been presented to him. "Oooh, you got the award,"

the hatcheck girl cried. "You must be Mr. Faulkner." "No, ma'am,"
said Bill. "I ain't Mr. Faulkner. I just saw this thing lying on the table
and walked off with it." "That's awful," she exclaimed. "I'll have to call
the house detective." So Bill and I slid out the side door and into a
taxi.[18]

Robert Coughlan also reported several such stories in his book
that resulted from the *Life* articles:

> With the success of *Sanctuary,* Faulkner had several invitations
> from Hollywood. A story goes that one studio baited its offer with an
> appeal to his chivalry, through the person of Tallulah Bankhead. . . .
> Miss Bankhead appeared, told him how much she admired his books,
> and asked him to come to Hollywood to write an original screenplay
> for her. Faulkner replied: "Well now, I'd like to help a Southern girl
> who's climbin' to the top. But you're too pretty an' nice a girl to play in
> anything *I'd* write. I wouldn't want to do that to you."[19]

> One time . . . a famous publisher appeared at a literary soiree to
> which Faulkner had been enticed, and upon being introduced
> launched into an effusive speech telling Faulkner how much he
> admired his works. He had a collection of them, the publisher went
> on to say, and had brought them along that day and would be honored
> if Faulkner would sign them. Faulkner listened without expression,
> puffing on his pipe, and when the man had finished answered curtly,
> "I only sign books for my friends."[20]

Sometimes his clever retorts bordered on pure insult. There was
the time that a visiting prima ballerina from the Soviet Union,
Alicia Markova, requested an opportunity to meet him while the
ballet troupe was in Oxford. When the invitation was conveyed to
Faulkner, he sent back the message, "Please give the lady my
regrets. I have a previous engagement to hunt a coon."[21] And
there was that widely disseminated retort to *Newsweek* when they
asked him why he had turned down an invitation from President
Kennedy to dine at the White House with fifty other American
Nobel Prize Laureates in 1962: "Tell them I'm too old at my age to
travel that far to eat with strangers."[22] That made great copy but
was hardly a respectful way to reply to the President of the United
States whose only intent was to do him honor.

Perhaps one of his most perverse exaggerations was to allow people to believe he was an alcoholic whose writings were the product of Old Crow and a morbid stupor. When his cousin, Sallie Murray Williams, asked, "Bill, when you write those things, are you drinkin'?," he replied, "Not always."[23] John reported in *My Brother Bill* that he "never did do as much drinking as he got credit for. He never tried to hide it but he did most of it at home. Whatever stories got out about it he never did deny. He simply paid them no mind."[24] There is no doubt, of course, that Faulkner had a drinking problem and making sport of it was an odd thing to do, although humor may have provided a healthy corrective. Hard drinking has always been considered a typical masculine pursuit in a backwoods society. What Hamilton Basso said after his death, however, I believe remains true: "Faulkner drank. We have heard many stories and probably will soon be hearing many more. I would only point out that the large body of his work, with its infinite variety and complexity, could not have been produced by a crock."[25]

Surely there is a good deal of conscious irony in Faulkner's insistence after he had won fame and fortune that he was really a mere farmer who wrote as a sideline. "I'm not a literary man," he would say. "I'm just a farmer who likes to tell stories."[26] As he said in an interview in Japan, "I am not really a writer in the sense you mean—my life was established before I began to write. I'm a countryman. My life is farmland and horses and the raising of grain and feed."[27] He seemed to deprecate the work that he obviously cared so much about when he said on another occasion, "Writin' has been a hobby with me, . . . like collecting stamps."[28] Given Faulkner's stature as a world class writer, this is one story that he can't foist off on us. I suspect we come nearer the truth as to how he felt about his accomplishment as a writer in something he once said to Robert N. Linscott while visiting his home in the Berkshires. He ran his finger along a shelf full of his own books in Linscott's library and remarked, "Not a bad monument for a man to leave behind him."[29] All of his self-deprecation as a writer can be viewed as another effort to create a public image—the igno-rant, red-neck farmer who happens to turn out in his spare time works of literary genius! Here exaggeration has been pushed beyond the limits of credulity.

It is not my intent to question the fact that Faulkner had a strong tendency to be reclusive or that he seriously believed in the rights of privacy and that the world had no right to encroach on his. When he told someone that at a party he was like a withdrawn hound dog peering from under a wagon, I'm sure that he was expressing a genuine discomfort in being at such occasions. And he honestly resented being quizzed about his work by over-zealous readers and critics.

Yet I also believe that he knew exactly what he was doing when he created an image for himself unlike any other among American writers. Rather than court adulation, he would scorn it. Rather than assume the role of a man of letters, he would pretend to be one of the salt of the earth, a mere peasant. Rather than discuss the hard labor and craftsmanship of his writing, he would make it out to be some stroke of luck or the primitive product of a Mississippi Grandpa Moses. He knew the American media and public well enough to understand that the result of this pose would be to fascinate us all the more and pander to our taste for the paradoxical and the bizarre. We would also buy some of his books, out of curiosity at first, only to be won over by their imaginative power and stylistic mastery. Faulkner knew popular culture better than most and how to use it skillfully in behalf of his art and creating a unique place for himself in the public world of letters.

NOTES

1. William Faulkner, *Sartoris* (New York: Signet/New American Library, 1964), 95.
2. Ibid., 48.
3. William Faulkner, *The Sound and the Fury* (New York: Vintage, 1954), 413–14.
4. William Faulkner, *Novels 1930–1935, Light in August* (New York: Library of Amer-ica, 1985), 479–80.

5. M. Thomas Inge, "Faulkner Reads the Funny Papers," *Faulkner and Humor,* ed. Doreen Fowler and Ann J. Abadie (Jackson: University Press of Mississippi, 1986), 153–90.

6. The undated card is copyrighted by Happy Time Greetings, Lingman, Kansas, and was purchased in 1974.

7. Michigan State University *State News,* 26 March, 1969, 22.

8. *Publishers Weekly,* 217 (11 April 1980), 61.

9. R. Fiore, "Funnybook Roulette," *Comics Journal,* No. 107 (April 1986), 41.

10. Mel Gussow, "Evoking the Funny Genius of Faulkner," *New York Times,* 16 June 1985, Section H, 3, 10.

11. Dale Rusakoff, "Faulkner and the Bridge to the South," *Washington Post,* 21 July 1985, Style Section, B1, B7–B8.

12, Robert Coughlan, *The Private World of William Faulkner* (New York; Harper and Brothers, 1954), 43.

13. John Faulkner, *My Brother Bill* (New York: Trident Press, 1963), 212–13.

14. Coughlan, 38.

15. Lenore Marshall, "The Power of Words," *Saturday Review,* 65 (28 July 1962), 16–17.

16. Coughlan, 24.

17. John B. Cullen, with Floyd C. Watkins, *Old Times in the Faulkner Country* (Chapel Hill: University of North Carolina Press, 1961), 54–55.

18. Robert N. Linscott, "Faulkner Without Fanfare," *Esquire,* 60 (July 1963), 36.

19. Coughlan, 106.

20. Ibid., 120.

21. Ibid., 104.

22. Joseph Blotner, *Faulkner: A Biography* (New York: Random House, 1984), 703.

23. Coughlan, 125. Cf. Blotner, 276.

24. John Faulkner, 148.

25. Hamilton Basso, "William Faulkner Man and Writer," *Saturday Review,* 65 (28 July 1962), 11.

26. Coughlan, 96.

27. *Lion in the Garden: Interviews with William Faulkner, 1926–1962,* ed. James B. Meriwether and Michael Millgate (New York: Random House, 1968), 169.

28. Coughlan, 101.

29. Linscott, 36.

Playing Hide and Seek with William Faulkner: The Publicly Private Artist

Louis J. Budd

We all remember the first time we collided with a disciplined case for the proposition that the human mind (treated with varying degrees of reverence) tends to select the reality that suits its wishes. Later we hear that what seemed a wall of logic is only a mirror too, that each wall of logic may in turn deconstruct itself. And so we are thrust *mise en abyme*. The infinitely regressive mirrors become disheartening, truly dispiriting when we are trying to reach through to the reflexive mind and personality of William Faulkner.

Therefore I pull back to a simpler problem, not Faulkner's mind but that of his admirers, in whom I do firmly detect a wishful reading of his biography. To reduce the risk of perceiving only the case I want to argue, I will try to incorporate the facts that Faulkner's personality was complicated beyond the typical human pattern of conflicting, changing desires and that, more specifically, he not only insisted eloquently and fiercely on his love of privacy but often turned away reporters and turned down rich offers to exploit his fame. However, a collective, vicarious pride in that latter fact hides what actually happened and keeps us from understanding both ourselves and Faulkner better.

The notion that Faulkner unconditionally resisted publicity hangs on as a snug commonplace. In a sophisticated critical biography, David Minter, as early as the preface, brings it up and then asserts: "Almost as deep as the shyness he felt toward strangers lay an aristocratic distaste for public exposure except on his own terms." Without even such refinements, Michel Gresset has recently expatiated on the much quoted passage from a letter to Malcolm Cowley in 1949 ("I will protest to the last: no photographs, no recorded documents.").[1] Gresset also used it as an epigraph for his Faulkner chronology in 1985, and Stephen B. Oates keeps it green in the latest biography. They make my search-and-destroy mission almost too easy.

But there are obstacles. The confirmatory, subjective mirrors are backed by a vocational consensus. Collectively, as the faculty of departments of literature, we are eager to elevate an author above his or her economic needs and the marketplace. (We still commit wishful thinking when we are willing to acknowledge an economy so simple as a marketplace today.) For years I believed that Willa Cather, though she had worked patiently under commercial realities as an editor, insisted as artist on being known solely through her fiction. I believed that because the headnotes in the anthologies of American literature say so. They say so because, in her later career, Cather said so and because the archetypical teacher of masterpieces wants to believe her. But even more than her admirers, the Faulknerians need to hear from a skeptic who will humanize their devotions.

An observer so knowledgeable, seasoned, and low-keyed as Malcolm Cowley could state in 1949: "Among the writers of his time, Faulkner was altogether exceptional in the value that he placed on privacy."[2] Is it fair today to quote Cowley's comparison from 1949? Won't any rebuttal depend on incidents after 1950, when Faulkner got the Nobel Prize and started to play the role of a personage? My skepticism applies to all phases of his career though it proves easily justifiable with his more and more forthright parading of himself as artist.

In the standard collection of interviews the editors comment benignly that, after the Nobel Prize, he "had clearly accepted . . . a measure of responsibility as a public figure."[3] In other words, they stick throughout with the spirit of their opening sentence: "William Faulkner's love of privacy and hatred of publicity lasted from the beginning of his career until his death nearly forty years later." They soon make their point more feelingly: "He held to the old-fashioned view that it was his duty to write books, someone else's to publicize them, and as a writer he refused to participate in the standard processes of publicity and advertising." (Notice the terms "old-fashioned" and "standard" and the implied "duty" of people to buy those books.)

It is justifiable to detect an emotional selectivity also when André Bleikasten, long a close observer of Faulkner materials, can declare as late as 1987 that he "remained fiercely jealous of his privacy to the very last. Yet in the course of the fifties he allowed himself to become a public figure and a spokesman for both his region and his nation." Bleikasten needs to invoke a different yet "strong sense of duty" that forced Faulkner into his "official roles" and also "the sense of 'noblesse-Nobel-oblige.'"[4] Cleanth Brooks updates the legend (or antilegend) into a trendier shape: "Faulkner refused to be one of the 'beautiful' people. Nor had he any wish to be one of those macho personalities such as a Hemingway or a Mailer."[5] Nonacademics have been much more objective. A fellow screenwriter from the 1940s, who did register Faulkner's "air of frigid inviolability, of preferred isolation," would protest, after the scholarship and criticism had piled high by 1980:

> All his friends, his relatives, his acquaintances, his admirers, and especially the professors, who teach Faulkner 1-A and 1-B in the universities, and who deleted everything they thought to be offensive, because they respected Faulkner's image more than they did the all too fallible man, distorted reality not so much by controlling what was said as by controlling what was not said. The logic was used that Faulkner believed that a man's work should be allowed to speak for him, that a man's private life was inviolable.[6]

The broadest crack in the image of an intensely private Faulkner comes from the quantity and, still more important, the intimacy of the interviews that he granted. My exploratory idea for the relations between Faulkner and popular culture was an analysis of the persona that he constructed in these interviews as he spoke both from his own needs and the cues that journalists fed to him. Though a few of those interviews are well-known, I was startled to discover how many he granted and, as I analyzed them, how trustingly the explicators have mined the favored ones. Joseph Blotner, whose honesty and alertness as a biographer I respect highly, was grateful for some clues the interviews reveal; also, as an eventually close friend, he felt a loyalty to Faulkner. Overall, Blotner is as cautious with, even suspicious of, the interviews as we have a right to expect. Yet he decided that the piece Jean Stein supplied to the *Paris Review* is "the most compendious, the best single Faulkner interview ever published." The editors of *Lion in the Garden* agreed, calling it "in many ways the most important and most influential of all Faulkner interviews."

Many critics have quoted from it with a gratitude matched only by their faith, and Oates's biography puffs it as "often profound." Blotner went on to praise its "polished anecdotes" and "comments that rang like epigrams."[7] Precisely so. Faulkner had worked with Jean Stein closely, day and night—a framing I'll come back to. My immediate point is that he had cooperated for weeks, in both Paris and New York City. He even drew a stylized head of himself as well as supplying the first page from the manuscript of *As I Lay Dying* for another illustration.

To imply that the subtexts of the *Paris Review* piece (let's stop calling it an interview) leap from the page is unfair. In the need to cope, at least some of us concentrate on the fixable meaning of texts, anxious to achieve as much communicability as possible. For me, anyway, to dig beneath the surface of interviews needed some pushes from broader theory. For example, I am Marxist enough to agree that economic pressures influence the highest-browed writers in spite of all denials by their mandarin coterie. Likewise, I have learned from sociology to perceive the individual as both formed and controlled collectively. The basic concept has had, of course, much refinement since August Comte, but even Peter Berger, who brilliantly dissolves social reality into man-made, arbitrary rules, does warn that those rules, once established, exert pervasive authority. Critics like Cleanth Brooks need to comprehend, before enshrining Faulkner's essay "On Privacy," that modern society molds subjectivity at least as powerfully as before.

Social psychologists disagree, of course, about diagrams of the molding process. Some like to start the modern round from William James, but I'm impressed more with George Herbert Mead, who reached his greatest prestige during the 1930s. We hear less now about Mead because his diagram resists embellishment by disciples. It's deliberately minimalist in demonstrating that the self is biosocial, emerging as the organism interacts with the physical as well as the human environment. Because, while sensitive to the circuits of language, Mead doesn't make it the quintessential force, he doesn't attract literary critics, nor would they have persuaded him to accept Faulkner's self-image of the born artist who cleaves to his destiny until the world honors him completely on his own terms. Mead forces me to watch for a personality that keeps reacting and adapting as Faulkner's career moves from the 1920s through the 1950s. If I wanted help from the depth psychologists I would consult the interpersonal school though Karen Horney and Harry Stack Sullivan, still important clinically, don't rate as fashionable today. So instead I'll invoke Erving Goffman, who has brilliantly deepened the analysis of role-playing as inescapable, universal, and incessant. His later work concentrated on "framing," that is, on the markers and constraints upon meaning through which we approach any matter or with which we present our own actions and words.[8]

It's superficial to quote the *Paris Review* piece without considering that Faulkner, in his drooping fifties, was trying to impress and then rather desperately to hold on to a young, sleek, and ambitious lover. Another interview with Loic Bouvard gets still more respect for its loftiness of mind. But we need to consider its physical frame—the Princeton campus—and, more influential, the frame projected by the interlocutor, who visualized—says Blotner—a "man of letters in the French sense who would try to answer with something of the same clarity and intensity. In a manner unique for him, Faulkner seemed to try to meet Bouvard on his own ground." That ground rested, in Bouvard's terms, on the conviction that he was communing with "one of the greatest artists of all time."[9]

The most famous groups of interviews can't be read intelligently unless, for example, we refocus for the Japanese expectation about Faulkner and, in turn, his expectations about them as well as his consciousness of speaking under the U.S. State Department logo to a recently defeated nation. The still more greedily mined sessions in Charlottesville were, among subtler factors, conditioned by his awareness of the Virginia tradition and, more culpably, of the fox-hunting society in the neighborhood. On his late visit to the U.S. Military Academy he was most determined to behave properly, indeed, ceremonially; he felt highly, gratifyingly honored. While traveling to West Point in a military plane, he may have worried, however, about his yarns glorifying his career in the Royal Flying Corps. The unselfconsciousness that observers sometimes reported was merely one more role—a common one that he could play better than most of us. His daughter has reminisced: "Living with Ma-ma and Pappy was like living on a stage-set. Everybody was playing a role."[10] Whether in private or in public, even when talking to a reporter with notebook open, Faulkner often dressed up the facts recklessly. Physically, he dressed up to the hilt for the West Point visit. Though his admirers like to feature his carelessness about clothes, he was frequently intent, as somebody has lately perceived, on staging his persona "right down to the dress costume."[11] One of his Oxford townsmen recalls tolerantly that Faulkner sometimes wore "heavy Harris tweeds" when they were "too heavy for this part of the country." Anybody who wants to can pile up examples for the point that Faulkner showed a far stronger concern for dress than we can allow a savagely private person. Likewise, we can find all kind of proofs (literally) for confronting the submyth that he shunned cameras. Secondary proof could start with the cordial memories of J. R. Cofield, photographer to Oxford. Surely the hero-worshippers need to push harder than Blotner's comment that he "may have hated photographs, but he could not have been unaware of how striking his often were."

Hero-bashing can serve constructive ends. But there's a more important problem entangled here. In 1987, with the nomination of Robert Bork to the Supreme Court, the right to privacy emerged as an issue that will stay prominent. Therefore it's constructive to question Faulkner's apologists because we need to understand that right as clearly as we can, and that includes challenging any inadequate approaches such as his own essay on the subject. Though the so-called right to fame or to celebrity— that is, to its profits—is now arousing litigation, that's neither vital for most of us nor directly informative here. Any flawed thinking, however, about the right to privacy leaves us more vulnerable to what will happen in the mainstream or, more appropriate, in the mainframe culture.

If some admirers concede a qualitative drop in Faulkner's hatred for publicity after the Nobel Prize, we shouldn't let them escape Madison Avenue by way of Stockholm. As early as the volume for 1928–29 his entry appeared in *Who's Who in America,* and he must have cooperated. He was laughably far from important enough to rate willy-nilly as an indispensable entry. But we don't have to guess about the interview that ran in the *Memphis Press-Scimitar* on 10 July 1931. While serving up homebrew, Faulkner had talked about producing *Sanctuary* and *As I Lay Dying.* He went on: "I haven't written a real novel yet. I'm too young in experience. It hasn't crystallized enough for me to build a book upon one of the few fundamental truths which mankind has learned. Perhaps in five years I can put it over. Perhaps write a *Tom Jones* or a *Clarissa Harlowe.*"[12] There was still broader-gauged talk; furthermore, he allowed photographs. The *Bookman* magazine used four when it published a longer version of the interview.

A few months later a college friend returned to Oxford to work up a "personality sketch." Though Faulkner gave him only half an hour, he did send him on to Phil Stone. The friend, who had aimed at the magazines, had to settle for the *Memphis Commercial Appeal*. Its editor, having sent a set of proofs to Oxford, soon informed him: "You may be somewhat surprised and certainly gratified to learn that I received a letter" from Faulkner "expressing his pleasure at your article and declaring it entirely satisfactory." The illustrated, full-page spread stressed that Faulkner "honestly dislikes," even "abhors," "literary people as a group" and gloated that his sudden rise to fame or at least notoriety had given him leverage for revenge on the editors who had rejected his stories before. Curiously, it also played up his temperance, which relaxed only for "mild semiannual libations."[13]

So what have I proved so far? Not much if Faulkner didn't have such a reputation for hatred of publicity. In fact he did begin in the 1930s to rebuff journalists icily. But Phil Mullen, associate editor of the *Oxford Eagle* from 1933 to 1951, generalized convincingly that Faulkner "liked the way I wrote about him, which was respectful without going overboard. Of course, Bill liked favorable publicity as much as anyone else." More pointedly, Mullen concluded: "Through the early years of his work, recognition came slow and hard. Critics were unfriendly; some of his homefolks made fun of him. So when fame did come, he rebuffed all efforts to lionize him, with withering iconoclastic humor and with cool refusal to be interviewed or photographed."[14] Though Mullen colors far too kindly the record after 1950, it is mixed rather than monochromic from any angle. Still, only Blotner's loyalty can justify his surprise that when, in October 1939, a friend took Faulkner to a football game in New York City, he made the "extraordinary gesture" of inviting along a journalist—who seized the chance to whip up an interview for the *New York Post*. It presented Faulkner as a "jolly little man who likes nothing better than telling droll yarns," especially about the Snopses, in a heavy Southern accent.

That *Post* story holds a basic marker. Even when journalists mean well, by the time they have filled their quota for jazziness any human subject looks slightly foolish at best. Only the hardened or else the fading celebrity who welcomes any sort of publicity can endure their tone. Of course, a touchy or just perceptive person writhes with embarrassment, swearing "Never again!" So in 1948, when Malcolm Cowley, by then a trusted friend, proposed doing a profile for *Life* magazine, Faulkner "wasn't happy about the intrusion into his life." However, "when we went back to the subject, after lunch . . . he gave what I interpreted as a sigh of resigned assent." They took a drive through the New England woods and "between comments on the landscape, Faulkner brought forth a good deal of information about himself, as if to help along my project."[15]

After the Nobel Prize, he made four tours abroad for the State Department. Though the People to People scheme sponsored by President Dwight Eisenhower fizzled and though Faulkner felt awkward about taking a lead in it, take a lead he did. His form letter that began, "The President has asked me to organize American writers to see what we can do to give a true picture of our country to other people," turned pixyish. But a second letter kept fully solemn.[16] On the same visit when he played the unapproachable "lion in the garden" at the Paris reception, he recorded fifteen pages from *A Fable* for the USIS. The devout or genteel rationale for such activities has invoked his general sense of "duty" or his "deep patriotic feelings."

Yet he was not performing solely for the State Department. Blotner, who entitles Book 11 of his biography "The Public Man," comments that his speeches "were getting not only more frequent but also longer." Pushing into the thick of the desegregation debate of the mid-1950s, he was so eager (or so felt a duty) to make his ideas count that he wrote to both *Time* and *Life*, in spite of cursing both magazines a few years before as cancers on the American brain. He sent a follow-up letter to *Life*, granted a politically loaded interview with the *London Sunday Times*, and joined in the Tex and Jinx radio show broadcast from the Waldorf Hotel.

Meanwhile, Phil Stone—who, to be sure, had grown envious and stood well to Faulkner's right on racism—had started growling by 1955: "The only way that I can figure out his habit of writing letters to the papers is that he is not getting as much publicity now as he did when he had just won the Nobel Prize. I know he insists that he does not want publicity, but I think he is about that, as I have told him, Mr. Greta Garbo." In July 1957 Stone wrote to Carvel Collins: "For some time now Bill has not been getting publicity. My prediction is that between now and October 1 he will do or say something startling that will again attract public attention." Stone made that "prophecy" to others, too, and he gloated to James B. Meriwether in September: "You may remember that I told you" that "Bill would do something to attract publicity since he has not been getting publicity lately." Stone enclosed a clipping of Faulkner's prointegration letter to the *Memphis Commercial Appeal*.[17]

We need to discount private envy and to avoid professional sardonicism or its masked partner, the superhuman ethical standards that some literary critics apply both to authors' own lives and the characters in their fiction. More positively, we need to honor any commitment to social conscience. So I am happy to hear David Minter argue that Faulkner had always held the ideal of serving his country and that he had come especially to admire André Malraux's "double life as novelist and statesman." More natively, Minter argues that "for years Faulkner had regarded himself as a person who had chosen art over the provincial values and prejudices that were a part of his heritage. Over the last several years he had been exploring the social implications of that self-conception."[18] By "natively" I mean this brings Faulkner back closer to the twentieth-century role of the American artist— like Floyd Dell or Sherwood Anderson or Edgar Lee Masters or Thomas Wolfe—trapped in local philistinism, which he subverts in either vengeful or constructive anger.

Because Faulkner was such a great artist I want to read his personal motives kindly—when, for instance, he gave the commencement speech at his daughter's junior college. I can join

Blotner in praising his loyalty to Howard Hawks by submitting to two interviews in New York City and another in Memphis (at a "cocktail party") that promoted a new movie in 1955.[19] I can appreciate the holiday spirit behind his taping of Irwin Russell's dialect poem "Christmas Night in the Quarters"—broadcast in December 1961 over local station WELK.

Nor do I condescend to his posing for a publicity shot when the Lux Radio Theatre adapted one of his short stories. And I hope he charged dearly for covering a hockey match and then the Kentucky Derby for *Sports Illustrated*. And I'm willing to believe that solely the cause of literature led him to cooperate for days on the filming of a seventeen-minute segment for the Ford Foundation's Omnibus Program. Cooperate he did, worrying ahead of time that he wasn't in good voice and entertaining the crew when they had finished. Phil Stone, playing a fat supporting role, wrote privately that "Bill was just as gracious and patient about this as possible." Faulkner even acted a scene in which he mildly grumbles before letting Phil Mullen through the door at Rowan Oak: "I don't see what my private life, the inside of my house, my family have got to do with my writing."[20] Though the classical rhetoricians already had a name for it, our media have perfected the gambit of pretending to deny the very fact they are affirming. Incidentally, that *Paris Review* piece begins: "Mr. Faulkner, you were saying a while ago that you don't like interviews."

But who can plead what benefit for literature when Blotner records that Earl Wilson interviewed Faulkner late in 1953? It would take a tolerant person to argue that Wilson's column of Broadway gossip was contemptible rather than despicable. And what benefit was served first by the letter in which Faulkner asks a British friend to draw up a mailing list that Jean Stein can use for that number of the *Paris Review?* The high point of comedy, however, came in 1957 on a football Saturday in Charlottesville, Virginia. Faulkner readily agreed to an interview at half-time by "Bullet Bill" Dudley, once so famous as a triple-threat that I still remember him though he didn't know who Faulkner was. Briefed hurriedly, Dudley introduced him as the winner of the "Mobile Prize." Then, according to Blotner, a regional network heard Dudley "talk literature" and Faulkner "talk football" for four to five minutes.[21] Though Faulkner allowed other unusual interviews after 1957, the danger of anticlimax warns me to stop. Besides, the West Point visit calls for a lengthy analysis. Until now, nobody had adjusted for how elaborately it was framed, in Goffman's sense, by the hosts. Faulkner, for his part, played a psychically reconstitutive role tied to his agonized efforts to get into uniform during World War II. I ask the explicators to stop dredging the West Point record for his tips about his works until they situate it within the two propositions I will finally lay out.

Before then I want to ask why Faulknerians interpret that visit so benignly or why they applaud his outrage over the profile that *Life* published in 1953. Supposedly he objected on principle, sight unseen, though Stone sneered, "I think he will read it and will pretend he has not."[22] If he did read it, I can suspect he was especially cut by the judgment that he was "a self-effacing but vain man who longed for recognition and rebuffed it when it came." His lifelong attitude toward publicity was ambivalent or just inconsistent or even erratic. The "Lion in the Garden" episode was balanced by an unusually friendly and relaxed interview in Paris. By 1956 and again in 1959 he was courting *Life* as an outlet—the second time on a purely personal matter. Likewise, in 1957 he sent a letter on foreign policy to *Time*, earlier the target of one of his most quoted rebuffs. As for hatred of cameras, he kept sitting even for studio photographs and would order seventeen prints of the one in pink riding habit to send to "friends all over the world."[23] Ultimately, he sat for an oil portrait.

But I'm not indicting Faulkner for the common sin of waffling. Rather I indict his admirers for any rigid faith in his insistence on privacy. After conceding him the right to inconsistency, to patriotism, to fatherly devotion, to human kindness, and to the need for making a living, I have to charge that they ignore the dun facts, just like the courtiers who pretend that the king is not bandy-legged or the queen is not pockmarked. They don't want to see that—to mimic Cowley's language provocatively and still more pointedly—among the major writers of our time Faulkner was altogether exceptional for the frequency and frankness with which he talked about himself as a artist-writer.

That conclusion could be fleshed out from the interviews even before 1950 along with his letter in 1927 to the Book Editor of the *Chicago Tribune* and the introduction for the Modern Library edition of *Sanctuary* (1932), which commented also that he had "written my guts" into *The Sound and the Fury*. The next year, when asked to supply an introduction for a reissue of the earlier novel, he struggled with it through three stages, telling his publisher, "I have worked on it a good deal, like on a poem almost, and I think that it is all right now." Blotner characterizes the latter part of the second stage as "intensely personal" and the third stage as marked "by a broader, more flamboyant style." [24]

The introduction mailed to New York City opens melo-dramatically: "I wrote this book and learned to read." Next, a bit indirectly, it lays claim on the term Art with a capital A. The second paragraph describes his "first ecstasy" of creating *The Sound and the Fury*: "that emotion definite and physical and yet nebulous to describe: that ecstasy, that eager and joyous faith and anticipation of surprise which the yet unmarred sheet beneath my hand held inviolate and unfailing, waiting for release." When finished, he felt that into it "I had already put perhaps the only thing in literature which would ever move me very much." The last paragraph or peroration began: "This is the only one of the seven novels which I wrote without any accompanying feeling of drive or effort, or any following feeling of exhaustion or relief or distaste." But, he revealed, he had started *The Sound and the Fury* only after giving up hopes of selling even minimally: "One day I seemed to shut a door between me and all publishers' addresses and book lists. I said to myself, Now I can write." His next sentence encapsulated a much longer passage in the preceding draft: "Now I can make myself a vase like that which the old

Roman kept at his bedside and wore the rim slowly away with kissing it."

Unfortunately for Faulkner's household, the Depression scotched the new edition. But when his publisher got ready to use that introduction in 1946, he objected that "I had forgotten what smug false sentimental windy shit it was."[25] Who dares improve that judgment? Faulkner had not, however, renounced the personal dramatics, even at so public a moment when, now famous, he accepted a gold medal from the American Academy of Arts and Letters. Here he recalled turning the age of fifty and looking back on his work: "I decided it was all pretty good—and then in the same instant I realised that that was the worst of all since that meant only that a little nearer now was the moment, instant, night: dark: sleep: when I would put it all away forever that I anguished and sweated over, and it would never trouble me anymore."[26]

During his own forties and the 1940s Faulkner had often wondered if he would get recognition in the United States—where it counted most, psychically. He burst out to his agent: "In France, I am the father of a literary movement. In Europe I am considered the best modern American and among the first of all writers. In America, I eke out a hack's motion picture wages by winning second prize in a manufactured mystery story contest."[27] When Malcolm Cowley asked for help toward a long essay, he answered candidly: "I would like very much to have the piece done. I think (at 46) that I have worked too hard at my (elected or doomed, I don't know which) trade, with pride but I believe not vanity, with plenty of ego but with humility too (being a poet, of course I give no fart for glory) to leave no better mark on this our pointless chronicle than I seem to be about to leave." After some practical details, he repeated: "I would like the piece, except for the biography part. You are welcome to it privately, of course. But I think that if what one has thought and hoped and endeavored and failed at is not enough, if it must be explained and excused by what he has experienced, done or suffered, while he was not being an artist, then he and the one making the evaluation have both failed."28

Put bluntly, expect no autobiography nor coaching on the explications. But both proved to be more often and more nakedly forthcoming, especially after Faulkner grew comfortable in the role of world-recognized, immortal artist that the Nobel Prize gave him beribboned right to play. The *Paris Review* piece encapsulates both lines of self-revelation. He topped his long record of yarning by explaining why "the best job that was ever offered to me was to become a landlord in a brothel." Deepening a motif struck in that 1944 letter to Cowley and then in his introduction to the *Faulkner Reader* (1954)—which set back to 1923 the vision that "my doom, fate, was to keep on writing books"—he expounded for Jean Stein on how the Faulknerian kind of "artist is a creature driven by demons" who make him "completely ruthless in their service." He also explained the motivation of most of his major characters.

Anybody who thinks I am mistreating Faulkner can conveniently reread the gathering of interviews and speeches given in Japan and Manila in 1955 or the hefty book that transcribes (not all of) the sessions at the University of Virginia in 1957. David Minter concedes that "sometimes he came close to pontificating" in Japan. Mostly framed, that is, keyed by questions he talked intimately about his fiction and attitudes, mixing humility with personal heroics. In Charlottesville he grumbled about how English Department types were pressing him to validate subtleties he had not suspected from himself. Yet he responded earnestly, sometimes enriching or else revising already famous fiction. Overall, decides Minter, Faulkner's "favorite picture of the artist emerged as a somewhat lush fin de siècle version of Romanticism's."29

Some patient Faulknerian should analyze how often he used the term "artist" instead of "writer" (much less "novelist"). Also, his creative "demon" by that name became increasingly prominent, relieved by touches of down-homeness—usually the pose of a dirt-farmer. Enroute to Stockholm he warned a critic-journalist, evidently without irony: "There is no use pretending." He went on, "I am not a literary man. I am a farmer that just likes to tell stories."[30] However, the heading of the story—"Faulkner Uneasy in His Nobel Role"—does suggest an excuse. The West Point record makes a fairer case study though a carpenter tends to elbow out the farmer.

Since I keep intimating skepticism I may as well charge that Faulkner could have shielded himself better from the media. A hundred years ago Henry James had quickly comprehended the new age of "newspapers and telegrams and photographs and interviewers." Though pursuit of him was neither fierce nor constant he did mount a steady defense. Willa Cather, who at first welcomed any exposure, managed more and more to seclude herself, right on Park Avenue in Manhattan. J. D. Salinger has been successfully reclusive, too successful perhaps—we can say with sympathy for Faulkner. If the public is goaded into getting interested in a personality for that very shunning of publicity, then the media see a chance for a running hunt. For *Newsweek* to label Faulkner "the world's most reticent author" was to make every ambitious reporter snatch up notebook and camera.[31] Still, there *are* writers—Thomas Berger or Thomas Pynchon or Anne Tyler—who keep a very low profile even in our own new age of high tech.

In several ways Faulkner actually justified the intrusions by the media. The need to frame himself impressively caused an alternating cycle. He would offer up some melodramatic pseudo facts about his past and then back away—in embarrassment or simply to avoid closer scrutiny. Why did he exclaim once: "Goddamit I've spent almost fifty years trying to cure myself of the curse of human speech." In certain moods he became indeed the "most reticent" of authors, rebuffing intruders stonily; but then he would unpredictably relent. Journalists felt they were rolling the dice when they tried an approach. Likewise, he intrigued them because he kept alternating roles. The smoothies at the State Department must have had trouble holding a straight face over his notion in 1955 that they present him abroad as a "simple private individual, occupation unimportant, who is interested in and believes in people, humanity."[32]

Publishing—note the root of the word—publishing over a signature is an intrinsically, aggressively public act, the antithesis of keeping private. Anybody who publishes avant-garde writing has especially to expect (and probably hopes for) curiosity along with some ridicule. Faulkner, I say reverently, knew he was a genius. He hungered for recognition of both the dense, oblique, and modernist artistry of his texts and of the mind and personality creating them. Robert Frost, who figured out the game of fame for the jackpot, must have smiled broadly at the bursts of Faulkner publicity, for, as his poem "Revelation" concludes:

> But so with all, from babes that play
>   At hide-and-seek to God afar,
> So all who hide too well away
>   Must speak and tell us where they are.

Since I also keep intimating the obviousness of my case, it's reasonable to ask why somebody hasn't already made it. Briefly and apologetically a few admirers have come close. For a recent collection of essays centered on the "late career," one critic arrives forthrightly at the position that "no matter how physically onerous many of the public appearances were, no matter how psychologically intrusive the attendant publicity was, Faulkner had a kind of ontological need for them."[33] Still, undermining the commonplace that he maintained his privacy as single-mindedly as Thomas Sutpen fought to establish a dynasty will take dogged effort—for at least four good reasons. Gertrude Stein liked to warn against the symbiosis, the mutual reinforcement that authors and their preferred audience can establish.

First of all, Faulkner did supply some vivid counterevidence, much of it heartfelt. Writers need privacy to work and even to think and feel toward their distinctive, original insights, undistorted by banal or sophisticated chatter. Especially during the middle phase of Faulkner's career, he abhorred discussions with literary esthetes, whose professional, Manhattan species irritated (or else threatened) him worst of all. Furthermore, with a kind of schizophrenia, he at times regarded his bound works as separate from his daily, private self. His actions or outbursts to that effect are well-known (far too well-known, according to me). Phil Stone believed in them so late as May 1950. That most often quoted outburst came in a 1949 letter to Cowley: "I will protest to the last: no photographs, no recorded documents. It is my ambition to be, as a private individual, abolished and voided from history, leaving it markless, no refuse save the printed books; I wish I had had enough sense to see ahead thirty years ago and, like some of the Elizabethans, not signed them. It is my aim, and every effort bent, that the sum and history of my life, which in the same sentence is my obit and epitaph too, shall be them both: He made the books and he died." That attitude understandably boiled into rage when his rebuffs to reporters made their own striking news. More substantively, he was often trying to escape being exploited for the stereotype of Southern decadence retailed by the Northern press.

The second reason, exemplified in that letter to Cowley, lies in Faulkner's rhetoric. To borrow a Southerner's tribute to eloquence from *Look Homeward, Angel*, he sure could "tie a knot in the tail of the English language." That recent critic distanced enough—he teaches in England—to see Faulkner's touch with a "dress costume" and his "ontological need for publicity" has warned about the University of Virginia transcripts: "We may not read them in the profoundly mesmerized state so often engendered by the novels, but nonetheless sometimes we read them—we have to—with a marked degree of fascination. And this applies not just to the highly wrought *speeches*. In my own experience it is the same with much of the Jean Stein interview."[34] As Faulkner's rhetoric keeps mounting like a cumulonimbus or elaborating its theme as sinuously as a snake charmer's flute, we are swayed by

emotion. When we are swept up by his arias we feel—as Leonard
Bernstein has said about hearing grand opera—enriched, enrap-
tured, and ennobled.

However—the third reason—rhetorical power grows hypnotic
only when we believe what it says and especially when we want to
believe. Some professional experts on literature or, more precisely, the great majority of those who savor expressive writers like
Faulkner fervently want to believe in the Romantic visionary
dedicated to Art's Sake. Or—to update my point—the drive of
Western literary criticism since World War II—"above all" and
beneath its wondrous feats of metaphysics—"reflects the need
. . . to maintain the creative entity of the self."[35] Magisterially,
Faulkner satisfied that need, and his increasingly emphatic admirers after 1950 confirmed his sense of an imperial self as artist.

When Faulkner insists to Cowley that he wants to be remembered only through and, indeed, only in his writings, his admirers
don't care to realize that a Freudian apprentice would grin at the
masking of an exceptionally piercing dread of oblivion. They are
charmed when he insists at West Point (and elsewhere) that "all"
the artist "really needs is a little whiskey and a little tobacco and a
little fun," that when you start thinking of royalties, "you are
sunk—you are gone, you have stopped being a writer. You must
be an amateur writer always."[36] To believe happily in this role
they have to ignore his haggling over the prices of his short stories
or the purpose of revisions made for the editor of a slick magazine.
Though they regret what supporting majestic Rowan Oak took out
of him—more, in psychic wear and tear, than the notorious
Hartford house cost Mark Twain—they don't care to contemplate
how he managed to pay taxes on more real estate within the city
limits of Oxford than anybody else. Their understandable love for
the works of art he left us blocks any realistic look at the all too
human sides of the creator's behavior.

A few Faulknerians find too easy reinforcement of their own
superiority or else their self-pity through his economic rhetoric.
They enjoy loftily his definition in 1955 of the artist as "everyone
who has tried to create something . . . with no other tools and

materials than the uncommerciable ones of the human spirit."
They feel vindicated by his jeer that American society regards the
"pursuit of art" as "a peaceful hobby like breeding Dalmations
[*sic*]" and feel more virtuous after his charge that "perhaps one of
the things wrong with our country is success. That there is too
much success in it. Success is too easy." They resonate both when
he spurns the commerciable and when it relentlessly spurns him.
So late as 1957 he told the American Academy of Arts and Letters
that "the fact the artist has no more actual place in the American
culture of today than he has in the American economy of today, no
place at all in the warp and woof, the thews and sinews, the mosaic
of the American dream as it exists today, is perhaps a good thing
for him since it teaches him humility in advance." [37]

Finally—the fourth reason—some Faulknerians are too eager
to feel that his privacy was uniquely violated. They will resent the
idea that Davy Crockett suffered more damaging intrusions from
the press than Faulkner. If only through a surrogate they yearn to
establish some kind of refuge from the industrializing roar, to find
a haven from the always swifter torrent we call society. Cleanth
Brooks praises to the hilt Faulkner's essay "On Privacy / The
American Dream: What Happened to It?" Although it hypnot-
ically towers into eloquence, it clouds the historical ground it
builds on, making a distinction between liberty and license without any evident sensitivity to its previous uses. Eventually we
mislearn that the "American sky" was "once the topless empyrean
of freedom, the American air . . was once the living breath of
liberty." But American society is now (in 1955, that is) "destroying
the last vestige of privacy," that is, is imploding the atomistic self
that reigned without role-playing and served as its own sanctuary
from sociocultural determinisms. Considering Faulkner's status
by then, his peroration rings hollow: "America has not yet found
any place" for the artist "who deals only in things of the human
spirit except to use his notoriety to sell soap or cigarettes or
fountain pens or to advertise automobiles and cruises and resort
hotels." [38]

After all my own broad strokes, I will settle for two fairly narrow but constructive goals. First, biographers and critics should cross-examine Faulkner's reputation for insisting on privacy. They will benefit from reconsidering whether he helped shape his public career deliberately, maneuvered for fame, or sometimes dreamed in terms of figuring as a great writer rather than of writing great novels. Academics today so resent the pull of media hype that they recoil from the idea that many classical authors have plotted their trajectory as a visible personage. Though we all at least fitfully contemplate our life curve and measure it against the patterns known to us, writers take on a specialized self-consciousness. As one impressively educated critic sets out to argue, "no poet becomes himself without inheriting an idea of what it means to be a poet" in the eyes of the world.[39] More specifically, anybody who ponders Leo Braudy's brilliant *The Frenzy of Renown: Fame and Its History* (1986) will recognize that the twentieth-century author carries on assumptions, sensitivities, and hopes about "what it means," writes Braudy, "to be public in Western culture," about winning and holding prominence. Faulkner's venerated outburst to Cowley denies both much of his own inescapable feelings and popular attitudes already registered in his boyhood.

Apart from the other spheres of his life, Faulkner tried on five different roles, each well-delineated in his contemporary milieu: (1) as an avant-gardist; (2) as a popular author, a comfortably self-supporting craftsman; (3) as a Romantic creator-isolato who resonated most to Keats while playing out the pageant of his bleeding heart like Byron; (4) as a high-culture, serious artist with an elitist, sophisticated audience; and (5) as a serious writer in the sense of a socially validated, humanistic voice of wisdom. These were not roles adopted on cue and dropped with the curtain but subconsciously, emotionally reinforced attitudes. Usually, Faulkner was drawn to or driven by two or three or more of these roles at the same time, and their competing tensions went into the making of his unique gifts to us. He gets a lead part in Jay Martin's *Who Am I This Time? Uncovering the Fictive Personality* (1988).

More relevant here, each of those five roles, along with their clashing demands, carried its own traps for privacy. Surprisingly—to me, anyway—Ronald Sukenick has coldly detailed the ambivalences hardening into dilemmas that avant-gardism incurs, and he grows sardonic toward what he labels the "cult of failure."[40] The self-supporting craftsman must of course cooperate with the publisher's tactics; Faulkner's letters to his agents in the 1930s and 1940s make fanciful his statement in Japan that it wasn't until he "got old and began to slow down" that he "became conscious there were people that read the books" he had signed. Here spoke the Romantic isolato who fumed to his agent that "I believe I have got enough fair literature in me yet to deserve reasonable freedom from bourgeoise material petty impediments and compulsion," who declared in Manila that an artist is "extremely lucky" because he had so "dedicated himself" that he "doesn't mind starving a little." Yet posturing in such striking terms attracts not simply an "Olé!" from some academics but also curiosity from the public. Likewise, the public that genuinely reads books will take hotter interest in the life of a writer who insists on the status of "serious." (I recently met a James Michener fan who couldn't quite remember his name.) Finally, a writer aspiring to the voice of cultural authority must give speeches and interviews. That's practically the name of the game.

So I come back to those interviews, which I had started to analyze for their framing and role-playing, for why they turned so anti-intellectual, even raunchy during the 1930s, so increasingly pontifical during the 1950s. Faulkner as novelist needed no warnings on the fact that we incorrigibly fictionize ourselves. His autobiographical comments, even without the egregious whoppers, can turn more deceptive than those of his famed contemporaries. Less urgently, the same warning applies to his commentary about his fiction and its characters. That volume of sessions in Charlottesville poses the most visible challenge. Faulkner stuck to some of his old yarns, like having been a bootlegger, but also courted the hunt aristocracy. He reached back to the 1920s to pose as a good ole boy from Mississippi who says "ain't" or, incongruously, as a wounded falcon of World War I; but, basically for the first time, he expatiated on symbols in his fiction and made his "demon" of a muse almost a daily presence. Actually, the preface by Frederick Gwynn and Joseph Blotner posts a caveat against literalist readers that they have ignored this far. [41]

The practical good news is that the interviews can furnish work-relief for the explicators, who gasp near a dwindling end for the major novels. Collectively, the interviews comprise a major new Faulkner text with deviously shifting, two-way frames and involuted, two-way roles. [42] During the last ten years, relatively unnoticed because of the pinwheels of metacriticism, there has been a flood of interviews, of "conversations" with living authors. Almost always, in what may not be a pun, these pieces pass at face value. [43] Critics haven't transferred to them the distinctions they have learned lately to make for autobiography as a genre. Faulknerians must work out a template, a software, with the brilliance and originality that their master forced them to bring to *The Sound and the Fury* and *Absalom, Absalom!*

NOTES

1. Michel Gresset, "Faulkner's Self-Portraits," *Faulkner Journal*, 2 (Fall 1986), 4. The title poem of Charles Nelson's *William Faulkner: The Anchorite of Rowan Oak* (mimeo. ed. by author, 1973) deserves mention somewhere in this essay.

2. Malcolm Cowley, *The Faulkner-Cowley File: Letters and Memories, 1944–1962* (New York: Viking Press, 1966), 71. For Cather's public self, see the two volumes of *Willa Cather in Person: Interviews, Speeches, and Letters*, ed. L. Brent Bohlke (Lincoln: University of Nebraska Press, 1986).

3. "Introduction," *Lion in the Garden: Interviews with William Faulkner, 1926–1962*, ed. James B. Meriwether and Michael Millgate (New York: Random House, 1968). See also James G. Watson, *William Faulkner: Letters and Fictions* (Austin: University of Texas Press, 1987), 156. The introduction to *Faulkner: After the Nobel Prize*, ed. Michel Gresset and Kenzaburo Ohashi (Kyoto: Yamaguchi, 1987), does comment (4) that "some American critics were cynical about Faulkner's change from an obscure but definitely authentic novelist who kept his integrity as an artist, to a world-famous Nobel Prize winner who began to assume an important role of message-giver to the world."

4. André Bleikasten, "A Private Man's Public Voice," in *Faulkner: After the Nobel Prize*, 45, 49.

5. Cleanth Brooks, "Faulkner's *The American Dream: What Happened to It?*" in *Faulkner: After the Nobel Prize*, 322; this essay under a similar title appears also in Brooks's

On the Prejudices, Predilections, and Firm Beliefs of William Faulkner (Baton Rouge: Louisiana State University Press, 1987).

6. A. I. Bezzerides, "Preface," *William Faulkner: A Life on Paper* (Jackson: University Press of Mississippi, 1980), 9.

7. Joseph Blotner, *Faulkner: A Biography*, 2 vols. (New York: Random House, 1974), 2:1594-95; see also the one-volume Blotner (1984), 619.

8. Erving Goffman, *Frame Analysis: An Essay on the Organization of Experience* (Cambridge: Harvard University Press, 1974), 573–74, concludes that the self "is not an entity half-concealed behind events, but a changeable formula for managing oneself during them. Just as the current situation prescribes the official guise behind which we will conceal ourselves, so it provides for where and how we will show through, the culture itself prescribing what sort of entity we must believe ourselves to be in order to have something to show through in this manner." In current polemics the gender-oriented analysts are stressing the social origins of selfhood (as did the antisegregationists like Kenneth B. Clark). Likewise, a fine starting point for rethinking the basic assumptions about privacy is Section II of Hannah Arendt, *The Human Condition* (Chicago: University of Chicago Press, 1958).

9. Blotner, *Faulkner*, 2:1440–41; for the Bouvard text, see *Lion in the Garden*, 68–73.

10. From an interview with Judith L. Sensibar. Professor Sensibar has kindly sent me a copy of her excellent paper (read at the 1987 Faulkner and Yoknapatawpha Conference), "'Drowsing Maidenhead Symbol's Self': Faulkner and the Fictions of Love."

11. Mick Gidley, "Explanation as Composition: Faulkner's Public Comments on His Fiction," in *Faulkner: After the Nobel Prize*, 266.

12. Unless noted otherwise, all interviews that I quote are reprinted in *Lion in the Garden*.

13. Louis Cochran, "A Front Steps Interview," in *William Faulkner of Oxford*, ed. James W. Webb and A. Wigfall Green (Baton Rouge: Louisiana State University Press, 1965), 101–7, 217–24; *Memphis Commercial Appeal*, 6 November 1932, Magazine Section, 4.

14. Phillip E. Mullen, "The Fame and the Publicity," in *William Faulkner of Oxford*, 162–63.

15. *Faulkner-Cowley File*, 107.

16. *Selected Letters of William Faulkner*, ed. Joseph Blotner (New York: Random House, 1977), 404; *Faulkner: A Comprehensive Guide to the Brodsky Collection / Volume 2: The Letters*, ed. Louis Daniel Brodsky and Robert W. Hamblin (Jackson: University Press of Mississippi, 1984), 201.

17. *Faulkner: Brodsky Collection*, 2:179–80, 217–19.

18. David Minter, *William Faulkner, His Life and Work* (Baltimore: Johns Hopkins University Press, 1980), 233.

19. Blotner, 2:1538; one-vol. Blotner, 599; *Memphis Commercial Appeal*, 14 June 1955, 17 (Faulkner "sparkled brightly")—none of these three interviews was reprinted in *Lion in the Garden*. Nor was Howard Thompson, "Through Faulkner's View-Finder," *New York Times*, 16 March 1958, Section 2, 7, which has Faulkner begin, "I'm always glad to do anything I can to help Jerry Wald." A cynic could point out that in 1955 he was helping promote *The Land of the Pharoahs*, for which he wrote the screenplay; in 1958 the film was *The Long, Hot Summer*, based on *The Hamlet*.

20. Blotner, 2:1438–39; *Faulkner: Brodsky Collection*, 2:95–99; Bezzerides, *Faulkner*, 109–11; Stephen B. Oates, *William Faulkner, The Man and the Artist: A Biography* (New York: Harper & Row, 1987), 258.

21. *Selected Letters*, 398; one-vol. Blotner, 575, 646–47; Blotner, 2:1678–79.

22. *Faulkner: Brodsky Collection*, 2:120.

23. J. R. Cofield, "Many Faces, Many Moods," in *William Faulkner of Oxford*, 112.

24. Blotner, 2:810–11.

25. *Selected Letters*, 235; "An Introduction for *The Sound and the Fury*," ed. James B. Meriwether, *Southern Review*, N.S.8 (Autumn 1972), 705–10. I follow Meriwether's judgment that this was probably the final version; the earlier version would suit my approach still better.

26. William Faulkner, *Essays, Speeches, and Public Letters,* ed. James B. Meriwether (New York: Random House, 1965), 206.

27. *Selected Letters,* 218.

28. Ibid., 182.

29. Minter, 235, 240.

30. Harvey Breit, "Faulkner Uneasy in His Nobel Role," *New York Times,* 8 December 1954, 27; not reprinted in *Lion in the Garden.*

31. Actually, the label of "most reticent" shed glory on the journalist who applied it; he or she did interview Faulkner, who "was very dressed up for a man who likes to consider himself a farmer" and who "talked of many things, nearly all deeply personal"—"Visit with the Author," *Newsweek,* 9 February 1959, 58.

32. *Selected Letters,* 234, 384.

33. Gidley, "Explanation as Composition," 265. Minter, 107, discussing *The Sound and the Fury,* comments that "Faulkner had never stopped needing recognition and money."

34. Gidley, "Explanation as Composition," 270. Another British observer distanced himself from the Charlottesville materials; in an otherwise glowing obituary he regretted that Faulkner had "allowed himself to become an academics' guineau-pig" there (J. W. Lambert, *London Sunday Times,* 8 July 1962, 25).

35. Art Berman, *From the New Criticism to Deconstruction: The Reception of Structuralism and Post-Structuralism* (Urbana: University of Illinois Press, 1988), 6.

36. *Faulkner at West Point,* ed. Joseph L. Fant III and Robert Ashley (New York: Random House, 1964), 83, 98, 99.

37. *Essays, Speeches, and Public Letters,* 143, 145, 153.

38. Ibid., 62–75.

39. Lawrence Lipking, *The Life of the Poet: Beginning and Ending Poetic Careers* (Chicago: University of Chicago Press, 1981), viii.

40. Ronald Sukenick, *Down and In: Life in the Underground* (New York: Beech Tree Books, 1987), 238–41, 249.

41. Frederick L. Gwynn and Joseph L. Blotner, eds., *Faulkner in the University: Class Conferences at the University of Virginia, 1957–1958* (Charlottesville: University of Virginia Press, 1959).

42. For recent, strong analyses of Faulkner's changing, divided self-images and of his role-playing see Louis Daniel Brodsky, "Faulkner's Life Masks," *Southern Review,* 22 (Autumn 1986), 738–65; Michael Grimwood, *Heart in Conflict: Faulkner's Struggles with Vocation* (Athens: University of Georgia Press, 1986); Watson, *Faulkner: Letters and Fiction.*

43. For a notable exception see Scott Donaldson's introduction for *Conversations with John Cheever* (Jackson: University of Mississippi Press, 1987), xi: the repetitious questions "reveal a great deal about the way Cheever and his work were perceived by various interviewers."

"When I Showed Him the Check, He Asked If It Was Legal": What William Faulkner Got and Gave Us from Pop Culture

George Garrett

The relationship of the American writer to popular culture has been and remains tenuous and difficult to describe, constantly changing. The role and station (status, if you will) of the American writer has changed radically in my own professional lifetime. And it has changed much since the prime time of William Faulkner's career. Truth is, it was changing all along, during his lifetime, too, though this is not something he would need to have noticed until late in life and late in his career. And evidently he did not notice it much. There are good reasons for that apparent inattention. For one thing he was much too busy trying to get his own work done, completed and published, and trying (somehow, day by day, month by month, year by year) to survive in order to be able to do his own work.

Among a good many other general impressions you can gain from reading Joseph Blotner's biography (the two volume or the one volume, no matter) or his edition of *Selected Letters of William Faulkner* is that Faulkner never had enough money, not until the very end of his life, to rest easy about money, that he was always wheeling and dealing, on a very polite and very small scale, just to make ends (briefly) meet.[1] And even at the end, when there was, at last, public honor and a modest measure of financial security, he could not easily come up with the necessary front money on his own to make a down payment on Red Acres near Charlottesville. This was at the peak of his reputation and his earning power. He could raise the money, but would go broke unless he could borrow it expeditiously.

You don't have to know much about money to know that even a sudden influx of money near the end of a lifetime career cannot make up for years and years of breakeven subsistence. Money does not work that way. Your own poverty claims you.

May I say, by way of a parenthesis, that the way money works, and that is generally understood, is part of our American popular culture now, perhaps the most important part, in that it is the *bonding element*, the universal glue that is shared by all the various and sundry activities which can be considered popular culture.

What Faulkner was desperately trying to raise in the summer of 1962, through his longtime publisher and through the collector Linton Massey, was $50,000 for the down payment on Red Acres. Considerable money now and even more then. Here is some of what he said in a letter of 29 June 1962, to Linton Massey: "I want to make an offer for Red Acres. I can make the offer as is. But if it is accepted, I will be broke. I will have to guarantee to write a book or books. I can earn about $10,000.00 or more a year from lectures etc. I will do this, write books or lecture [notice, at his age and stage, he doesn't promise to do both], to own Red Acres, but I dont want to have to guarantee to."[2] He offered his manuscripts as security if need be.

As an example of changes in the scene, may I be so bold as to mention some figures from 1988? Recall that Faulkner in 1962 guessed he could make about $10,000 for a year's worth of lecturing. In 1988 the asking fee for a single lecture by Margaret Atwood was $7,500; Toni Morrison, $10,000; Ann Beattie, $12,500; Tom Wolfe, $16,000. And those figures are peanuts compared to the fees asked for and received by the likes of Henry Kissinger and Timothy Leary and G. Gordon Liddy. Since Faulkner's day the public lecture has become an odd little part, a cranny of popular culture. And, of course, there has been the great inflation, everywhere, even in the world of literature. But as I understand it, inflation has multiplied prices by about eleven times since 1900, not since 1962.

We should also notice that William Faulkner believed he could raise $50,000 in 1962 by signing on to do a book or *books* plural.

Compare that with the situation of novelist James Jones only two years later in 1964. Two publishers, Dell and Pocket Books, made offers to win him away from Scribner's. Here I quote from my own biography of James Jones: "Each was a complex, stepped contract with various escalator clauses, offering bonuses and increases according to the size of sales. Essentially, Dell offered an advance of $350,000 for the first book and $150,000 each on the second and third plus all the complexity of 'steps.' His royalty was to be 17 percent in hardcover and 10 percent in paperback. Pocket Books came up with something similar—$300,000 for the first book, $200,000 for the second, and $150,000 for the third."[3]

One thing, among others, which this discrepancy means is that Faulkner had been so busy writing he was somewhat out of touch with the contemporary literary scene. He said as much to the students at the University of Virginia, admitting that "there was a gap of about twenty-five years during which I had almost no acquaintance whatever with contemporary literature."[4] However, Faulkner also told University of Virginia undergraduates: "I think the artist is influenced by all in his environment. He's maybe more sensitive to it because he has got to get the materials, the lumber that he's going to build his edifice."[5]

That image of lumber puts me in mind of how in 1599 James and Richard Burbage took down the lumber of the old playhouse, the Theatre in Shoreditch, and put it up on Bankside as the brand new and improved Globe. Somewhere in a back closet of your consciousness, keep Shakespeare in mind—a writer who had tried his hand first at high art and culture, but who was deeply involved in pure popular culture for most of his working life. So often our greatest literary artists, submerged in the present, get and guess wrong, either or both, their past and future. Certainly Faulkner, like most of the rest of his generation, really, honestly believed (at least for a long time) that he lived in roughly the same literary world which had recently been inhabited by the likes of Henry James and Conrad, even by Twain, Melville, and Dickens; believed that there was a kind of continuum, that the new generation was, essentially, up to the same thing the earlier ones had been, faced with similar problems and challenges. And, just so, my generation of American writers has awkwardly assumed that we still somehow belong to the same literary world as William Faulkner and the masters of his generation. The evidence is overwhelming that we do *not* live or belong in the same world. If we could be more objective than we are able to be, I am convinced that we would see clearly that not only is the world we live and work in radically different from Faulkner's but also that what we are doing, the *writing* we are doing, is by definition and design, something else, something quite different from what he and his generation were up to.

Be that as it may, Faulkner's generation was the last one in America which could plausibly, sanely accept the illusion that the so-called serious novel had any prospect of general popularity. It is a matter more of irony than anything else that Faulkner and Joyce and Hemingway (and many others) began as writers wishing and hoping to earn some form of conventional popular success; that such a goal seemed entirely possible and plausible. And that in the end the masters, of that generation of masters, had as much to do as anybody else in removing the so- called serious novel from the realm of popular culture.

Other factors were at work, not the least being the kinds and forms of literacy, the nineteenth century had (briefly) known. But nevertheless when, one by one, the masters saw that their art form was likely to endure, if at all, only as a kind of high art rather than part of popular culture, they embraced the inevitable and thus bear a full share of the responsibility of and for the decline in simple popularity of their kind of modern novel. I say their kind of novel because what we now call the *genre* or public novel—novels of suspense, of fantasy, of romance, even the cult of celebrity—is now enjoying an enormous, blooming, though small-scale success. There are some greatly gifted writers, playing other artistic games by other rules, who are doing very well indeed in our time, who are closely involved, to the extent that anything in print still can be, in popular culture. Very few critics and scholars, with the notable exception of our own inimitable Leslie Fiedler, have demonstrated the courage and the chutzpah necessary to deal seriously with these works. But it seems at least likely that the last half of the American literary century may be said to belong more to (for example) Elmore Leonard and John D. Macdonald, Harlan Ellison and Arthur Clarke, Stephen King and Alexandra Ripley than, say, to Pynchon or Coover, or Gass or Gaddis, or even Roth.

Which does not mean that the *finest* of the modern masters are in much danger of losing place and/or face, but that some of the lesser lights of high art may very well find themselves in a similar situation to some of the earlier (and now lesser) Elizabethans—people like Barnabe Barnes and Sir John Davies and Michael Drayton, Fulke Greville and George Tuberville. Sidney and Spencer and Chapman were justly regarded as great writers in and of their age, but by now have to give way and precedence to the likes of Marlowe and Jonson and Shakespeare. Which tells us only that there are both upward and downward mobility in the arts as well as real life.

Faulkner's generation began by imagining that somehow they could be, at one and the same time, serious artists and popular novelists. They could—if they were both good and lucky like Faulkner, or Scott Fitzgerald, earn some kind of living with *literary* popular art—short stories and screenplays. Sooner or later, they were entitled to hope, their novels would catch on.

Among the many snarls of irony in the celebrated and much-discussed, and often-misunderstood, introduction to *Sanctuary*, one of the threads of irony in that introduction, is that it constitutes a farewell to the hope (not the idea or ideal but the *hope*) of the novel as popular art. In the heart, the dead center of the Great

Depression, in (of all places!) America, William Faulkner begins with an apology for even entertaining the vague idea that he might possibly earn some money from writing this book, any book. And he ends with a parodic commercial: "So I tore the galleys down and rewrote the book. It had been already set up once, so I had to pay for the privilege of rewriting it, trying to make out of it something which would not shame *The Sound and the Fury* and *As I Lay Dying* too much and I made a fair job and I hope you will buy it and tell your friends I hope they will buy it too."[6] That the complex introduction was and still is widely misunderstood and that *Sanctuary* was a success, but that Faulkner was not able, at the time at least, to enjoy the full fruits of that success, compound the ironies associated with this book, this time in Faulkner's life. It is surely debateable, but it seems to me that after *Sanctuary* Faulkner never really or seriously imagined being a conventionally *popular* novelist again. He would do various kinds of popular and solidly commercial writing, with various kinds of success. But I think his "Introduction" to *Sanctuary* can be taken as a personal valediction, a farewell to the novel as an artifact of popular culture.

Can we return to Shakespeare for a moment? It is relevant (at least to myself) because I can and do consider William Faulkner to be an artist of the kind of magnitude, depth, and breadth of William Shakespeare. Allowing for many obvious things in which they are widely different, there are some less obvious things which they have in common. For instance, at the outset of their extremely productive professional careers both of these artists believed that they were working in popular art forms. With some differences—the Elizabethan stage was a fairly new medium; the novel, though not by any means fully explored or exploited, was aging fast. The plays of Shakespeare, though early and often praised, did not acquire the patina of intellectual respectability in his lifetime. Faulkner lived to see the novel, at least his kind of novel, become for better and for worse a form of highbrow art, the texts of novels actually studied, investigated, and explicated, in the groves of academe.

In March of 1958, in an informal session at the house of Professor Willard Thorp of Princeton University, the following exchange took place and was remembered and reported.

> Student: "Mr. Faulkner, how do you feel about having your books studied in classrooms and people writing Ph.D. dissertations about you and your work?"
> Faulkner (lighting pipe, *Puff Puff*): "Well, (puff puff) I expected it."

Which may indeed be true. William Shakespeare had a confident and ingrained sense of his past, a vision of it, but Shakespeare had no real sense of the future at all— if he had, even a hint of it, the short term future (Revolution, regicide, end of the theatre as he knew and imagined it, Reformation) or even longer term, it would probably have stunned him into perfect silence.

Faulkner, though he knew and could imagine the past as well as any artist and seems to have understood everything about the past except his own place in it, Faulkner had an amazing prescience, a prophet's dreamlike flashing awareness of what future time was most likely to bring. There are many examples of this characteristic—and it is something we are going to come back to—but here and now I just want to remind you of one superb example of his prophetic powers. In 1935, in a book review of *Test Pilot* by Jimmy Collins, Faulkner turned to the idea of a folklore of speed, a folklore of the future which (as you can see) certainly encompasses the apocalyptic environment we have since come to live in, a world at home with such concepts as Mutual Assured Destruction: "It would be a folklore not of the age of speed nor of the men who perform it, but of the speed itself, peopled not by anything human or even mortal but by the clever willful machines themselves carrying nothing that was born or will have to die or which can even suffer pain, moving without comprehensible purpose towards no discernible destination, producing a literature innocent of either love or hate and of course of pity or terror, and which would be the story of the final disappearance of life from within the earth. I would watch them, the little puny mortals, vanishing against a vast and timeless void filled with the sound of incredible engines within which furious meteors moving in no medium hurtled nowhere, neither pausing nor flagging, forever destroying themselves and one another."[7]

That flash was more in the line of genre fiction in 1935. If you listened carefully you heard even a hint of futuristic *literary* criticism—a prophecy that out of the *folklore* of the future, that is the popular culture, would come a nonjudgmental, flat-affected, spare, and unengaging literature (what, for lack of better terms we now call minimalism and metafiction)—"a literature innocent of love and hate and of course of pity and terror."

Something else contained there, in that visionary passage, is an awareness of how popular culture constantly changes as the whole culture is also changed. No generation of Americans witnessed more obvious and radical changes in the whole texture and fabric of our society and culture than William Faulkner's own generation. It is in his lifetime that automobile and airplane, electricity, telephone and radio and motion picture and television changed and evolved, rapidly, from newly invented oddities (the "passing fancies" Rogers and Hart identified in "Our Love Is Here to Stay"), changed from odd and interesting inventions to universal, entirely mundane, and somehow, finally, necessary commonplaces.

And bear in mind, also, the fantastic changes wrought by World War II—the end of the grinding Great Depression, the end not only of international isolation, but of national isolation and immobility. With the new mobility came the possibility of more uniformity than this society or culture had ever known or even known that it wanted. Simultaneously with these huge changes came such sometimes contradictory forces as what the late Rene Dubos used to call regionalism by choice and, at the same time, the new Federalism, redefining the national constitution and greatly limiting, severely diminishing, both the independence and the power of local and state governments, of whole regions of the nation.

All of these changes surface somewhere in the works of William Faulkner.

Prior to World War II, then, American popular culture tended to be much more regional, localized, thus (his term was correct) more a matter of *folklore* and custom and tradition than anything else. Locally there were the events and adventures in the pulpit, in the courthouse, on the political stump, events and adventures at once defined and maintained by local gossip and memory. All these things shape Faulkner's language and his subjects. The world came calling in other ways, in the revivals, carnivals, fairs, football games, all of which Faulkner wrote about.

Yes, there were the funny papers and Faulkner surely seems to have read them, alluded to them, used them. Yes, there was the radio—though here Faulkner's use of the familiar elements of radio shows seems to me minimal for the era. There were the national magazines that he depended on as a potential marketplace for his short stories—for example the *Saturday Evening Post, Collier's,* and *Liberty* (we should keep in mind that the first full-fledged example of the now dominant form of illustrated journalism, *Life,* came on the scene, and tentatively enough, on 23 November 1936). Ross's *New Yorker* and the old *Vanity Fair* existed, not yet making any serious claims on more than their own sophisticated local consciousness. And I don't recall many incidents involving the wild improbability of one of Faulkner's authentic Mississippi characters being aware of or any way interested in such things. There is the celebrated and significant exception—the picture of Candace Compson, brought by the spinster county librarian of Jefferson, in 1943, to the attention of Jason Compson: "a picture, a photograph in color clipped obviously from a slick magazine—a picture filled with luxury and money and sunlight—a Riviera backdrop of mountains and palms and cypresses and the sea, an open powerful expensive chromium-trimmed sports car, the woman's face hatless between a rich scarf and a seal coat, ageless and beautiful, cold and serene and damned; beside her a handsome lean man of middleage in the

ribbons and tabs of a German staff general."[8] It is absolutely
appropriate that the only person in Jefferson in 1943 who would
have ever seen and noticed and clipped and folded the photo in
the slick magazine would be the librarian. Try to imagine the
difference, what kinds of attention in all forms a beautiful and
well-born Mississippi woman in the company of an enemy general
would attract in 1988.

The *New York Times* and the old *Herald Tribune* were at the top
of the national newspaper heap; but even in the limited world of
literature, they had far less power than they now have come to
possess. And, anyway, any news they brought to the South, the
Midwest, the West, arrived days late. Local papers, still mostly
independently owned, if not noticeably independent, were pretty much all that mattered. Newspapers and reporters figure in a
variety of Faulkner's works, in a folkloric kind of downhome *Front
Page* fashion. That is, they were a useful stereotype in popular
culture, one which could be at once exploited and revised, as in
Pylon.

In his last years, the years of his fame and, as well (as he saw it),
of his service—travelling the world for the nation, speaking out in
many ways on many issues, he became increasingly aware of the
inherent and implicit, as well as the overt and explicit dangers of
what we now call the media. We have some idea of what his bitter
and ironic thoughts were concerning television from the answer
he gave in November 1958 to J. Robert Oppenheimer's question—"I wonder what you think of television as a medium for the
artist."[9] To avoid serious offense, I won't repeat Faulkner's answer
here out of a complex context; but even with all its contextual
ironies, it does not suggest an enthusiastic appreciation of the
artistic possibilities of television.

We know more of Faulkner's reaction to the growing power and
pervasive influence of journalism in the two published essays out
of the five or six he once planned to be a book, tentatively titled
"The American Dream: What Happened to It." And especially
from the one more personal essay, "On Privacy," recounting some

part of his own unhappy experience with contemporary journalism and his awareness of the deeper dangers of its ruthless
impact upon liberty and equality and, as he put it, "hope for the
individual man."[10]

Speaking of the American Dream (and note that it has nothing
to do with the dream of upward mobility advanced by both
political parties in 1988 as a desirable purpose and goal in life), he
wrote in 1955: "It is gone now. We dozed, slept, and it abandoned
us. And in that vacuum now there sound no longer the strong loud
voices not merely unafraid but not even aware that fear existed,
speaking in mutual unification of our one mutual hope and will.
Because now what we hear is a cacaphony of terror and concilia-
tion and compromise babbling only the mouthsounds; the loud
and empty words which we have emasculated of all meaning
whatever—freedom, democracy, patriotism—with which,
awakened at last, we try in desperation to hide from ourselves that
loss."[11]

Faulkner was dead and gone before the aspect of popular
culture now called the cult of celebrity had fully come into focus.
There was not yet a *People* magazine or "Lifestyles of the Rich and
Famous," or, for that matter, personal posters and t-shirts; no
bumper stickers except for political campaigns; no vanity license
plates except by pure accident. Yet he sensed very strongly the
direction things were taking: "Perhaps it is impossible now for any
American to believe," he wrote, "that anyone not hiding from the
police could actually not want, as a free gift, his name and photograph in any printed organ, no matter how base or modest or
circumscribed, in circulation."[12]

What he, as an artist, died without having to know and to deal
with was the present situation wherein it can be seriously argued
that the reputation and success or failure of contemporary American artists, of popular art or, as Saul Bellow names it, private art,
of literature as well as rocking and rolling, depend not much at all
upon the inherent quality of the work or indeed upon any perception of quality by others, but purely and simply upon the publicity

one way or another engendered or aroused by the artist. Thus a Truman Capote, a Norman Mailer, a James Dickey, a Joyce Carol Oates, in their ceaseless struggle to gain and hold public attention (that is, to get publicity) though they are opposites to William Faulkner in almost every way conceivable except that all are, in Capote's case were, workers with the word, wordsmiths, different as they may be and have been, they could argue that if he had the bad fortune to live in their world and their time he would have to make his intricate *persona* even more a matter of public record and curiosity than he did, would have to spend more time cultivating his image and somewhat, maybe a good deal less, cultivating his art and craft.

Come on down to the next generation, our very youngest writers here and now, and you'll have to agree that if a meeting between William Faulkner and, say, Jay McInerney or Tama Janowitz were miraculously possible it would not be a meeting of like human beings, but a classic close encounter of the Third Kind. Among the very young and new writers only one that I know of so far, Madison Smartt Bell, though he speaks with the tongues of our own *fin de siècle*, has a fully realized sense of the American literary tradition, including the masterwork of William Faulkner.

It needs to be pointed out that even our discussion of the matter of popular culture is rich with ironies. If the novel—or at least a certain kind of novel—is at home in academic enclaves, so also (as we here bear witness) is popular culture. You can now get a Ph. D. in popular culture in many places, which really ought to be the death knell of much popular culture, but may not be. It takes one to know one, so it shouldn't surprise you that the journalists have been having a field day lately writing about the study of popular culture. For the deadly serious side there is the *Washington Post's* Jonathan Yardley whose "Pop Culture: The Academic Undiscipline" (13 June 1988) is a one-thousand word feature rage against "this trend toward trivialization" and "lazy professors and lazy students, permitting the standards of academic life to be undermined by people whose interests lie not in genuine scholarship but in careerism and self-indulgence." More fun—and maybe more typical are pieces like this one from the 26 July 1988 *New York Times*, "Academics Analyse TV/As If Soaps Were Opera." But the place of popular culture in the scheme of things is also a matter of millions of dollars. Here, a little over a week ago *(New York Times*, 25 July 1988) is S. I. Newhouse, Jr., head of many newspapers, head of Random House, and, in the magazine world, head of Conde Nast Publications. Announcing that it is now time to "reposition *Vogue* for the 90's," he offers some serious predictions for the coming decade: "He characterized coming cultural changes as 'profound' and said they included 'increasing informality' and a blurring of the rigid guidelines of what is high art and kitsch, all of which, he said, would be manifest in fashion."

Emblematic of the elaborate interchange of high art and kitsch is the much-publicized career of writer Bobbie Ann Mason, who was first of all a Ph.D. with a dissertation on Nabokov, next the author of a book in the popular culture field—*The Girl Sleuth: A Feminist Guide* (1975), and more recently a novelist of the New South, rich with brand names and flaky characters and as essentially cute as anything Disney ever dreamed up.

The one area of American popular culture which, in the end, engaged a great deal of Faulkner's time and attention and energy was of course the movies. The thing itself, the movies and going to them, doesn't play a large part in his fiction. His people don't have the time or spend a whole lot of it going to the picture show. But, in the absence of support from academe, the possibility of which arrived for the American writer just as Faulkner's life was coming to a close, and must have been yet another culture shock, he earned a lot of his living writing for the movies. Bruce Kawin has done some wonderful work on the subject in *Faulkner and Film* and I strongly recommend it to you. He is especially fine in indicating subtle interconnections—how the nature of film clearly influenced William Faulkner's fiction in a variety of ways and how, in turn, Faulkner's novels have been an important influence on a lot of film makers, especially among the Europeans. And, in addition, Kawin has contributed some good, solid scholarship, information which is greatly helpful to all of us.

There isn't a lot I can add to what has already been done by him and others. Except, maybe, to call to your attention a couple of things. One is that, in a relative sense, according to the times when he was working, William Faulkner worked on a lot of screen projects—more than most "outsiders" (writers whose primary form was not screenwriting) and more than many full-time screenwriters. Then and now there are whole successful screenwriting careers based on a lot less work. There may have been a lot about film, as art and craft, he did not know, but there simply could not have been a whole lot about *screenwriting* in America that he didn't know except how to get rich at it. Screenwriting, especially in the days of the big studios, but always really, is a very important activity but only a very small part of film making. They can't get very far without a writer, true; and it is also true that no film is likely to be a whole lot better than its treatment and its shooting script. But it is, most of the time, deeply frustrating and unsatisfying work. Faulkner figured that out pretty early. Writing screenplays teaches any writer of fiction some new things to do with narrative and language. These are the positive lessons. The negative ones are things you don't ever want to have to do again in your own work. I can see signs of both the negative and the positive reactions in William Faulkner's work after he began to write screenplays for money.

But there is something else. Except in a very few cases— *Intruder in the Dust* is one prime example of the exception to the rule—Faulkner's work is almost impossible to adapt faithfully to the screen in its own terms. Story line seems so wedded to the way of telling that translation is virtually impossible. I believe that he didn't want them hacking away at his work; but I think there is something else. Jelly Roll Morton somewhere described the elaborate and intricate harmonies he and his friends used in Gospel quartets at wakes in New Orleans. The primary motivation for the difficult harmony, he said, was to make it impossible for anybody else to jump in and join the singing. Unlike a lot of writers, Faulkner from the beginning showed a willingness to adapt his own work for film. Not much came of it; but his thinking was sound. I like to think, anyway, that he made books that he alone was capable of adapting, in spirit if not in precise detail, for the screen. That is where the money, the desperately needed money, was and would be—in selling the "property" and then in writing the screenplay for it.

I think in some of the books there are marvelous moments where we get more than a hint as to what he might have done with his own material in a screenplay adaptation. Meantime, though, he took the hack work and did it as well or better than could be expected.

There is another seldom admitted fact about working for the movies. Because it is a specialized and group enterprise, you can only learn your own part of it really well, well enough. The problem for many writers (Fitzgerald, surely, for one) was trying to learn everybody else's craft also. Faulkner knew better than that. But he also learned what everybody in the business learns sooner or later—that this astonishing new art form arrived on the scene almost fully formed. That, *essentially*, Griffith and Eisenstein did everything that could be done with film right at the outset. As Hitchcock put it more than once, the only real difference between the early films and later films is the introduction of sound. And the only difference there is that you can now hear what you had to imagine hearing. Film keeps changing all the time, but it is like a deck of cards dealt out in different hands, different arrangements. Old timers will tell you that there is probably a clear precedent for everything that can ever be done with film by 1919 or a little later.

Here, then, is the restless artist William Faulkner. No two of his novels are alike in ways and means. They may have the same voice or voices and the same complex of characters, but every single one of them has a completely different way of telling a story. Maybe if Faulkner could have exercised the power of Irving Thalberg or

Sam Goldwyn or even Harry Cohn he might have made some great films. There are enormous odds against it, however, as the odds are against all film makers.

Perhaps if one or another of the great buccaneer producers of the age had been able to recognize the genius of William Faulkner . . . who knows? But never mind. What we do know, and all that we need to know is this—that he was the man who wrote the books. And that they live.

NOTES

1. My title comes from an incident reported in Joseph Blotner, *Faulkner: A Biography*, 2 vols. (New York: Random House, 1974), 1:768.

2. *Selected Letters of William Faulkner*, ed. Joseph Blotner (New York: Random House, 1977), 461.

3. George Garrett, *James Jones* (San Diego: Harcourt Brace Jovanovich, 1984), 142.

4. *Faulkner in the University: Class Conferences at the University of Virginia, 1957–1958*, ed. Frederick L. Gwynn and Joseph L. Blotner (Charlottesville: University of Virginia Press, 1959), 243.

5. Ibid., 57–58.

6. *Sanctuary: The Corrected Text* (New York: Random House, Vintage Books, 1987), 339.

7. William Faulkner, *Essays, Speeches, and Public Letters*, ed. James B. Meriwether (New York: Random House, 1965), 192.

8. *The Portable Faulkner: Revised and Expanded Edition*, ed. Malcolm Cowley (New York: Viking, Penguin, 1987), 712–13.

9. *Faulkner: A Biography*, 2:1705.

10. *Essays, Speeches, and Public Letters*, 63.

11. Ibid., 65–66.

12. Ibid., 68.

Pop Goes the Faulkner: In Quest of *Sanctuary*

Leslie Fiedler

Though I had never stopped reading and rereading Faulkner and attempting to come to terms with his achievement in the privacy of my own head, as the eighties came to a close I realized that I had published almost nothing about any of his books for more than a quarter of a century. During that time, to be sure, my interest had shifted from the art novel to popular fiction: novels which please the many who prefer their reading pleasure unmediated and unexamined, like *Gone with the Wind*, rather than those, like James Joyce's *Ulysses*, which provide opportunities for classroom exegesis and analysis to the few who get their kicks out of such second-hand responses to literature. But I had begun by thinking of Faulkner as a kind of American Joyce; as how could I not in light of the fact that I had been introduced to him by critic-pedagogues who taught me to read *The Sound and the Fury* and *Absalom, Absalom!* as modernist masterpieces, modelled on *Ulysses*.

Disconcertingly, however, as I have since discovered, Faulkner may well have never read *Ulysses* at all; and though certainly he did not read *Gone with the Wind* either (his only recorded comment on it is that no story should take a thousands words to tell) certain Hollywood producers recognized affinities between his work and Margaret Mitchell's. For a while, at any rate, they considered trying to use the nostalgic and sentimental stories about the Old South, eventually gathered together under the title of *The Unvanquished*, as the basis for a film which they hoped would rival, or at least share in the spectacular box-office success of, *Gone with the Wind*. It was a hope for which there seemed some warrant, since most of those short fictions had appeared originally in the *Saturday Evening Post*, most popular of all the family slicks.

To be sure, for this very reason perhaps, Faulkner was never proud of them; or, in any case, he pretended not to be, referring to them in private correspondence as "pulp" and "trash." Clearly he was embarrassed at being able to produce stories which pleased both the editors and readers of a journal in which he appeared side by side with such critically despised panderers to popular taste as Fannie Hurst, Edna Ferber, and Octavus Roy Cohn—and was well paid for doing so. It was, indeed, precisely that embarrassment which prompted the infamous and ambiguous introductory note to *Sanctuary* in which he apologized for its weakness, describing it as "cheap because it was deliberately conceived to make money."

Yet all the same, he continued intermittently throughout his career to try to make it commercially—driven not only by economic pressures, as he found it easy to confess, but, as he found it harder to admit, by a desire, a need to communicate with the mass audience he affected to despise. Even less easily was he able to come to terms with the fact that he was good at doing so. Not only could he compete with the pros on the pages of the slicks; he could hold his own with veteran Hollywood hacks in turning out viable film scripts. Of the movies he helped write, *To Have and Have Not* and *The Big Sleep* have achieved the status of minor classics, and other well-crafted but uninspired Class B films like *The Last Slaver* continue to be replayed on cable off prime time.

In any case, both in print and on the screen, Faulkner provided pleasure to a large audience, most of whom would be unwilling to pick up except on assignment, and incapable of understanding, unless guided through them in the classroom, his denser, more complex and more critically esteemed fictions, like *The Sound and the Fury* or even *As I Lay Dying*. Finally, as I was moved to observe many years ago, Faulkner managed to please "two audiences, each unaware of the fact, much less the grounds, of the other's appreciation."

The little review essay in which I first made this observation was prompted by the appearance in 1948 of Faulkner's *Collected Stories*, most of which (as well as his extravagantly admired "The Bear") had first been published in popular family magazines. But though I have reprinted that essay twice in the years since, it seems to have made almost no impression on the Faulkner critical establishment; which is, I suppose, why I am moved once more to try to make clear the sense in which Faulkner's "pop" stories (and by the same token, his "pop" novel, *Sanctuary*) represent not works of the left hand, irrelevant or peripheral, but the essence, the very center of his achievement.

In them, certainly, we can find a clue to what is less apparent in his more involuted and pretentious fictions: the fact that Faulkner is more like such nineteenth-century popular entertainers as Dickens and Twain than such alienated authors of our own century as Proust, Mann, and Joyce. We must not be misled by Faulkner's own attempts to conceal this by identifying himself with the pioneers of modernism—particularly in the speeches which late in life he gave to academic audiences, from whom earlier on he had fled. In them, drop-out that he was, he assured the Ph.D.'s assembled in his honor that he considered Mann and Joyce the greatest authors of the age, and the former in particular the founder of a literary tradition to which he himself belonged. But such remarks seem to me to have been prompted by a kind of second-hand cultural snobbism from which Faulkner never quite recovered, after having picked it up early in life—first from his friend and mentor, Phil Stone, and then from the highbrow bohemian types with whom he associated briefly in New Orleans, Greenwich Village, and Paris.

Despite what he said and thought, however, I myself can find no evidence at all of the influence of Mann on Faulkner, and little enough of Joyce—beyond that of his poetry, which was as immune as Faulkner's own to the impact of modernism. To be sure, Faulkner sometimes uses the narrative mode called "stream of consciousness," so spectacularly exploited in *Ulysses*; but by the late '20s such interior monologues had become standard features even of the most provincial fiction. Besides, as I have already noted, Faulkner on at least one occasion asserted that he had never read *Ulysses*. To be sure, he is also on record as having asserted that he lied when he said so; so that it is finally impossible to know (he is a notoriously unreliable source of information about himself) whether or not he was lying about having lied in the first instance.

What we do know for certain is that when toward the very end of his life he accumulated a library for his residence in Charlottesville, Virginia, he included in it none of the master works of high modernism which he had publicly touted, but instead the novels of Cervantes, Hugo, Tolstoy, and even Mark Twain's *Tom Sawyer* and *Huckleberry Finn*; though while still in the full throes of his youthful snobbism, he had described Twain as "a hack writer who would not have been considered fourth rate in Europe." But it was, of course, with the complete works of Dickens that he began—as how could he not? It was, after all, from that immensely popular Victorian novelist that his mother had read to him as a boy, and it was from his books too that he had read to his own daughter. *Martin Chuzzlewitt*, in particular, seems to have possessed his imagination. Indeed, Sairy Gamp, the obese and drunken midwife, nurse, and layer-out-of-the-dead, who steals that novel from its major characters, is reembodied in Madame Reba, the comic-grotesque brothel keeper, who makes her first appearance in *Sanctuary* and her last in *The Reivers*, two of the most popular—in part for that reason perhaps—of all Faulkner's books.

Yet Faulkner himself nowhere that I know of confesses his indebtedness to Dickens; nor do the major critics of his work acknowledge it. Indeed, in the index to Cleanth Brooks's otherwise exhaustive study of the Yoknapatawpha fictions the name of that earlier novelist does not even appear. Albert Guerard, to be sure, in *The Triumph of the Novel* deals with the affinities between Faulkner and Dickens and Dostoevsky. What interests him, however, is what he takes to be the antimimetic, ludic, nonrepresentational narrative mode of their novels, the sense in which they can be understood to have established an alternative to what F. R. Leavis called "the Great Tradition": a countertradition which climaxes in our own time in the postmodernist fictions of Nabokov, Pynchon, Burgess, Hawkes, Barth, and Barthelme. He therefore never pauses to reflect on the fact that both the popular nineteenth-century forerunners of Faulkner, quite unlike their alienated twentieth-century successors, were shamelessly cliché-ridden and unabashedly sentimental; and that it was this, indeed, which kept them unalienated from the mass audience.

But so (despite his ambivalence about making it in the marketplace) is Faulkner. Like Dickens before him—and unlike more recent writers who prefer irony to pathos—the sentimental is for him a prevailing mode. This is conspicuously true of his war stories, whether of World War I or the War between the States, in which the soupiest platitudes of self-sacrifice, blind courage, and honor are unabashedly exploited. But it tends to overwhelm him, too, whenever he deals with wide-eyes small boys, sturdy yeoman farmers, and faithful black servants. It manifests itself even in *The Sound and the Fury*, where, despite the nihilism suggested by the Shakespearean quotation evoked in the title ("a tale told by an idiot . . . signifying nothing"), the final word in it is given to the believing Christian—as true blue as she is true black—Dilsey. It is a last minute cop-out reinforced by the phrase devoted to her in the appendix (an instant cliché, if there ever was one), "They endured."

Much admired by the flintiest-hearted elitist critics—afraid perhaps that to denigrate her might seem "racist"—Dilsey seems to me a dismayingly stock character, an Aunt Jemima type, scarcely distinguishable from the Black Mammy in whose arms Scarlett O'Hara seeks refuge at the end of *Gone with the Wind*; or for that matter, from Harriet Beecher Stowe's equally pious and faithful Uncle Tom (the gender difference is irrelevant, since both are essentially sexless). But finally, of course, almost all of

Faulkner's females are stereotypes, though few of them are as benign as Dilsey. Beside Black Mammies like her, the only women in Faulkner rendered sympathetically are certain safely postmenopausal white old maids and widows. Fully sexed women are typically regarded with horror; except—in the opinion of many readers, including not a few academic "specialists" in Faulkner—Ruby Lamar: that cliché Whore with a Heart of Gold, who seems to me always on the verge of breaking out into a tearful chorus of "He's my May-un." It should be remembered, however, that Horace Benbow, closest thing to a spokesman for the author in *Sanctuary*, finally turns in despair from Ruby, describing her as just another "stupid mammal."

In any case, all the other women in that profoundly misogynist novel, like most of their sisters everywhere in Faulkner's oeuvre, are products of the flipside of Faulkner's sentimental attitude toward their sex: his nauseated rage at them for refusing in "reality" to live up to the idealizing stereotypes of them as inviolate temples, sanctuaries of innocence. As in Dickens, the pejorative antistereotypes cued by that rage in Faulkner become, without ceasing to be stereotypes, caricatures, grotesques, at once horrific and comic. Think of Madame Reba once more—and specifically of the truly Dickensian scene after Red's funeral, in which she and two other brothel keepers weep for the indignities of their sex—while a young relation of one of them drinks himself silly on the beer he has snitched behind their sobbing backs. It is perhaps because we are asked to laugh at rather than weep over such characters that even those of us totally committed to the esthetics of modernism continue to find them acceptable. Certainly, ever since Oscar Wilde, the critical establishment has refused to be moved by the plight of such stereotyped monsters of incredible innocence as Little Nell, but has felt no qualms about responding to that of such equally stereotyped monsters of malevolence as Sally Brass and Quilp.

If Faulkner has proved easier for modernists to come to terms with than his Victorian master, this is because though there are in his work Quilps in great plenty (most of them called Snopes) and not a few Sally Brasses, there are no Little Nells. Even little Caddy in *The Sound and the Fury*, whom he once rather disconcertingly described as his "heart's darling," he does not kill off before the fall of puberty as Dickens did Little Nell, but permits to grow up and lose her mythological innocence; as, indeed, he had foreshadowed from the very start by portraying her in "muddy drawers." In any case, throughout his earliest and best fiction (late in his career he tries, unconvincingly I think, to redeem them) Faulkner vilifies women, drawing on the copious stock of misogynist platitudes current in his time and place.

"No Jiggs and Maggie cliché of popular anti-feminism," I wrote nearly thirty years ago in *Love and Death in the American Novel*, "is too banal for him to use; he reminds us (again and again) that men are helpless in the hands of their mothers, wives and sisters . . . that females do not think but proceed from evidence to conclusions by paths too devious for males to follow . . . that they possess neither morality nor honor . . . that they are capable of betraying without guilt, but also of inexplicable loyalty . . . that they enjoy an occasional beating at the hands of men . . . that they are unforgiving and without charity to members of their own sex." What I did not then add, perhaps because I was not yet ready to confront head-on *Sanctuary*, of which it is the declared theme, is the final item of this pop misogynist credo: "women are completely impervious to evil."

With such views of the second sex, quite obviously the stereotypical Happy Ending of Boy-Gets-Girl, so dear to the hearts of the popular audience, is unavailable to Faulkner. Indeed (as Albert Guerard has so persuasively contended) consummated heterosexual passion is for him a taboo, a forbidden form of love. But in this regard he is scarcely unique among American writers, on all levels from the highest of high novelists to the purveyors of the sleaziest pop, who have managed (as I have been pointing out throughout my critical career) to provide an alternative happily-ever-after, which has pleased many and pleased long: joining together in the wilderness two males, one a white man or boy in flight from the world of white women, the other a nonwhite, red, black, or brown, but in any case at home in the wilderness.

Such interethnic male bonding is to be found not only in our classic literature from Cooper to Melville and Twain; but it constitutes the erotic or sentimental center of latterday youth bestsellers like *One Flew Over the Cuckoo's Nest*. It has become finally a stereotype reimagined over and over in Hollywood movies, like *The Fortune Cookie* or *The Defiant Ones*; and it is a cliché reembodied on television, especially on the Cop Shows in which a salt-and-pepper pair ride side by side in a squad car or back each other up on the streets, as, for instance, in current favorites like *Spenser for Hire* or *Miami Vice*. Needless to say, it is also to be found in Faulkner's most popular works, including *Intruder in the Dust, The Reivers,* and, especially, "The Bear," which has the dubious distinction of being considered by high-tone critics among the best of Faulkner's stories and at the same time having pleased the middlebrow editors and readers of the *Saturday Evening Post*.

Beneath such frozen stereotypes of interethnic male bonding (as Faulkner no doubt intuited) there lies a genuine myth of love, whose archetypal resonance no travesty ever quite destroys. To be sure, its primary appeal is to males; yet females too respond to it, despite its misogynist overtones. After all, though Melville once expressed doubts that any woman could read *Moby Dick* with pleasure, many have—or at least have claimed to; responding positively also to *Huckleberry Finn* and, apparently (some 80 percent of the readers of the journal in which it first appeared were women) "The Bear" as well.

From the very beginnings of our literature, however, writers—principally but not exclusively females addressing a female audience—have exploited another myth of love, as appealing as that of interethnic male bonding to boys and men, or that of Boy-Gets-Girl to readers of both sexes. This is the theme of Brother-Sister incest in all its variations: witting and unwitting, narrowly averted or tragically consummated. Its classic formulation is found, of course, in Edgar Allan Poe's best-loved story, "The Fall of the House of Usher"; but long before Poe, it had been exploited over and over in certain best-selling women's novels of the late eighteenth and very early nineteenth centuries. Moreover, realizing its appeal, Melville made it the archetypal erotic center of *Pierre*, the only book he ever deliberately wrote to attract the female audience. It is scarcely surprising then to find it recurring over and over in Faulkner, who instinctively, as it were (it is a talent shared by all truly popular writers) realized how deeply it lay embedded in the collective unconsciousness of America. Not only is it present in *Flags in the Dust, The Sound and the Fury,* and, most notoriously, in *Absalom, Absalom!* but it persists even in *Sanctuary,* especially in its first inchoate version, in which Faulkner had not yet disentangled the Popeye-Temple story from the Sartoris saga.

Neither of those two primary erotic myths, however, is to be found in the master works of high modernism, in which they tend to be replaced by the self-serving secondary myth of the *poete maudit,* the unloved alienated artist, alternatively portrayed as symbolically killing his bourgeois father or wandering through the nighttime city in quest of him. Such portraits of the artist as a rejected and disaffected young man are conspicuous by their absence in most of Faulkner's fiction. The closest thing to it, perhaps, is Horace Benbow, who is specifically characterized as an artist in *Flags in the Dust,* but not, interestingly enough, in either version of *Sanctuary.* Quentin Compson, to be sure, seems an artist in embryo in *The Sound and the Fury,* but we know, of course, that he commits suicide while still short of maturity. And though Horace survives into middle age, he disappears from the continuation of his story in *Requiem for a Nun,* being replaced by Gavin Stevens, who typifies the "intellectual" mouthpieces in Faulkner's later novels. Like Horace, he is an overeducated lawyer with a degree from an elite university; but unlike him, he can swap yarns with the old boys on the front porch, sporting a Phi

Beta Kappa key which none of them recognizes. He seems to me, finally, to symbolize the nonalienation of the popular artist: functioning not as a distrusted creator of fictions ordinary people cannot understand or as a prophet intruding into the larger community uninvited and unwelcome; but as an amateur detective called upon in moments of disaster and confusion—in short, not merely accepted but *needed*.

It was in large part for this reason that of all pop genres the detective story proved most attractive to Faulkner, who prized it, too, because it preserved the traditional Aristotelian plot structure, which is to say, told a "story" in the old-fashioned sense of the word. But such linear narratives, with a last minute recognition and reversal (the "O. Henry hook" they called it contemptuously) had been disavowed by modernist novelists, who preferred to it the climaxless "epiphany" perfected by James Joyce. Certainly, Faulkner exploited that pop form not only in later works like *Knight's Gambit* and *Intruder in the Dust*, but in *Sanctuary*, his first truly popular book, which outsold everything he had written before it and stayed in print during the long years of critical eclipse when almost everything else he had written had ceased to be available except in libraries. It was *Sanctuary*, in any case, which first made Faulkner's a familiar name to the general reader, and persuaded Hollywood not just to hire him as a scriptwriter but to make a film version of that book. That movie, in which he himself had no hand, proved to be very bad indeed, its horrific details euphemized to the point of incoherence, and has been deservedly forgotten; but his versions of the work of others, which its sale helped make possible, were often quite good—best of all (as might well have been expected) his screenplay of Raymond Chandler's detective story, *The Big Sleep*.

It was not, however, only such factors, plus Faulkner's ambivalent yearning to reach the mass audience, which attracted him to that pop genre. Two older writers, whom he admired and emulated, had also tried their hand at it: Dickens, of course, to begin with and his great-grandfather, as well, with whom he shared a name and sought desperately to identify. The "Old Colonel," it should be remembered, had been not only a heroic warrior, which Faulkner sometimes pretended to be but could not help acknowledging finally was beyond his power; he was also the author of a best-selling novel called *The White Rose of Memphis*, which was a murder mystery, complete with detectives, disguises, false accusations, and the final exposure of the guilty; and here his grandson could hope at least to emulate him.

Faulkner, moreover, seems clearly to have been influenced by two of the most popular American detective story writers of the 1920s, S. S. Van Dine and Dashiell Hammett—the former of whom he must have read in hardcovers, while the latter came to him via the pulp magazines which we know he used to read. The evidence is less clear that Faulkner ever bought any of the novels of Van Dine; but it is hard for me to believe he did not; since he had been introduced by Phil Stone to *The Creative Will*, a critical study which Van Dine had published under his true name, Willard Huntington Wright. It must surely have tickled Faulkner to realize that the author, who under that name had written a book attacking all popular art as the refuge of the vulgar and ignorant, under his pseudonym had grown rich and famous by writing mysteries for precisely that despised audience. In those books, moreover, Philo Vance, the amateur sleuth who is their hero, echoes the elitist sentiments of *The Creative Will*, thus compounding the ironies. Finally—in one more turn of the screw— Faulkner seems to have modelled his own favorite sleuth, Gavin Stevens, on Philo Vance, making him, like his prototype, a supersophisticated, garrulous, and grandiloquent amateur given to mouthing highminded platitudes about philosophy, politics, psychology, and esthetics.

In *Sanctuary*, however, Gavin Stevens is absent—except as dimly foreshadowed in the self-pitying, ineffective figure of Horace Benbow, who moves through an underworld milieu of pervasive corruption and violence much like that in which Hammett's pitiless and effective Private Eyes operate successfully. The style of *Sanctuary*, moreover, except when Horace's drunken babbling spills over into its text, consists of short declarative sentences, without subordination, more like those of Hammett than Van Dine, whom, Hammett, in fact, had excoriated in print for his stylistic pretentiousness. The language of *Sanctuary*, too, is more like Hammett's: lean and mean, close to the tight-lipped, hard-boiled speech of the streets. Nor does Faulkner's pop novel resemble Hammett in style and diction alone. Its final ironic plot twist, in which Popeye, who has escaped hanging for murders he has actually committed is executed for one which he has not, is so closely anticipated in one of Hammett's Continental Cop stories, that it is difficult to believe Faulkner had not read and remembered it.

In any case, insofar as *Sanctuary* is a detective story, it is one in the tradition of lowbrow pulp *schlock à la* Hammett, rather than of the kitschy middlebrow slicks so congenial to S. S. Van Dine. Yet Hammett—though he had by that time met Faulkner in Hollywood and they had become mutually destructive drinking buddies—when he finally got around to reading *Sanctuary*, did not esteem it very highly. "Mr. Faulkner," he wrote, "is over-rated by such people as have read him at all. He has a nice taste in the morbid and the gruesome, but doesn't seem to do much with it." Faulkner, on the other hand, has left no recorded response to any of Hammett's fiction, only a strange comment on his character, an incredible valedictory which shocked Lillian Hellman, to whom he observed, "He drank too much."

Nonetheless, even as Hammett and Faulkner expressed such distrust of each other, certain eminent French authors like André Malraux and Albert Camus were touting them both, associating them with each other as presumably neglected American geniuses who had redeemed the *roman policier* by raising that pop genre to the level of Greek tragedy. Yet, as Malraux himself was moved to remark, *Sanctuary* is an odd sort of *roman policier*, being a detective story without a proper detective. Horace Benbow, it is true, equivocally identifies himself as such at one point, when he is asked, "are you a detective?" and answers, "Yes . . . yes. No matter. It doesn't matter." But he is really of course only a small town lawyer, and not a very good one at that, who spends more time worrying about the indignities of being married to a woman married once before and wrestling with his incestuous attraction to his step-daughter and his sister than in solving the case of murder and rape in which he finds himself involved.

His single real feat of detection is discovering that Temple Drake has been present at the scene of the crime and locating her in her whorehouse retreat. But though he seems for a moment to have persuaded her into testifying on behalf of his falsely accused client, Lee Goodwin, she finally clinches the prosecution's case by deliberately lying on the witness stand; thus exculpating Popeye, who is actually guilty, and condemning Lee—not just in the eyes of the jury who sentence him to death, but the larger community who torture and lynch him. To be sure, as we have already noticed, Popeye does not finally escape scot-free either, eventually committing a kind of suicide by refusing to defend himself against charges of having committed another murder of which he is innocent. The reasons for his complicity in his own death, Faulkner never makes clear; but they are (I am convinced) somehow connected to his ambiguous relationship with the woman whose lying testimony has seemed initially to deliver him from hanging. In the end, the only major character in *Sanctuary* who is left not merely undestroyed, but untouched by guilt is that woman herself, Temple Drake, though she is, directly or indirectly, responsible for all the deaths that occur in its pages.

The final effect of *Sanctuary* is, in any event, precisely the opposite of that created by the detective story in its closed middlebrow form, at least as that effect is described by W. H. Auden in his immensely persuasive essay "The Guilty Vicarage." Its resolution, that is to say, does not restore the community in which the crime has occurred to a state of Edenic innocence—by identifying a single source of guilt and thus exculpating all the initially suspected others. Instead, that entire community is revealed as

guilty along with the nominal criminal, who is merely a scape-
goat ritually punished for its sins; and the question therefore of
who is "really" guilty turns out to be irrelevant. But if *Sanctuary*
is, in this sense, an antidetective story, so also are most of Hammett's as well as those of his disciples and imitators from Raymond
Chandler to Mickey Spillane.

Many critics have, of course, realized the sense in which *Sanctuary* is such a detective, or rather antidetective story, and not few
have recognized as well its indebtedness to the gangster novels
and movies, which possessed the imagination of the mass audience in the era of Prohibition, bootlegging, and the Valentine
Day Massacre. It is hard, indeed, to miss its affinities to that form;
ending as it does with the expected, almost required death of the
gangster-in-chief—and evoking along the way most of the stereotypes associated with the genre. Certainly, its criminal characters
are stereotyped, from Popeye himself, the gunsel whose phallic
power resides only in the killing machine holstered under his
arm, to the standard crew of scarcely articulate hard guys who
protect him and run his booze—including Red, the handsome
stud he engages to pleasure Temple and finally murders. And
lurking in the background is the predictable shyster mouthpiece:
"the Jew lawyer from Memphis," who apparently orchestrates the
final courtroom scene.

Few, however, seem to have realized that *Sanctuary* includes a
potpourri of almost *all* the popular genres of the late 1920s. Yet
Faulkner himself boasted in his introduction of having put into it
everything that "a person in Mississippi would believe to be
current trends"—meaning, of course, not what would be considered chic in the realm of high art, but whatever was currently
fashionable in the well-paying slicks and the penny-a-word pulps.
Notable among these is the tale of "Flaming Youth" or "Our
Dancing Daughters," immensely popular in a time when appalled
parents stared across a widening generation gap at their jazz-age
offspring—liberated by "coeducation," the automobile, and the
sexual revolution. Certainly Temple Drake, whatever she finally

becomes, enters the scene in the guise of a typical longlegged teenaged flapper, as played by Clara Bow or the young Joan Crawford; a co-ed *demi-vierge* in scandalously short skirts, who might well have been drawn by John Held, Jr., the favorite cartoonist of the period. Similarly, Gowan Stevens is a standard collegeboy type, a callow youth who cannot hold his drinks and learns it the hard way.

The two of them seem, indeed, almost comic characters in quest of an appropriate comic denouement. But this, of course, they do not find; even though, as the book moves toward its close, it becomes more and more humorous. One could, in fact, extract from its otherwise grim pages a collection of "funny stories," which constitute another enduring pop genre. These range from the rather hackneyed, but much admired (*over*admired, I am convinced) "Stupid Rube in the Big City" anecdote, in which a pair of Snopeses take a brothel for a hotel, to the Dickensian vignette of the three Mourning Madams and the drunken small boy. My own favorite, however, is the brutally hilarious scene at Red's wake, in which his coffin is upset by his drunken comrades (even as the band plays "Sonny Boy"), and his body is flung to the ground, dislodging the wax plug which had concealed the bullethole in his forehead. It is a classic example of what we have come only recently to call, though we did not invent it, "black humor": the kind of joke in bad taste which recurs in the last sentences of *Sanctuary*'s penultimate episode, in which Popeye—with the noose already around his neck—says to the sheriff, "Fix my hair, Jack," and the sheriff answers, "Sure . . . I'll fix it for you," springing the trap.

But at this point we are on the borderline between nausea and laughter which is to say, between humor and horror. And this should remind us that still another pop genre much on Faulkner's mind as he wrote and rewrote *Sanctuary* is the Horror Story as practiced from the time of Poe to that of Lovecraft and Stephen King. "Horrific" is, indeed, the word he customarily used to describe that novel—and horrific it is in good faith. Indeed, there is scarcely any of the stock effects of the horror genre, audio or video, which it lacks: from the tap-tap-tap of a blind man's stick to the rustle of rats in a corncrib, the ominous thud of a muffled gunshot off scene, the crackle of flames from the lynch-mob's bonfire, and the barely audible whisper of blood in Temple's ravaged body. So, too, do the standard grotesques of the Gothic Romance abound: "crips" and "feebs" and freaks, not least of which is Popeye himself—more monster than human, more shadow than substance. "The black man," Temple and Horace call him, aware perhaps that this is a traditional American name for the Devil. And there is, too, of course, the infamous bloody corncob, an ikon of unspeakable evil, for which *Sanctuary* is remembered even by those who have never read it; though Faulkner alludes to it only briefly at a point where his horrific tale is nearly told.

But finally—and essentially—the novel which Albert Camus believed to be the greatest of Faulkner's fictions belongs to the most disreputable and unredeemable pop genre of all, being pornography, as the dictionary defines that pejorative term, "a portrayal of erotic behavior designed to cause sexual excitement." Though there are many such portrayals in Faulkner's work of "erotic behavior," including such kinky subvarieties as pedophilia, necrophilia, incest, and bestiality, *Sanctuary* was the only one of his books which its intended publisher refused at first to publish, presumably as too "dirty." Yet it is in some ways the softest of soft porn—avoiding not only what were then still considered "dirty" words, but explicit descriptions in any words of the sex act itself. The brutal violation of Temple, for instance, is rendered solely in terms of her fantasies, climaxing in her hallucination of turning into a boy—popping a teeny-tiny penis; though, of course, that male organ is called by none of its grosser street names.

Nonetheless, however soft, *Sanctuary* is sadomasochistic porn in the tradition of the divine Marquis's *Justine* and *Juliette*, ambiguously and disturbingly blurring the distinction between murder and desire, violence and passion, *thanatos* and *eros*. Its central image of love therefore (after all, insofar as he can, Popeye loves Temple, and in her way Temple loves him) is Rape. But Rape, however abhorrent in fact, is an image of true archetypal resonance, which has provided a mythic erotic center for a large number of works which have pleased many and pleased long. These include not just banned books like de Sade's, but many classics and longtime family favorites ranging from Shakespeare's *Titus Andronicus* and Samuel Richardson's *Clarissa* to *Gone with the Wind*, the Tarzan series (in which everyone she encounters attempts to rape Jane), and those currently popular Women's Romances, whose beautiful protagonists not infrequently end up marrying the balefully attractive males who began by ravishing them.

All such stories represent, in any case, latter-day avatars of the ancient archetype of the *donna fuggiata*, the Pursued Woman: a primordial image which, no matter how the actual relations of the sex may change, persists in the deep unconscious of us all. Faulkner, however, ironizes and at the same time heightens the titillation implicit in that archetype by making his rapist impotent, which is to say, not-quite-male, and portraying his intended victim as not-quite-female. Not only do both of Temple Drake's names hint at her androgynous nature, but the sexual role she plays is finally mythically "masculine." Beginning by running always in the wrong direction or not fast enough to foil those who pursue her in lust, then ceasing to run at all—she ends by becoming the sexual aggressor, the pursuer rather than the pursued. So at least she seems, in her last sexual encounter with Red, in which—as Faulkner describes it "she sprang like a bow, hurling herself upon him, her mouth gaped and ugly like that of a dying fish as she writhed her loins against him"; and we seem to be there watching, at once fascinated and repelled.

"Watching" is the operative word; since *Sanctuary*, like all true pornography, is essentially voyeuristic in its appeal. When reading it, that is to say, we do not typically identify with its erotically active characters, rapist or raped; but with the Peeping Tom author, who compels us to keep our eye glued to the keyhole, ashamed but unable to withdraw—as the author himself seems to have been in the first place. Certainly, Faulkner confessed as much in his shamefaced public apology for his novel; suggesting, to me at least, that pornography only really works for us when at some level we feel that the pleasure it provides us with is disreputable; or in any event are uncomfortably aware that others, whom we otherwise respect, consider it so—some indeed wanting to ban or burn it.

But Faulkner made such guilt-ridden voyeurism the subject as well as the mode of apprehending the novel, in which from start to finish someone seems always to be watching someone else watching him or her. Think of Popeye and Benbow staring at each other for two hours across the spring at Frenchman's Bend; or Benbow once more watching in one mirror Little Belle watching him in a reflecting other. The climax of such reflexive voyeurism, however, comes in Faulkner's rendering of the scene in which Popeye slobbers over the bed in which Temple and Red copulate at his command. That scene is represented not directly, but as reported by a black maid who has watched Popeye watching; thus putting us as readers in the position of voyeurs at a fourth remove— watching the author watching her watching them. It is this which makes *Sanctuary* unique: the first (and as far as I know, the only) piece of metapornography for which I have, for reasons I hope I have made clear, long been ashamed to confess my inordinate fondness; and which therefore, I believe, no one who reads it properly can ever be proud of liking.

Photographs in the 1929 Version of *Sanctuary*

DAVID MADDEN

In Knoxville, Tennessee, in August 1948, fifteen-year-old Jerome O'Madden—for that was my pen name of the moment—sits at a desk he shared with his two brothers until one ended up in the prison and the other in the reform school, on the back porch, enclosed and converted into a room the size of a jail cell, a room half full with his iron cot, almost one-fourth full with an icebox whose drip pan he too often forgets to empty, almost one fourth occupied by the desk, leaving a space as large as a baseball home plate to stand in, the walls covered with his drawings of writers and scenes from his own stories and movie stills he collected as a child or stole when he ushered at the Bijou, a shelf on the wall filling up with second-hand paperbacks, including *Short Stories* by his first hero Thomas Wolfe and *A Portrait of the Artist as a Young Man* by James Joyce, a hero new to his pantheon, and in this room—which he calls his Sanctuary because in a movie he saw years ago, a cathedral provided sanctuary for a romantic fugitive hero—he rides the crest of his inspiration and finishes a lyrical short story called "In the Summer They Slaughtered Cattle," set in the slums under the bluff along the Tennessee River.

Having long been fascinated in life, and having now recreated in literature, the world of the poor white trash and Negro slums, he is drawn to the actual scene. Leaving his own lower-class house, he walks in the blazing sun past the tobacco warehouse, through the Negro neighborhood, where two years ago he hawked the extra that headlined the dropping of the "Adam" bomb on Japan, and past the Bijou, the courthouse, the monuments, the jail. He walks Front Street and then climbs the path up the bluff, and enters a rat-infested store, jam-packed with second-hand books and magazines. Once an infamous saloon, the book-store reeks of stale beer and piss and tobacco, perches on stilts above the kudzu-laced bluff at the end of the Gay Street Bridge above the Tennessee River, run by an old lady with the help of her circus side-show fat son.

He looks at each greasy magazine and dusty hardcover and paperback book in the store *once more,* and is drawn again to James M. Cain's *Serenade.* As a writer who is still not sure he won't also become an artist—or a private detective—he is drawn again to the bizarre art work on the cover of *Sanctuary* by William Faulkner, as he had been repeatedly attracted to the high art tone of the Penguin and Signet covers of the *Short Stories of Thomas Wolfe* and *A Portrait of the Artist as a Young Man*—and earlier to Erskine Caldwell's *God's Little Acre,* the first novel he ever read. He sees that all four covers are by the same artist, Robert Jonas, one of the few who signs his cover art.

Jonas's cover art conveys what he knows is the public attitude about this writer and this book, that *Sanctuary* is dirty, full of violence, sex, corruption, perversion, insanity, incest, death, that it is morbid, squalid, pessimistic, grim, obscure, decadent, bizarre, revolting, that it has all the notorious qualities of a trashy pulp detective story and is a cheap exploitation of the characteristics of the works of Edgar Allen Poe. But in the "About the Author" note on the back under a photo of Faulkner, showing a weak mouth and chin that suffers comparison with the godlike writer image of Thomas Wolfe and the black-patch genius image of James Joyce, and in the "About This Book" note inside the front, many of those negative words are used in a bewilderingly approving way.

> Faulkner has been called the modern master of the Grand Guignol. His novels are as full of rape, incest, violence, death and corruption as the plays of Webster and Tourneur. And he has been placed with Bierce and Poe in the category of the horror story.
>
> *Sanctuary* is his most violent work. On the surface it is a story of

action, a gangster story. The plot evolves around Popeye, the impotent killer, as around some monstrous spider. . . .

Perhaps his unique contribution to American literature, though, is his ability to convey feeling—the below-the-conscious stream of horror, suspense, despair—the emotional complex of illiterate characters. Faulkner describes the indescribable: insanity, intoxication, the moment of love, the moment of death, the secret, unplumbed depths of the soul. Like Webster, he "sees the breastless creatures underground lean backward with a lipless grin."

Jerome O'Madden's own private feelings about Faulkner's public reputation are ambivalent—that he is sordid and sleazy but somehow artistic—attraction and repulsion simultaneously. He is drawn himself to the sordid elements in his observations of life in the slums and in his own writings—"In the Summer They Slaughtered Cattle"—but he is also in the throes of a recent religious conversion and *Sanctuary* reeks of the forbidden, maybe the blasphemous. He is afraid of this book, as if it were *a thing*, contagious to the touch. And the cover art embodies all these conflicting feelings. His general impression is that it is a trashy illustration like those on many willfully trashy-looking magazines and books, but he senses an artistry about it, that it is not simply a dashed-off illustration, that it illustrates a deliberate conception.

The red and green on the top and bottom borders is dominant in the decayed green, pocked wall, splattered with blood, and in the photograph of a woman in a mauve kimono stuck to that wall with a hat pin. The photo is ripped violently around the edges and across the woman's body at the waist and again, slashed aslant her belly just above her groin. One arm is behind her head, the other across her face, obscuring it as if she is profoundly ashamed of what she does in the book itself.

I pick it up as I once picked up, when I was a little boy, a discarded condom on a creek bank, with deep repulsion and fascination.

Because the public disapproves of this writer, even scorns him for his sensational, money-making greed and because there are signs he is also somehow an artist, I feel an affinity with him even as I sneer with the rest of the world at him. I buy the used copy of *Sanctuary* and walk out into the August light, holding it in my grimy hand, as I hold it before you at this very moment, reverently preserved like Lenin or Snow White in its own encasement.

I walked back through the Faulknerian landscape and cityscape of Knoxville, Tennessee, to my cramped sanctuary, where I read again the opening page: "From beyond the screen of bushes which surrounded the spring, Popeye watched the man drinking."

To the degree that photographs in Faulkner's fiction are important, the two published versions of *Sanctuary* offer the most interesting examples for study.

What I paid almost no attention to at all when I first read the 1931 version of *Sanctuary* and reread it years later was Faulkner's use of photographs. I missed it again when I read the 1929 manuscript version that was published in 1981. Even so, my response to the invitation to talk to the popular culture emphasis in Faulkner's work was instant—Faulkner and photographs. Given the fact that I had to scan all of Faulkner to conclude that only in *Sanctuary* does Faulkner make significant use of photographs, why did I think so readily of photographs? Because in the 1929 version of *Sanctuary* Faulkner makes repeated and complex use of the photograph of Horace Benbow's thirteen-year-old step-daughter Little Belle—enhanced by a long description of many portrait photographs and snapshots on the wall beside Miss Jenny's bed. It is Horace Benbow who contemplates these photographs as refuge from the complexities of dealing with Little Belle and other women *in the flesh*. That there is also a photograph of Narcissa (63) and metaphorical "pictures" of Belle enhanced the impact of the seven passages devoted to Little Belle's photograph.

In the 1931 version, the one that most people have read, and that Leslie Fiedler took as his text last night, Horace's final response to Little Belle's photograph—as he vomits, his consciousness fuses with that of a woman having sex—is in-

Cover by Robert Jonas, Penguin edition, *Sanctuary*

comprehensible, as is much of the rest of that version of the novel. A major consideration is this: it is commonly assumed that Horace's consciousness merges with Temple's because Faulkner refers to the corn shucks upon which she was violated but in spite of the fact that the vague pronoun "she" was used. The 1929 version makes extensive and deliberate use of male and female pronouns to create ambiguity; given Horace's consciousness as the context, I am convinced that readers are to suppose that Horace's confusion and fusion of identities satisfies some psychic need. "He tried to think of his sister, of Belle. But they seemed interchangeable now" (27). The three women Horace observes making "unabashed toilets" in public suggest Belle, Narcissa, and Ruby (66).

Faulkner's use of the photograph in the 1929 version is the best place to begin for anyone who, like myself, would argue that the 1929 version is the superior version.

Looking again this year at Robert Jonas's cover art for the 1947 paperback edition of the 1931 version of *Sanctuary* that most people revere or revile, I was astounded to see that he, unknowingly, had chosen an image from the novel that captures the concept of the 1929 version far more effectively than the 1931 version. It was the 1931 version that Robert Jonas read, but it is an example of the inadvertent, accidental wisdom of popular culture that his paperback cover art conceptualizes the 1929 version.

Forty years later I suddenly realize what that cover captured. That is proof either that I have done the longest double take in the history of human perception or that what is most effective and enduring is what is least obvious and most suggestive.

Robert Jonas seriously read every book for which he painted a cover and tried to conceptualize that book, not just illustrate a scene from it. Through some fault of memory, he has offered on the *Sanctuary* cover a photograph not of Little Belle but of *a* woman. There is no photograph of Temple Drake in the novel. Most of the passages in which Horace responds to the photographs of Little Belle, Faulkner cut out of the 1931 version. One might expect then that a serious illustrator would hardly notice the two remaining descriptions of the photograph itself, would certainly not feature a detail so incidental on the cover, and certainly not in a way that would make Horace, by implication, the main character. In the 1931 version, Horace is no longer the meditative hero. But the passage in which Horace goes from looking at a photograph of Little Belle to merging his own consciousness with that of a woman being raped had such a profound effect on the consciousness of this serious modern painter that he offers a ripped-up photograph of a woman, face obscured. For the 1931 version, this figure emblemizes four people, all of whom are facets of Horace's psyche: Little Belle-Temple and Horace-Popeye.

My own guess is that despite his intellectual and emotional fidelity to his work, Jonas has expressed quite unconscious associations that are perfectly true to Faulkner's intention—but *in the version of the book Jonas didn't read,* still latent in the revised one that he did read; in his own painterly technique, he illustrated Faulkner's direct use of photographs in *Sanctuary* and the complex effects achieved by that use.

July 21, 1988, at seven and at eight o'clock: I stopped writing to call Robert Jonas in Brooklyn. I asked him what he remembered about creating the cover. He said he would dig up a copy and call me back. He did. He had only a few of the books he illustrated left now, he said, and *Sanctuary* was one of them, but he no longer had the original drawing. "My good friend William DeKooning, a great painter, said it was the best cover I ever did. I am a poet, not an illustrator. I never *illustrated* a cover. I was never literal. I used symbolism or metaphor. I have not looked at this cover in years. I was amazed. The photograph seems to have been ripped up and hidden away, and then somebody has pinned it to a wall as if to remember the time in which it was taken. The wall is bloody. This is what I find astonishing," he said. "The wall is pocked as if it were a damaged membrane, symbolizing the rape of Temple." Nothing Jonas said made me feel that he had *consciously* tried to conceptualize the way Horace—to Jonas's perception—merged the thirteen-year-old Belle with the seventeen-year-old Temple.

A new Signet cover came out only one year later, 1949, by an anonymous hack; it was very crude, very trashy, and, above all, but typical, misleading: Popeye on the left is eyeing Temple, who appears to be already a prostitute soliciting him. The concept is all wrong, but the emphasis on Popeye and Temple is true to the narrative thrust of Faulkner's 1931 version.

Faulkner opened the 1929 version with a condemned black man framed in the barred window, observed by Horace. At the end of the novel, Popeye falls through a windowlike opening, a rope around his neck. The literal descriptions of photographs in *Sanctuary* are enhanced by these photographlike symbols and metaphors.

There are numerous instances throughout *Sanctuary* of Horace and others motionless, framed, looking out of windows of cars, houses, jails, and other buildings, and of Horace observing people framed by windows or doorways. The effect is like that of a framed photograph. Horace and Miss Jenny watch through the window as Narcissa, her boy, and Gowan walk in the garden (35). In a letter to Narcissa near the end, Horace's final words, referring to Ruby and Goodwin, are: "She's there now, in front of the jail with that child, standing where he can see them from the window: have I not seen her there a thousand times?" (283).

Horace has a compulsion to perceive or conceive of himself and others frozen in time and space.

> And he thought at the time of the two of them—Popeye and himself—facing one another across the spring. Only the water seemed to move, to have any purpose. . . . Not only the air, but time, sunlight, silence, all appeared to stand still . . . . the two figures facing one another decorously, were isolated out of all time. . . . (23) Popeye and Goodwin and the woman. . . .three figures fixed forever in the attitudes in which he had left them, waiting for him to return. . . . (26)
> Presently all sense of motion ceased. The truck seemed to be suspended motionless. . . . (30)

Those are three of several instances in the first thirty pages. Near the end, Horace thinks, "I can't even face the picture" (260). Even when he satisfies a need to fix life in a "picture," he cannot face the picture itself.

Six pages before he looks at his own and Popeye's reflections in the spring, Horace embraces Little Belle between two mirrors: She calls him "Shrimp," then recants, "flinging herself upon him in a myriad secret softnesses beneath firm young flesh and thin small bones. 'I didn't mean that! Horace! Horace!' And he could smell that delicate odor of dead flowers engendered by tears and scent, and in two mirrors he saw her secret, streaked small face watching the back of his head with pure dissimulation, forgetting that there were two mirrors" (15). Literal mirrors of glass or water as a mirror appear frequently throughout *Sanctuary*, images caught as in photographs. There is a blackened, broken mirror in the Goodwin house; Temple uses a mirror in the whorehouse.

Four pages later, Faulkner describes for the first time the framed snapshot of Little Belle. It sits on his desk in his study.

> On the desk sat a photograph in a silver frame. Within the frame the small, soft face mused in sweet chiaroscuro. He looked at it quietly, wondering at what age a man ceases to believe he must support a certain figure before even the women at whose young intimacies he has made one: counsellor, handmaiden, and friend. Upon the silence there seemed to lie the reverberant finality of the slammed door, and he thought of Little Belle beyond it, lying face-down on the bed probably, in that romantic despair, that dramatic self-pity of the young . . . . From the desk he took a pipe and tobacco pouch. Then he tried to slip the photograph inside his breast pocket, but the *frame* was too wide. He worked it free of the frame and it went in. (19, my italics)

Horace takes it out if its frame as he leaves the house to move into his mother's empty house. So the photograph is probably in his pocket when he stares at Popeye across the spring five days later.

The image that has stayed with me over the years is of Popeye and Horace staring at each other for two hours across that spring.

In 1948 I did not realize how important to the overall conception of the 1931 version that first photographlike image at the
spring was. It is far more important in the 1929 version.

Two pages after the first description of the photograph of Little
Belle, now twenty-one pages into the novel, Faulkner slips into
the scene at the spring, but the point of view in this 1929 version is
always Horace's, not first Popeye's and then Horace's, as in the
1931 version.

> . . . a bird sang. He listened to it as he knelt his face into the reflected
> face in the water, hearing the bird above the cool sound of his
> swallowing. When he rose, the surface of the water broken into a
> myriad glints by the dripping aftermath of his drinking, he saw among
> them the shattered reflection of the straw hat.
>
> The man was standing beyond the spring, his hands in his coat
> pockets, a cigarette slanted from his pallid chin. . . . he had that
> vicious depthless quality of stamped tin. (21)

In both versions, Popeye and Horace seem to be polar opposites in many ways—obviously in that Popeye carries a concealed pistol, Horace a concealed book. But the 1931 version
places the emphasis on the relationship between Popeye and
Temple, subordinating Horace and Little Belle. The 1929 version
makes Horace's psyche the focus, and what Faulkner develops
throughout the novel is our awareness of similarities between
Horace and the impotent, voyeuristic, possibly homosexual
Popeye.

Horace himself senses a "kinship" with Popeye: "You'd think
there'd be a kinship between two people who looked on death at
the same time, even though it was from opposite sides" (52). The
two seemingly different men who watch each other across their
reflections in the spring watch other men. Popeye watches Red
copulate with Temple in the whorehouse. She taunts Popeye:
"Dont you wish he was the one watching us instead of you?" (228).
Much less obviously, Horace watches many women with their
men. Faulkner uses "pictures" to suggest that Horace and Popeye
are to be compared at every opportunity. Near the whorehouse "a

fat man in a dirty apron with a toothpick in his mouth . . . stood for an instant out of the gloom with an effect as of a sinister and meaningless photograph poorly made" (167). One thinks of Popeye with that cigarette in his mouth. Horace sees above the mantel in the whorehouse, "draped in black, the photograph of a meek-looking man with an enormous moustache" (210). The photograph suggests "meek" Horace himself.

The changes Faulkner made weakened that powerful image of Horace and Popeye at the spring. To get the action started and to focus on the story of Popeye and Temple Drake, Faulkner opened the 1931 version with the image of Popeye and Horace at the spring from Popeye's point of view.

In the 1929 version the image may have less immediate impact, but it is already more complex by implication, having been set up in earlier, parallel images that will be even further developed, and this Horace-Popeye image also will be further developed more than it was is in the 1931 version.

The 1929 version opens with twenty pages devoted to Horace's meditations on the condemned man's face in the jail window and on the women in his life—his wife, Belle, his stepdaughter, Little Belle, and his sister, Narcissa, and others, all of whom will appear in literal or metaphorical photographs.

Horace and Popeye staring at each other across their mirrorlike, but shattered reflections in the spring where Horace was drinking is the photographlike image that the literal photographs enable us to experience more fully.

> Then he would go to his room . . . where Little Belle's photograph was propped against a book on the table. He stood for a while before it, looking at the soft, sweet, vague face, thinking quietly how even at forty-three a man. . . . (59)

Horace contemplates the various types of photographs on Miss Jenny's wall.

> The first was a faded tintype in an oval frame. A bearded face stared haughtily across the neck-cloth of the '50s, buttoned into a frock coat.

The man was in the full flush of maturity's early summer; the whiskers virile, the nose high-bridged, the eyes quick-tempered and overbearing, and turning his head Horace saw a delicate replica of it above Miss Jenny's shawl, beneath the silver coronet of her hair, serenely profiled by the fire, and a shadowy, faintly sullen promise of it leaning against the mantel. He looked at the portrait again. Beside it hung a second and more hasty one, in the field: the same man in a long gray tunic with the awry shoulder-straps of a Confederate colonel. His trousers were thrust into dusty boots, his gauntleted hands rested upon the hilt of a sabre, the bearded face shadowed by a broken plume.

"What are you doing?" Miss Jenny said. "Looking at the Rogues' Gallery?"

. . . .

Next was a conventional photograph dated fifteen years ago. The man was about sixty, going bald, the mouth shaded by a thick moustache. . . .

The next was also light-stained, faintly archaic. . . . The face above the broad collar, the puffed cravat and the high lapels of the early 1900's was that of a sick man.

Next was a photograph of two boys with long curls in identical velvet suits. They were not long definitely out of babyhood yet. . . . already there was a distinction between them, although they were obviously twins.

The next three were in a row. The middle one was a painted miniature, the face that of a boy of seven or so. . . .

The curls were still there, the eyes bold and merry, the mouth sweet. It was flanked on one side by a hasty snapshot. Both operator and subject appeared to have been moving when the camera was snapped, for the picture was both lop-sided and blurred as well as out of focus. The subject's head emerged from an elliptical manhole in a tubular affair on the side of which the effigy of a rabbit projected its painted ears into the picture. To the front arc of the pit a narrow screen curved tightly, and two struts slanted upward into a flat surface at right angles in horizontal perspective, from which the pistol-grip of a machine gun tilted. The face, beneath a wild thatch, was in the act of turning when the camera snapped. It was full of movement, travestied by the dead celluloid, the eyes squinted and the mouth open, as though he were either shouting or laughing.

On the other side of the miniature was another conventional photograph. In uniform, with orderly hair, he lounged in a deep chair placed cleverly to bring the subdued light onto his bleak, humorless

face, and again Horace looked toward the fire, at the boy leaning
there. . . .

The next row consisted of nine photographs of the boy, one for each
of his years, ranging from that in which he sprawled naked on a fur
rug, through his various avatars in rompers, velvet; as an Indian, a
cowboy, a soldier, a groomsman in a diminutive tailcoat, to the final
one in which he sat the pony, erect, hand on hip, a salvaged revolver-
frame in his waist-band, a small negro perched like a monkey on the
withers of a gaunt mule in the background. . . .

Narcissa entered, with a newspaper. She drew a chair up and
opened the paper and began to read aloud, lurid accounts of arson
and adultery and homicide, in her grave contralto voice. (41– 44)

To see photographs very similar to the ones on Miss Jenny's
wall, see *William Faulkner: The Cofield Collection*. Horace is
living in his mother's empty house. Horace again contemplates
the photograph of Little Belle, for the third time.

"It's when I think of Little Belle; think that at any moment . . ."
Against the book on the table the photograph sat under the lamp.
Along the four edges of it was the narrow imprint of the missing
frame. . . . He began to whisper Damn him, damn him, tramping
back and forth before the photograph. . . . Tramping back and forth
while the soft, bemused face blurred and faded in and out of the
photograph. (143, 145)

Fleeing the house, and the photograph, he remembers the
photograph vividly.

He discovered then that he had forgotten the book. The photograph was still propped against it—the very thing which had driven
him from bed to walk four and three quarters miles in the darkness—
and his inner eye showed it to him suddenly, blurred by the highlight, and beside it his freshly loaded pipe. (149)

Clarence Snopes tells Horace he can find Temple Drake in a
Memphis whorehouse.

When he had gone Horace entered the house and turned on the
light, blinking after the subtle treachery of the moon. Little Belle's
photograph sat on the mantel. He took it down, looking at it. The light
hung on a shadeless cord, low; the shadow of his body lay upon the

photograph. He moved it so that the light fell upon it, then drew it back into the shadow again. The difference was too intangible to discern, even by its own immediate comparison; the white still white, the black still black, the secret, musing expression unaltered. Delicate, evocative, strange, looking up out the shadow with a crass brazenness, a crass belief that the beholder were blind. (205)

Unable to cope with complex contradictory female flesh, Horace turns from the active sensual Little Belle to her effigy in the photograph. She is a changeless, almost sexless symbol of innocence that offers no threat to his masculinity or his effete romanticism. But the flesh, in the form of one man or another, intrudes. "Damn him, damn him." The "him" is always ambiguous.

In pursuit of his purpose to transform the meditative 1929 version into the 1931 novel of action, Faulkner cut most of the passages describing Little Belle's photographs, leaving only an establishing description and the climactic passage in which Horace becomes a woman being raped. He also cuts the photographs on Miss Jenny's wall. What he has done here is to turn a meditative picture gallery into a motion picture. But even in the 1931 version, the cinematic technique is not one of flowing images, but the juxtaposition of static images, characteristic of Faulkner no matter how slow or fast the narrative pace may be.

Having just returned from listening to Temple Drake's story of sexual depravity in Reba's whorehouse in Memphis, Horace looks at Little Belle's photograph for the fifth and final time, becomes nauseated, vomits, merges his consciousness with a woman being raped.

> He found the light and turned it on. . . .
> Then he was looking at the photograph, holding it in his hands. Enclosed by the narrow imprint of the missing frame Little Belle's face dreamed with that quality of sweet chiaroscuro. Communicated to the cardboard by some quality of the light or perhaps by some infinitesimal movement of his hands, his own breathing, the face appeared to breathe in his palms in a shallow bath of highlight, beneath the slow, smoke-like tongues of invisible honeysuckle. Al-

most palpable enough to be seen, the scent filled the room and the small face seemed to swoon in a voluptuous languor, blurring still more, fading, leaving upon his eye a soft and fading aftermath of invitation and voluptuous promise and secret affirmation like a scent itself.

Then he knew what that sensation in his stomach meant. He put the photograph down hurriedly and went to the bathroom. He opened the door running and fumbled at the light. But he had not time to find it and he gave over and plunged forward and struck the lavatory and leaned upon his braced arms while the shucks set up a terrific uproar beneath her thighs. Lying with her head lifted slightly, her chin depressed like a figure lifted down from a crucifix, she watched something black and furious go roaring out of her pale body. She was bound naked on her back on a flat car moving at speed through a black tunnel, the blackness streaming in rigid threads overhead, a roar of iron wheels in her ears. The car shot bodily from the tunnel in a long upward slant, the darkness overhead now shredded with parallel attenuations of living fire, toward a crescendo like a held breath, an interval in which she would swing faintly and lazily in nothingness filled with pale, myriad points of light. Far beneath her she could hear the faint, furious uproar of the shucks. (220)

It is a serious distortion of the 1929 version to attribute the "she" only to Temple. Little Belle, Belle, Narcissa, Ruby, Temple, and other women bring out facets of Horace's mental and sexual problems. In the 1929 version, vicarious sexuality in reversed sex roles is developed in a complex series of variations (Temple imagines herself a boy), all facets of Horace. Popeye makes love to Red vicariously through Temple, watching them copulate, and few of Horace's vicarious relationships with men through his many women are lost in unintentional ambiguity. Throughout the 1929 version, Horace vicariously becomes *all* the women in his life at that moment when he imagines a man violated each of them. And the scene in which the photograph of Little Belle triggers Horace's shift to a woman being raped is the major instance; seventy pages before the end of the novel, it is the climax of Horace's story; all the rest only further clarifies it by parallels to it.

Horace's preoccupation, which became an obsession, with photographs in the 1929 version helped to produce Faulkner's technique of the frozen moment in which everything is implied; the photograph is a rather clear objective correlative to that technique. And that technique expresses Horace's deeply psychic need for a way to stop time, to defy mutability: he needed to make the world he knew or imagined hold still so he could contemplate it, perhaps capture it, in a permanent image, the way a photograph does.

With photographs in Faulkner's fiction, as with most of the elements in Faulkner worth experiencing, what you see is not what you get. It is what is implied that offers the richest experiences. What matters is not literal descriptions of photographs but the effect of photographs indirectly on our responses to Faulkner's fiction. Even more importantly, it is Faulkner's most characteristic technique—the frozen, static, image—and the juxtaposition of images—that is so like a photograph in its lingering effect, that gave me the impression, that his literal or direct use of photographs is far more pervasive than the Concordances to his novels will prove.

Key moments in Faulkner's fiction are often those in which he freezes an image; note the frequency of his use of such words as "immobile," "frozen," "static," "motionless," "transfixed," "statutelike," "as in a painting," "as if in a photograph," "as if in a slow motion movie." The most violent action in Faulkner reaches a moment of stasis.

Faulkner himself seems to have a compulsion to create such images. The reader's response to such photographic, frozen moments is somewhat like young Ike McCaslin's slow perception of the bear's footprint in the mud in "The Bear" in the *Go Down, Moses* version (weakened for the *Saturday Evening Post* version).

> . . . seeing as he sat down on the log the crooked print, the warped indentation in the wet ground which while he looked at it continued to fill with water until it was level full and the water began to overflow and the sides of the print began to dissolve away. Even as he looked up he saw the next one, and, moving, the one beyond it. . . . then he

saw the bear. It did not emerge, appear: it was just there, immobile, fixed. . . . (208–9)

Most of Faulkner's narrators or main characters obsessively reach for those moments of stasis, especially Horace Benbow in *Flags in the Dust* and the *Sartoris* revision and in the 1929 version of *Sanctuary* and even in the 1931 version, and, more than any of Faulkner's characters, the autobiographical Quentin Compson.

I agree with Noel Polk when he argues, in the afterword to the 1981 publication of the 1929 manuscript version of *Sanctuary*, that Faulkner's famous remarks in the Modern Library edition about writing *Sanctuary* to make money do not refer to the 1929 version that no buyer of trashy books would buy or could even read, that far from being a book that would shame *The Sound and the Fury*—the problem with the 1929 version was that Horace Benbow resembled Quentin Compson too closely. Afraid to seem to repeat himself with a book that was not really as good as *The Sound and the Fury*, Faulkner recast the novel in galleys. If we accept the notion that Quentin Compson is Faulkner's most autobiographical character, and that Horace resembles Quentin Compson, we can imagine Faulkner wanting to de-emphasize a character who might betray a kind of self-hatred on Faulkner's part.

Pop Culture Invades Jefferson: Faulkner's Real and Imaginary Photos of Desire

Judith L. Sensibar

William Faulkner is the South's first great writer. Before his advent, as Anne Goodwyn Jones has shown, real Southern men did not write; in fact, for historical and political reasons, all forms of art were deemed an exclusively amateur and female pastime.[1] Yet despite this well-documented tradition and despite Faulkner's great-grandfather's careful trivialization of his own poetry and fiction,[2] this relative is still routinely cited as the novelist's chief familial artistic progenitor and model.[3] That Faulkner showed little interest or skill in emulating the Colonel's polemical literary style, his much admired legal and financial wizardry, or his public physical violence is simply ignored. Colonel Falkner succeeded because he fulfilled the ideals of his community. Faulkner succeeded despite ignoring or violating them in important ways. Most importantly, he dared to assume a woman's role in order to become an artist.[4]

By declaring himself an artist, Faulkner openly threatened one of his culture's most firmly entrenched gender classifications. This is not to argue either that he was a feminist or that he wished to appropriate feminine space in order to extend the patriarchy's hegemony. Faulkner's ambivalence towards the feminine manifests itself frequently in both life and art.[5] But his fiction is immersed in gender issues and, as I have written elsewhere and will elaborate here, his response to patriarchal definitions of those issues was extremely complicated.[6]

Hugh Kenner's romantic assertions notwithstanding, genius

does not spring full blown from the brow of Zeus.[7] For American Southern writers, the journey to authentic speech, the difficulty of freeing themselves from a culturally imposed requirement to serve as polemicists for Southern patriarchal values, "to pacify the autocratic voice of [the] ruling classes or established ideas," was especially pronounced.[8] Anne Jones and Louis D. Rubin, Jr., have detailed and analyzed the cultural pressures placed upon both sexes not to create at all or, at most, to write fiction and poetry reflecting the fantasies of the South's Narcissa Benbows, Ellen Coldfields, and Drusilla Sartorises. Such propaganda, which passed for art, was relegated to women "in the equation of woman, beauty, literature, and irrelevance."[9] Since the Civil War, writers who forthrightly questioned the status quo had been judged traitors and banished. Through the examples of her fictional artists, Madame Pontellier and Mlle. Reisz, Kate Chopin shows what happened to Southern women who took their talents seriously: they were silenced as hysterics or marginalized as insane.

A Southern gentleman knew better than to be an artist. "The *forte* of the Old Dominion," said a pre–Civil War news editor, "is to be found in the masculine production of her statesmen . . . who have never indulged in works of imagination."[10] While, as Jones notes, imaginative realms were off-limits to Southern males, the three respectable occupations for genteel white women were teaching, sewing, and writing. In fact, the South praised and venerated their women writers, for the most part, because they conformed to cultural strictures that guaranteed "a fundamentally nonserious literary tradition." Paradoxically, however, the disruption of Southern patriarchy began in the South's historical endorsement of women writers.[11] I draw your attention to this paradox because such connections between creativity, the feminine, and patriarchal values play importantly in Faulkner's artistic beginnings, particularly in his use of real and imaginary photographs.

And I suggest that we can arrive at a more fruitful understanding of the relation between gender issues, creativity, and desire in

Faulkner's fiction if we start where he did—with his assumption that, for a Southerner, art was an exclusively female occupation. Practically, what did this mean? Because my space here is limited, I will focus on one way in which this issue manifested itself in Faulkner's work throughout his career—his experiments in expressing illicit longing by merging language with, first, his own drawings and photographs and, later, with fictional photographs. In these experiments Faulkner uses drawings and photographs to figure desire in ways that challenge conventional language and the binarism of gender and to explode patriarchal tenets and assumptions about difference. Not surprisingly, it is here also that his debt to the lived and the imaginative realities of two of the first artists in his life, Maud Butler, his mother, and Estelle Oldham, his wife and childhood friend, reveals itself most clearly.[12] For they taught him how to mask his subversive activities and use marginalization to his advantage in order to enjoy serious art's forbidden pleasures.[13]

ACTUAL AND FICTIONAL PHOTOGRAPHS

In a recently released film, a Cajun woman uses her photograph album to tell their family's history to her city cousin, a New York journalist. Consistently, one person's face has been blanked out. The city cousin asks who he is. "My boy, my oldest boy. He went bad," the Cajun mother answers. "But he is your son! He is one of your children!" protests her city cousin. "He does not exist," the Cajun mother says stonily. We watch the two women's expressions; we look at them looking at the album, open across their laps; we see the city cousin's shock. There is something violent and taboo about destroying a photograph. To destroy it is to erase that irrefutable proof of what was: "A photograph is at once the past and the real."[14]

Memory is flawed: it distorts, it forgets. I cannot recall my beloved grandmother's face. I can hear her voice, taste her wild plum jam, remember the feel of her fingers lifting the skin of my scalp as she braided my hair; but her features blur when I try to call them up.

My father-in-law comes to visit. He is eighty-three and has a hole in his heart. I take over a dozen photographs. Constantly I frame father and son, grandfather and grandson—shoring up against the end, the not exist. After he leaves, I finish the roll and open our camera. It is empty. Instantly, intensely, I feel bereaved. It is irrational. Still, I grieve.

Photographs don't lie. Our great-aunt says she needs her hip replaced. "I don't want a second opinion. I saw the X rays. Even a lay-person could see my pelvis is like tissue paper." Legally, she is blind. But she believes (sees) the X ray.

Barthes asserts that no writing can authenticate as definitively as a photograph: "language is, by nature, fictional; the attempt to render language unfictional requires an enormous apparatus of measurements: we convoke logic, or, lacking that, sworn oath; but the Photograph is indifferent to all intermediaries: it does not invent; it is authentication itself; the (rare) artifices it permits are not probative; they are, on the contrary, trick pictures: the photograph is laborious only when it fakes." A photograph can lie about its referent's meaning but never about its existence; "the power of authentication exceeds the power of representation." [15]

Clearly, as those who write about photographs and our own experiences have shown us, the actual photograph encodes the essence of the modernist and postmodernist experience of knowing, or rather, not knowing.[16] Its teasing false reality (in contrast to other frankly interpretive mimetic forms), its use as a device for fragmenting reality; as a tool of aggression, acquisition, power; as witness, evidence; its surrealistic ability to freeze time—"The reading of a photograph is always historical"[17]—and yet blur the lines between art and life as it demarcates the chasm separating sight from speech; its unquestioned ability to testify to, as Barthes says, "what has been;"[18] its outrageous voyeurism that "makes everyone a tourist in other people's reality and eventually in one's own"[19] and, paradoxically, its ability to do all this *without language*—to speak with its body—are some of the qualities that make the photograph, particularly the photograph of desire, so compelling to us and to Faulkner's fictional men and women.

In general, those who have written about photographs and photography focus on actual photographs.[20] If, like Sontag, they allude to fictional photographs, they do not distinguish between the actual and the imagined.[21] Even Wright Morris, who illustrates some of his novels with real photographs, has never explored the epistemologically dazzling vista presented by the fictional photograph.[22] But it is precisely this vista that Faulkner's fiction exploits. Since his photographs are fictional rather than actual, we never literally see them. A step is left out; their episteme is further complicated. We know that for their fictive spectators, the people pictured exist or existed, but for us this information is only connoted. With the literal camera image removed, we are denied the "objective" record with which to measure for ourselves the reflections of each spectator/speaker's desire, his or her wish for what will be or what was. Only the actual photograph can denote. But as we read fictional photographs, we are not aware of this absence, lack, gap; the fictional spectator's gaze has become, for the moment, our own.

Photographs seem to exert tremendous erotic power in Faulkner's fiction. In "The Leg" (1925), an early short supernatural tale, a photograph created by a jealous lover's ghost drives his girlfriend mad, nearly causes his rival's murder, incites the girl's brother to murder, and causes the brother's death. In the first Yoknapatawpha novel, *Flags in the Dust* (1926), Bayard Sartoris burns the photograph of his dead twin brother in a desperate effort to free himself from his obsession with his idealized double. *Sanctuary* (1931) and *Absalom, Absalom!* (1936) are Faulkner's most stunning invocations of the photograph's multiplicity of meanings and its wordlessness to figure desire in ways which transgress and thus transcend patriarchy; there it becomes a subversive presence, challenging the boundaries of language and the binarism of gender. In these novels the force of this image reaches beyond the conventions of the literal photograph. The epistemological issues double as he uses this trope to question and critique phallocentric ways of seeing, speaking, and acting out desire. In *Sanctuary* Horace Benbow's forbidden fantasies of lust, incest, and pedophilia all coalesce as he gazes on a stolen photograph of his nubile young step-daughter. In *Absalom, Absalom!* Rosa Coldfield articulates the essence of absence and desire encoded in a picture of someone else's lover. Throughout Faulkner's work, even as late as *A Fable* (1954), fictional photographs are tropes for epistemological conundrums of forbidden love.[23]

The origins of Faulkner's interest in the fictional photograph suggest that it was an extension of his earliest emotional and aesthetic solutions to writing beyond sexual difference. As he explores the ontology of this image, one that, at its deepest level, merges the antithetical imaginations of two of the women artists (avowed primitives) with whom he lived his life, he recovers and articulates their imaginative visions to create the tension between the real and surreal that is central to his own art.[24] The strength he derives from identifying with, then merging with, and finally separating from them moves his fictional representations of desire beyond traditional notions of culturally imposed gender distinctions.[25] The presence of this mimetic visual image in Faulkner's earliest imaginative creations reveals, in part, why it served so well to challenge the prescribed binary boundaries of the lives of his fictional characters and why men *or* women who see desire with the gaze of patriarchy are silenced, while those who challenge it can speak and become artists of the word.[26]

The photograph's power is its epistemological ambiguity, an ambiguity doubled—for us—by its fictionality. Objectively, literally, the photograph is an undistorted, frozen mirror image of what has been. Unlike a painting, the photograph is no obvious imitation of reality, nor is its reality fleeting and instantaneous, like a mirrored image. Yet, paradoxically, in the act of possessing the photographic image, of giving meaning to it with words, the viewer's vision begins to blur and distort. Faulkner understands this precisely. As the failed artist, failed lawyer, failed lover Horace Benbow gazes hungrily at a photograph of his step-daughter's "small face," it "seemed to swoon in a voluptuous languor, blurring still more, fading, leaving upon his eye a soft and fading aftermath."[27] And Barthes confirms, "photographs are signs which don't *take*, which *turn*, as milk does. Whatever it grants to vision and whatever its manner, a photograph is always invisible: it is not it that we see."[28] Instead, the spectator's words (the captions) record a visual image that replicates the carnival theater of emotions released by his/her desire to possess the image in the photograph. Language transforms the photograph from a record of an external reality of the other (its subjects) to an image of the speaker/perceiver's internal reality and so seems to confirm the impossibility of an objective perception of reality. There is a shift in meaning from what the photograph denotes to what the spectator connotes: Barthes claims that "in no other treatment does connotation assume so completely the 'objective' mask of denotation."[29] How the Faulknerian spectators transform this carnival image and what they do with it signals, first, the extent of their bondage to patriarchal constructs of desire and, second, their ability to speak effectively.

Faulkner often uses the fictional photograph to disrupt patriarchal dogma and assumptions about difference. With it he questions certain culturally gendered erotic responses and probes the reasons for their being gendered. In his novels, our not being able to actually see the photograph—its fictionality—gives it a greater intensity than either straight fantasy or an actual photograph. Faulkner's characters capitalize on the photograph's multiplicity of meanings and its wordlessness to imagine desire, and use it or fail to use it to either challenge or accept the prescribed binary boundaries of their lives.

HISTORICIZING FAULKNER'S FICTIONAL PHOTOGRAPHS

"Seeing comes before words."[30] It is a long way from Faulkner's imitative 1920 dream-play *The Marionettes* to *Sanctuary* and *Absalom, Absalom!*, but this play, which Faulkner illustrated with his own drawings that swerve dramatically yet silently from his written text, signals the beginning of his revolt. To write or paint challenged the status quo. In writing, illustrating, binding, and selling five copies of *The Marionettes*, Faulkner did both. His drawings here are perhaps the most subtle challenge, for they say, in concrete images, what he cannot say in words.[31] A fictional photograph serves a similar purpose for Faulkner's fictional characters: it offers them the chance to free themselves from silence, without imprisoning themselves in language.

As I've noted elsewhere, *The Marionettes'* central protagonist is Pierrot, that amoral, often inebriated hero of the nineteenth-century French pantos whom modernist novelists and poets adopted and reinvented to serve their own imaginative yearnings. At the opening and throughout *The Marionettes* Faulkner has drawn him sprawling side-stage, his head resting on a spindly café table. There, immobilized and insensible and thus not morally responsible for his thoughts, he dreams the two dreams that are this play. These uninhibited "fermented" dreams and the drawings that often turn from their text reflect truly how Pierrot/Faulkner sees and says himself in the world. They may be thought of as his way of appropriating the language of the body—his mother's tongue. For he says here, with his drawings of Pierrot's, his "moon-mad" mother's, and Marietta's bodies what he dares not say in words.[32]

Pierrot's unspoken dreams are explicitly about sexual longing and unappeasable desire. The drawings reveal that the young Faulkner's favorite persona, Pierrot, wants to merge with and possess the two artists in his life—his mother, who controls the power of "song," and a young virgin, who offers adult passion. The drawings also show that he knows that such coupling will kill his lover and leave him voiceless, staring solipsisticly in a mirror (see figure 1). That Faulkner has appropriated Maud Butler's and Estelle Oldham's imaginative language is clear. These drawings

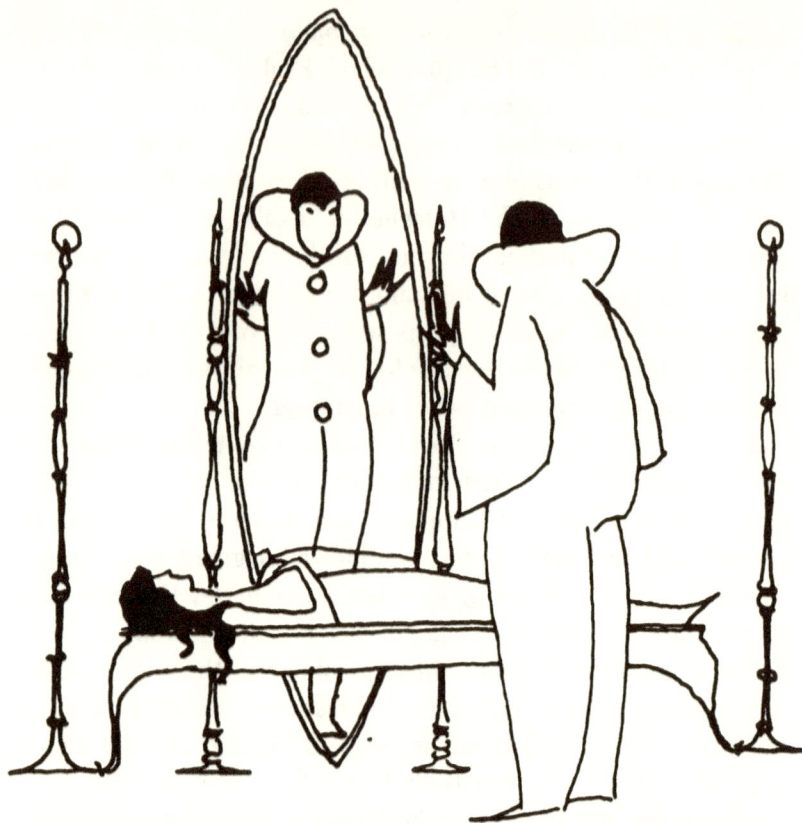

Figure 1: Pierrot, his mouth erased, stands beside the dead Marietta but Stares at Himself in the mirror. From William Faulkner's *The Marionettes* (c.1920). Courtesy of Jill Faulkner Summers and the William Faulkner Collections (Acc. No. 627Iaj), University of Virginia Library.

reflect, in part, the ways in which he has been stimulated by and has attempted to merge both women's antithetical imaginative realities. Maud's paintings were deliberately realistic—she speaks of herself as a realist; Estelle's "dream" paintings, as she calls them, are impressionistic and sometimes, surreal.[33] In speaking of her brother-in-law John, who painted in the same realistic style as his mother, Maud, Estelle clarifies, "The difference between John's style and mine is that he painted trees as trees and little negro cabins like little negro cabins. He was a realist. My paintings are not realistic. . . . All my subjects are unconscious things. All are pure fantasy."[34] Five years later she said, "I never paint from nature. . . . I never paint still-lifes. I think God can make flowers better than I can."[35] While Faulkner's highly stylized Beardsleyesque *Marionettes* drawings are self-consciously antirealistic, Marietta, the play's female protagonist whom Pierrot seduces and abandons, bears an uncanny resemblance to contemporary photographs of Estelle Oldham (see figures 2 through 5). Thus surrealism masks realism, creating the play's hidden psychological tension; his drawings' nonserious imitative style screens a deeply serious and disruptive content—Pierrot's desire to be an artist and to become that by possessing the imaginative language of both mother and lover.

Faulkner's early experiments with actual visual images extended to photography as well. As early as 1918 he had begun what was to be a lifelong manipulation of the camera-eye as he played with the power of actual but trick photographs to alter viewers' perceptions. Posing for a series of snapshots of himself as wounded war hero, Faulkner constructed a firmly masculine body, an acceptable front behind which he could practice his art (see figure 6). Here he used photographs to manipulate reality to his own advantage, to appear as he wished to be viewed by his family and fellow townspeople.[36] But the military cover was not sufficient for his purposes. He needed, as well, to play the fool. Thus he alternated his flier's pose with the ridiculous costumes of dandy and tramp. I know of no photographs of Faulkner in these other roles, but the nickname they earned him—Count No 'Count—a linguistic photograph attesting to the success of his posing, survives. His deliberately outrageous but essentially harmless behavior distracted his townspeople's attention from his more potentially disturbing pursuit—one that threatened proscribed gender classifications: becoming an artist. These experiments in altering his own visual image, while simultaneously teaching himself to write and draw, show Faulkner moving from

Figure 2: The virgin Marietta watched over by Pierrot's "moon-mad" mother. From *The Marionettes.* Courtesy of Jill Faulkner Summers and the William Faulkner Collections (Acc. No. 627Iaj), University of Virginia Library.

Figure 3: Estelle Oldham Franklin, c. 1920. Photograph Courtesy of
Jill Faulkner Summers.

Figure 4: Pierrot and Marietta. From *The Marionettes*. Courtesy of Jill Faulkner Summers and the William Faulkner Collections (Acc. No. 627Iaj), University of Virginia Library.

Figure 5: Estelle Oldham Franklin holding her son, Malcolm
(c. 1927). Courtesy of Jill Faulkner Summers.

Figure 6: William Faulkner (above and opposite page) posing in his various military costumes, 1918-20. Photographs Courtesy of Jill Faulkner Summers.

the relatively powerless position of actor/fool in spectacles of frustrated desire to creator of actors in spectacles of desire.

READING FAULKNER'S FICTIONAL PHOTOGRAPHS

Barthes speaks of the power of the camera's eye to make him feel like an imposter and (thus) specter:

> In front of the lens, I am at the same time: the one I think I am, the one I want others to think I am, the one the photographer thinks I am, and the one he makes use of to exhibit his art. . . . I do not stop imitating myself, and because of this, each time I am (or let myself be) photographed, I invariably suffer from a sensation of inauthenticity, sometimes of imposture (comparable to certain nightmares). In terms of image repertoire, the photograph (the one I *intend*) represents that very subtle moment when, to tell the truth, I am neither subject nor object but a subject who feels he is becoming an object.

In this "parenthesis," he says, "I am truly becoming a specter."[37]

Barthes's choice of verb voice pinpoints the difference between his response to being photographed and Faulkner's. Barthes feels manipulated by the camera—"I am (or let myself be) photographed." Even though he plays a role in front of it, it (the photographer) is in charge of him. Faulkner's staged photographs elicit the precise opposite sensation. He fakes for the camera lens to provide and control the spectacle—to occupy a different in-between space. He deliberately plays the eerily Chaplinesque figure of the wounded war hero or fool—Count No 'Count—to clear space for his forbidden career. To the people of Oxford he was a joke.

It is no accident, then, that Rosa Coldfield, an expert at reading photographs of desire, appears to the doomed Quentin and his lost father as a joke as well. They view her as a foolish old spinster caught in a forty-three-year old time-warp by an insult to her maidenhood. Rosa Coldfield understands the role she is supposed to play as Jefferson's penniless and slightly mad piece of "lonely thwarted old female flesh," a role confirmed as we view her through Quentin's eyes in the opening paragraphs of *Absalom, Absalom!*[38]

There she sits like a life-sized puppet, "bolt upright in the straight hard chair that was so tall for her that her legs hung straight and rigid as if she had iron shinbones and ankles, clear of the floor with that air of impotent and static rage like children's feet" (7). Dehumanized, infantilized, treated as property by her father and as a potential broodmare by her brother-in-law, Thomas Sutpen, Rosa Coldfield uses the one title/function she has garnered because she *is* so marginalized—poetess laureate of Yoknapatawpha—to move from silence into speech and from object of spectacle to projector of spectacle. Cast by the patriarchal values of her family and community in the role of fool (foolish child and hysterical virgin) she becomes self-conscious fool, thereby taking control of the text of the house of Sutpen and releasing it, in all its madness and frenzy, to the world at large.[39]

Like a photograph, whose function in the play and tug of desire she so perfectly understands, Rosa was there and can testify to what has been. The novel is filled with photographic imagery and loaded with theatrical and cinematic scenes that for Mr. Compson are "just incredible. It just does not explain. . . . They are there, yet something is missing; they are like a chemical formula; . . . you bring them together again and again and nothing happens: just the words, the symbols, the shapes themselves, shadowy inscrutable and serene" (100–1).[40] For Compson and the rest, the scenes don't add up because they do not understand the relation of the scenes to their meaning. These scenes, like photographs, "offer appearances—with all the credibility and gravity we normally lend appearances—prised away from their meaning. Meaning is the result of understanding functions."[41] Rosa's marginalized position as artist and fool paradoxically privileges her intelligence and her voice. She does not know everything but she knows and understands a great deal more than any fictional listeners or many real readers have given her credit for because they look at her and listen to her from Quentin's, Mr. Compson's, and Shreve's perspectives.

One indicator of Rosa's brilliance and clarity of imagination is her ability to read a particular kind of Faulknerian photograph of desire. While the town of Jefferson makes her a subject for jump-rope ditties—as she says herself, "Oh yes, I know: 'Rosie Cold-field, lose him, weep him; caught a man but couldn't keep him'" (168, 170–71)—she is busy inventing serious art, the story she tells Quentin. Like Faulkner, and many Southern women, she conceals her art-making with masks: "I was not only a Southern gentlewoman but the very modest character" (169).[42] She appears as a proper lady, producing quantities of polemical art, over 1,000 poems—"odes, eulogies, and epitaphs"—to fallen Civil War heroes (11, 83). These "beautifully safe and patriotic productions"[43] establish her as "the poetess laureate" of Yoknapatawpha before she tells the tale that questions all the values those polemics support. Furthermore, she makes sure that her real art will have national circulation. A pauperized spinster, *she* may not leave the South, but she can tell her story to a young man who is leaving:

"Because you are going away to attend the college at Harvard they tell me," Miss Coldfield said. "So I don't imagine you will ever come back here and settle down. . . . So maybe you will enter the literary profession as so many Southern gentlemen and gentlewomen too are doing now and maybe someday you will remember this and write about it." (9–10)[44]

Rosa cannot escape the physical confines of her culture and is locked in other ways within its patriarchal constructs. But her imagination is free and she uses it to communicate and question.

Quentin recognizes part of Rosa's motivation, *"It's because she wants it told."* But he fails to see that (as the narrator notes in a rare intrusion) Rosa has the "cold, implacable, and even ruthless" attributes Faulkner claims are essential for a great writer (10).[45] Rosa can tell a good story; her personal life may be a shambles but, still, she is a successful artist who uses fantasies evoked by a photograph of desire to elicit new meanings. By understanding the content of a photograph of desire, Rosa Coldfield lays claim to her own reality and enlarges ours. Articulating to another the absence in her life leads her to understand it and then use it to create art. Thus, while Rosa's life remains circumscribed—the novel's other narrators nourish the melodramatic belief that she dies because the source of her outrage has been destroyed—her story takes on a life of its own. In similar circumstances Horace Benbow will use language to obfuscate; here Rosa uses language to create and illuminate:

> I had never seen him (I never saw him. I never even saw him dead. I heard a name, I saw a photograph, I helped to make a grave: and that was all). . . . (I did not love him; how could I? I had never even heard his voice, had only Ellen's word for it that there was such a person) . . . because I had not even seen the photograph then. . . .
>   . . . because I did not love him. (How could I have, when I had never seen him?). . . .

As she talks to Quentin, her inner vision begins to clarify:

> I dont know even now if I was ever aware that I had seen nothing of his face but that photograph, that shadow, that picture in a young

girl's bedroom: a picture casual and framed upon a littered dressing table yet bowered and dressed (or so I thought) with all the maiden and invisible lily roses, because even before I saw the photograph I could have recognized, nay, described, the very face. But I never saw it. I do not know of my own knowledge that Ellen ever saw it, that Judith ever loved it, that Henry slew it: so who will dispute me when I say, Why did I not invent, create it?

Rosa has raised the question, is the existence of the photograph material? That is, if the feelings that it evoked in her and she describes feel true to the listener, isn't that emotional reality more valid than a physical object? And, of course, this is what she is asserting as she then describes her marvelous invention:

—And I know this: if I were God I would invent out of this seething turmoil we call progress something (a machine perhaps) which would adorn the barren mirror altars of every plain girl who breathes with such as this—which is so little since we want so little—this pictured face. It would not even need a skull behind it; almost anonymous, it would only need vague inference of some walking flesh and blood desired by someone else if only in some shadow-realm of make-believe. (146–47)

At first Rosa asserts to her audience—Quentin—that she could not have loved Charles Bon because she only knew him from his photograph. But as she describes what Bon's picture connotes, she realizes why his photograph both created and fed her desire. This realization allows her to move on to an elegant and imaginative insight about the kinds of people who crave this kind of desire, what its essence is—absence and illicitness—and what lack it fills. We never know what Bon looks like—his features, hair color, his eyes. These are facts and they don't interest Rosa. All she cares about are how and why photographs work as they do upon the spectator's imagination. Rather than losing herself, like Horace, in lustful fantasies of illicit, forbidden, incestuous, and unattainable desire, she frankly acknowledges her wishes to her audience and then uses them and her own experience to abstract and generalize. Her idea is wonderfully playful, amusing, and true. It's also an accurate reading of adolescent sexuality. As Sontag notes,

> The sense of the unattainable that can be evoked by photographs feeds directly into the erotic feelings of those for whom desirability is enhanced by distance. The lover's photograph hidden in the married woman's wallet, the poster photograph of a rock star tacked up over an adolescent's bed . . .—such talismanic uses of photographs express a feeling both sentimental and implicitly magical; they are attempts to contact or lay claim to another reality.[46]

Unlike Horace, Rosa is not fantasizing silently and alone in a dark and empty house. She shares her feelings as she creates a story she knows cannot be written in the South. In doing so, she demystifies this kind of desire. Unlike Horace, she *wants* to communicate and she wants to understand relationships. Mastery of the photograph's message renders Rosa's telling a success. She achieves a coherence Horace never can experience. Rosa's tale disrupts because, in its larger sense, it demystifies the polemics of conventional Southern fiction. In doing this, it causes its hearers to rethink the racial and gender distinctions imposed by Southern patriarchy. By telling her tale to Quentin, Rosa breaks forty-three years of silence.[47]

Both Horace Benbow's and Rosa Coldfield's talismanic use of photographs of desire question, frustrate, and disrupt gendered notions of sexuality. For each, the photograph is a trope for a thematics of desire that feeds on frustration, absence, incestuous wishes, and voyeurism. But while Rosa's response, and her intent, is (in this instance) to demythologize desire for herself and her listener, Horace's is opposite. Rosa, who imagines herself as Macbeth and Hamlet, at first seems to appropriate Judith's photograph of Charles Bon, as Horace has Little Belle's. But Rosa never literally steals Judith's photograph. She doesn't need to because what she really wants to appropriate is an understanding of her desire. Possessed of that, she does indeed become "all polymath love's androgynous advocate," an artist (146).

Much has been written about *Sanctuary* as a Wasteland novel. The unnoticed "wasteland" Faulkner paints here is that wrought by culturally imposed class, race, and gender distinctions. Each major character represents a Type in the panorama, but a Type developed to its logical and most horrendous extreme. Thus Narcissa, draped always in white, is the ice maiden, that aristocratic image of the Southern Lady "born in the imaginations of white slaveholding men" and therefore "linked directly to fundamental southern questions of race, class, and sex."[48] Horace is the Southern Gentleman, sworn from birth to protect and worship but never have sexual thoughts about this maiden ideal; Temple and Little Belle, the dark side of the virgin image, the Southern Lady turned whore; and Popeye, the "black man," that Other through whom Faulkner ironically caricatures the patriarchal myth of blacks' unbridled licentiousness and sexual potency. Horace's reading of Little Belle's photograph reveals the desires and fears those culturally imposed gender distinctions are designed to mask and control. His designs on the photograph he steals are purely pornographic, onanistic, and acquisitive. But because Faulkner's purpose is to question Horace's way of seeing, Horace's designs are disrupted.

Speaking of the convention of the female nude in Western painting and photography, John Berger argues that "women are depicted in a quite different way from men—not because the feminine is different from the masculine—but because the 'ideal' spectator is always assumed to be male and the image of the woman is designed to flatter him." In these nude scenes,

> the principal protagonist is never painted. He is the spectator in front of the picture and he is presumed to be a man. Everything is addressed to him. . . . It is for him that the figures have assumed their nudity. But he, by definition, is a stranger with his clothes still on . . . the picture is made to appeal to *his* sexuality. It has nothing to do with her sexuality. . . . The woman's sexual passion needs to be minimized so that the spectator may feel he has the monopoly of such passion.[49]

Horace—and Popeye, his underworld double—fit this description exactly. These are Horace's expectations. But they are constantly being frustrated. For example, Little Belle's gaze
continually eludes him: "He stood before it [the photograph],
looking at the sweet, inscrutable face which looked in turn at
something just beyond his shoulder" (162). While he owns her
photograph, he cannot own her gaze. Like Rosa, he makes the
photographed object less, not more, real. But unlike her, he
doesn't realize what he's done, that "a photograph is both a
pseudo-presence and a token of absence."[50] If he were to understand, his desire would be too threatening.

Horace dramatizes the destructive power of the patriarchal
gaze—for both the gazer and the gazed upon. In a novel where
everyone sees or is seen in frames, Horace's act of unframing and
snitching, not his wife's, but his step-daughter's picture as he flees
to his sister's "sanctuary" may be seen as the first step that leads to
the greatest frame-up in the novel—Lee Goodwin's lynching. In
this sense Horace destroys or maims everything his eyes touch.
He tries to use his position as spectator-owner of Little Belle's
photograph in a traditional way. But Horace's appropriation, like
Popeye's voyeuristic framing of Temple to sate his hunger (Temple develops a passion for Red that Popeye can't control), fails.
Horace's gaze triggers fantasies of desire that literally make him
sick. Desire cannot be contained or framed. Faulkner's phallic imagery here is wonderfully ironic. With the thick smell of honeysuckle writhing "like cold smoke" outside his darkened bedroom window, Little Belle's face "appeared to breathe in his palms
in a shallow bath of highlight, beneath the slow, smokelike
tongues of invisible honeysuckle."[51] The "infinitesimal movement of his hands, his own breathing" make her "small face seem
to swoon in a voluptuous languor, blurring still more, fading,
leaving upon his eye a soft and fading aftermath of invitation and
voluptuous promise and secret affirmation like a scent itself"
(215–16). Like Rosa, Horace never describes this voluptuous
promise. Little Belle's actuality holds no interest for him. Her

photograph's function is to stimulate masturbatory fantasies. Horace next transforms Little Belle into an image that conflates her with Temple Drake and Emma Bovary. But his fantasied rape of this object ends in vomiting, not orgasm, as (now transformed to Popeye) he

> leaned upon his braced arms while the shucks set up a terrific uproar beneath her thighs. Lying with her head lifted slightly, her chin depressed like a figure lifted down from a crucifix, she watched something black and furious go roaring out of her pale body. She was bound naked on her back on a flat car moving at speed through a black tunnel, the blackness streaming in rigid threads overhead, a roar of iron wheels in her ears. The car shot bodily from the tunnel in a long upward slant, the darkness overhead now shredded with parallel attenuations of living fire, toward a crescendo like a held breath, an interval in which she would swing faintly and lazily in nothingness filled with pale, myriad points of light. Far beneath her she could hear the faint, furious uproar of the shucks. (216)

Horace's gaze is undermined as a potential feast becomes a violent retching scene. His spectatorship leaves him totally unmanned— and empty. His words will also prove empty, for he loses his case, his client is lynched, and the uncomprehending Horace remains trapped within the confines of a power structure he claims to despise. Silence results from using others as objects.

Rosa succeeds where Horace fails not because she is a woman and he, a man. She succeeds because, although she turns what we would call a masculine gaze upon Judith's photograph of Charles Bon, a gaze which transforms Bon from subject to object, her gaze is, finally, self-conscious. This self-consciousness, her desire to know why she sees the way she does and to analyze her motives and to abstract and learn about this gaze, and then to share her knowledge with another, questions all the premises upon which such objectification is based. It changes her and makes us, if we listen to her voice, see desire in a way that questions the conventions of Rosa's (as well as our own) culture. Faulkner may be suggesting that because Rosa is a woman, she is better equipped to make that challenge. But her gender alone is no assurance of success, and her success is very limited because, in so many other ways, her behavior meets cultural expectations. But Rosa is unlike either her sister Ellen, who retreats into a harmless and highly acceptable madness, or Temple Drake and Eula Varner who, like Horace, know how to use language creatively but choose instead to become exemplars of various patriarchal sexual myths. In contrast, Rosa uses one of those myths—that of the sex-starved, hysterical spinster—to camouflage her subversive voice.

Faulkner's portrayal of Rosa's and Horace's desire is complicated and compelling. The roots of its complexity lie deep in his own, always very self-conscious, conception of himself as an artist in a culture devoid of and hostile to homemade art, a culture so hostile that it had relegated what art it did foster to its women. As a young man claiming to be an artist, Faulkner threatened tightly held convictions about masculinity and femininity, and so put his own gender classification at risk. We see him exploring his anxiety and fear of being silenced/feminized in early poems like "After Fifty Years" or in *The Marionettes* where a young man is imprisoned by the stories or music of crazy old women. We see his fear more subtly imaged, and better understood, in the men obsessed by Caddy's voice in *The Sound and the Fury* and in the men obsessed by Rosa's in *Absalom, Absalom!*

Many writers begin as visual artists. Experiments in several media and genres are not unusual. Nor was feminization of American artists limited to our Southern regions—one has only to read Emerson or Hawthorne to see the anxiety such labeling produced in nineteenth-century New England. But as Jones and Rubin have shown, and as Faulkner himself observed, this attitude reached its extreme in the South.[52] What is unusual was Faulkner's imaginative response. In the beginning of the second decade of this century, when he began his career as an artist, he cared as much about exploring the visual arts as he did about becoming a poet. Like literature, painting and music were also feminized. Faulkner's mother and maternal grandmother (who lived with them) were, perhaps, gifted. Both are remembered for the intensity with which they sculpted and painted.[53] Maud's mother, Lelia Swift Butler, was, apparently, offered an art scholarship abroad in 1890.[54] She could not accept it as her husband had gone bankrupt and deserted her. Her daughter then dropped out of college. Mother and daughter moved to Texarkana where Maud worked as a stenographer to support them (58). Lelia Butler was reduced to sculpting laundry soap at home, the only medium she could afford. Maud often came home to unmade dinner and unwashed dishes. Her mother had spent the day working. Opposition to Lelia Butler's art began in childhood. According to one of her grandsons, her father was a Baptist "of the hard-shell variety, for he thought any creation which came out of thin air, like a painting, was the work of the devil." He took away her paints and told her "never to touch them again." But she defied him. With new materials, she rowed out in the middle of a nearby lake and painted in secret.[55] That Maud Butler Falkner passed on this story to her own four boys suggests the value she placed on her mother's iconoclasm and talent.

Maud Butler married late—at twenty-five. Within a year she bore William, the first of her four sons. As far as is known, Maud did not paint again until she was in her sixties and living, finally, on her own. And then she painted almost full time until her death. Estelle Oldham Faulkner's career as an artist follows a similar chronology. While their culture classified them, safely, as amateurs, both women were, in fact, primitives, in John Berger's sense of these terms.[56] Their art (and in more subtle ways their lives) displays the strengths of that origin—an individualism and freedom from convention and tradition that they apparently passed on to Faulkner. While Berger's remarks are intended to describe European male primitive artists, they work equally well for describing Maud Butler and Estelle Oldham. Like most primitive painters, both began painting in late middle-age. Therefore, as Berger notes, "their art derives from considerable personal experience and, indeed, is often provoked as a result of the

profundity or intensity of that experience."[57] Because their paintings were the creations of a mature vision, they also reflect fully
formed and somewhat stabilized perceptions of reality, and so can
be read as an accurate summation and ordering of how the world
seemed to these two women. Equally important, because primitive artists are either self-trained or trained in maturity, they have
adapted to being marginalized as different or other: "The primitive begins alone; [s]he inherits no practice. . . . [S]he does not
use the pictorial grammar of the tradition—hence [s]he is un-
grammatical." [S]he refuses the tradition "because [s]he knows
already that [her] his own lived experience which is forcing [her]
him to make art has no place in that tradition. . . . [S]he knows it
because [her] his whole experience is one of being excluded from
the exercise of power in h[er]is society, and [s]he realizes from the
compulsion [s]he now feels, that art too has a kind of power. The
will of primitives derives from faith in their own experience and a
profound skepticism about society as they have found it." Berger
also notes that primitive art is saying what "was never meant,
according to the cultural class system, to be said."[58]

The years during which first Maud Butler and then Estelle
Oldham painted occurred long after their actual painting could
have had any effect on Faulkner's fiction. But their aesthetic
values and perceptions, their means for coping in a culture that
suppressed and trivialized art, and their privileging of art as a
vocation were a constant that dated from Faulkner's earliest childhood. It was from them that he learned how to use literal visual
images to first say with bodies what he could not say with words,
how to expect and cope with marginalization as the price of being an artist, and, finally, to encode what he had learned in
these fictional photographs in novels that constantly undermine
culturally imposed racial and gender classifications. Faulkner's
imaginative training begins in and is supported by this female
tradition. And it is striking to me that Southern women writers,
black and white—Carson McCullers, Eudora Welty, Toni Mor-

rison, Flannery O'Connor, Alice Walker, to name only a few—
have been among Faulkner's most creative readers.

NOTES

1. See her excellent summary, analysis, revision, and extension of Louis D. Rubin's, Eugene Genovese's, and Lewis Simpson's explanations for this anomalous situation and its resulting "flawed literature"—"the literary Sahara that was the South" in *Tomorrow Is Another Day: The Woman Writer in the South, 1859–1936* (Baton Rouge: Louisiana State University Press, 1981), 42 and 43.

2. Judith L. Sensibar, *The Origins of Faulkner's Art* (Austin: University of Texas Press, 1984), 41–42.

3. See, for a recent example, Stephen B. Oates, *William Faulkner: The Man and the Artist* (New York: Harper and Row, 1987).

4. For an opposing view of Colonel Falkner as an ego ideal for his great-grandson see *Origins*, Chapter 4. The Colonel's attitude towards his writing confirms Ellen Glasgow's observation that "literature was almost an avocation to the [male] Southern writer before the Civil War, something that he did for ladies' books." Jones says, "It is plausible that a man's taking literature seriously would threaten still more profoundly his already ambiguous sense of sexual identity, an ambiguity whose anxiety he staved off by worshipping woman and deferring to her mysterious beauty and goodness" (42).

5. For example, see Joseph Blotner, *Faulkner: A Biography* (New York: Random House, 1974 and 1984); Michael Grimwood, *Heart in Conflict: Faulkner's Struggles with Vocation* (Athens: University of Georgia Press, 1987); David Minter, *William Faulkner: His Life and Work* (Baltimore: Johns Hopkins University Press, 1980); Gail L. Mortimer, *Faulkner's Rhetoric of Loss: A Study in Perception and Meaning* (Austin: University of Texas Press, 1983); and Judith Wittenberg, *Faulkner: The Transfiguration of Biography* (Lincoln: University of Nebraska Press, 1979).

6. Sensibar, *Origins* and "'Drowsing Maidenhead Symbol's Self': Faulkner and the Fictions of Love," *Faulkner and the Craft of Fiction*, ed. Doreen Fowler and Ann J. Abadie (Jackson: University Press of Mississippi, 1989), 124–47.

7. Hugh Kenner, "Genius Came Later," *New York Times Sunday Book Review*, 12 August 1984.

8. Louis D. Rubin, Jr., quoting from George W. Cable's 1883 commencement speech. See *The Writer in the South* (Athens: University of Georgia Press, 1972), 10. Rubin notes that until Faulkner, the only writers who seriously challenged the status quo—Samuel Clemens and Edgar Allen Poe—left the South. Faulkner's male friends who wished to be artists and writers—Ben Wasson, Lyle Saxon, Bill Spratling, and Stark Young—followed their example. See also Anne Goodwyn Jones, *Tomorrow Is Another Day*.

9. Jones, 44.

10. Rubin, 12, quoting from a Virginia newspaper editor's welcoming speech to Charles Dickens, 1842. See also Jones, 42.

11. Jones, 34, 44, and 45.

12. An equally important teacher was Faulkner's black nurse, Caroline Clark Barr, who lived with him from his birth until her death in 1940. Her aesthetic legacy is oral. For a brief discussion of Barr's contribution, see Sensibar, "'Drowsing Maidenhead Symbol's Self.'" A longer treatment is included in a book now in progress. See also Sensibar, *Origins* and the above article for discussion of Southern women artists Faulkner chose as friends and lovers.

13. In her book Jones shows how certain Southern women writers used similar tactics. Concerning self-representation, see also Erving Goffman, *The Presentation of Self in*

Everyday Life (New York: Doubleday Anchor, 1959). For a discussion of the role the-
atricality played in Faulkner's life and art, see Sensibar, "'Drowsing Maidenhead'" and
Origins, Chapters 1 and 4.

14. Roland Barthes, *Camera Lucida: Reflections on Photography* (New York: Hill and
Wang, 1981), 82.

15. Ibid., 87, 89.

16. The critical literature on the aesthetics, practice, and power of photography is vast
and varied and derives from a rich variety of disciplines. A partial listing of books and
articles I found useful for understanding how and speculating why Faulkner used both
actual and imaginary photographs in his life and art includes the following: Richard
Arnheim, "On the Nature of Photography," *Critical Inquiry*, 1 (September 1974), 149–161;
Roland Barthes (see references to various essays throughout this article); Walter Benjamin,
"A Short History of Photography," in *Classic Essays on Photography*, ed. Alan Trachten-
berg (New Haven: Leete's Island Books, 1980), 199–216; John Berger (see references to
specific essays and books throughout); Jefferson Hunter, *Image and Word: The Interaction
of Twentieth-Century Photographs and Texts* (Cambridge: Harvard University Press,
1987); W. J. T. Mitchell, *Iconology: Image, Text, Ideology* (Chicago: University of Chicago
Press, 1986); Neil Walsh Allen and Joel Snyder, "Photography, Vision, and Representation," *Critical Inquiry*, 2 (Autumn 1975), 143–69; Susan Sontag (see references throughout); Alan Spiegel, *Fiction and the Camera Eye: Visual Consciousness in Film and the
Modern Novel* (Charlottesville: University Press of Virginia, 1976); Wendy Steiner, *Pictures of Romance* (Chicago: University of Chicago Press, 1988); John Szarkowski, *Looking
at Photographs: 100 Pictures from the Collection of the Museum of Modern Art* (New York:
The Museum of Modern Art, 1973) and *The Photographer's Eye* (New York: The Museum
of Modern Art, 1966); as well as numerous novelists and poets. While many of these critics
and artists disagree about what a photograph is/does/signifies, all concur on its centrality to
current arguments about aesthetics, mimesis, representation, and cognitive perception.

17. Roland Barthes, "The Photographic Message," in *A Barthes Reader*, ed. Susan
Sontag (New York: Hill and Wang, 1983), 206–7.

18. Barthes, *Camera Lucida*, 85.

19. Susan Sontag, *On Photography* (New York: Farrar, Straus and Giroux, 1977), 57.

20. I have found little discussion of the fictional photograph as a distinctly separate
aesthetic, political, and perceptual question. Françoise Meltzer's exploration of how and
why literature plays with portraiture begins to touch on some of the questions I think
fictional photographs pose. See particularly her chapter "Still Life" in *Salome and the
Dance of Writing* (Chicago: University of Chicago Press, 1987), 113–58.

21. See Sontag, *On Photography*, 161–67, and *passim*, and Alan Spiegel, *Fiction and the
Camera Eye*.

22. Henry James's New York Edition is perhaps the most famous example of the use of
actual photographs to illustrate fiction. But as James himself points out, the purpose of
Coburn's photographs was very different. Speaking disdainfully of traditional means of
illustrating literature, James wrote, "the frame of one's own work no more provides place
for such a plot than we expect flesh and fish to be served on the same platter. One welcomes
illustration, in other words, . . . with the emphatic view that . . . it would quite stand off
and on its own two feet and thus, as a separate and independent subject of publication,
carrying its text in its spirit, just as that text correspondingly carries the plastic possibility,
become a still more glorious tribute" (James, Preface to *The Golden Bowl*, quoted in Ralph
F. Bogardus, *Pictures and Texts: Henry James, A. L. Coburn, and New Ways of Seeing in
Literary Culture* (Ann Arbor: UMI-Research Press, 1984), 52. The twenty-four plates for
the New York Edition were to serve as "complementary, non-interfering, and generalizing
illustrations" for his novels and short stories and "to stand on their own as beautiful
pictures" (5). While James's intentions and their results are a fascinating aspect of the larger
subject—the relations between fiction and actual photographs—they are not directly
relevant to a discussion of how Faulkner's or any other novelist's or poet's fictional
photographs function. James's own fictional photographs are another matter entirely and
relate directly to questions raised by Faulkner's fictional photographs.

23. Discussion of these other novels is included in the book I am now writing.

24. I use primitive here in John Berger's sense of the term. He argues that it has been traditionally used "to put in its place the art of men and women . . . who did not leave their class by becoming *professional* artists." Primitive artists are not trained in the conventions of their medium and their art is treated as an "'eccentricity'. . . because they refused, or were ignorant of, the fact that all artistic expression has traditionally to undergo a class transformation," so as to conform to "the main European tradition of secular art, serving that same 'civilized' ruling class." Primitive artists "are quite distinct from *amateurs*— most, but not all of whom, came from the cultured classes" ("The Primitive and the Professional," in *About Looking* (New York: Pantheon Books, 1980), 64–68). Clearly, Maud Butler saw herself as a primitive—not a professional or amateur. She was irate when Robert Coughlan wrote in *Life* magazine that she was an amateur painter: "He said I was a church-goer—I haven't been in a church in ten years, except for funerals. As for my painting, I am not one of these little old Southern ladies who paints porcelain or greeting cards. Women come to me to have their china painted or to get greeting cards. I tell them to go somewhere else. I am a picture painter. I *sell* my paintings; I make money on them" (Maud Butler Falkner, interview, summer 1953. Quoted in James Dahl, "A Faulkner Reminiscence: Conversations with Mrs. M. F. Faulkner," *JML*, 3 [April 1974], 1028).

25. Gender in Faulkner's fictional world is a slippery affair. The constant sexual and racial transformations in *Light in August* and *Absalom, Absalom!* are two obvious examples. Most characters know neither who nor what they are. A major source of confusion is their blind belief in the strict racial and gender classifications imposed by their culture. In *Within the Plantation Household: Black and White Women of the Old South* (Chapel Hill: University of North Carolina Press, 1988), Elizabeth Fox-Genovese includes a valuable chapter on this subject. See, "Gender Conventions," 192–242.

26. This is an interesting turn on the longstanding argument in aesthetics concerning the genders of pictorial versus verbal representations. For an excellent summary and further extension of this argument see W. J. T. Mitchell's *Iconology: Image, Text, Ideology.*

27. William Faulkner, *Sanctuary* (New York: Vintage Books, 1931, 1958), 215–16; subsequent citations to this edition are given in the text.

28. Barthes, *Camera Lucida*, 3.

29. Barthes, "The Photographic Message," 200.

30. John Berger, *Ways of Seeing* (London: British Broadcasting Corporation, 1972, 1987), 7.

31. For a more detailed discussion of this point, see *Origins*, 19–40.

32. Pierrot/Faulkner's intensely erotic relationships with both mother and lover figures are discussed in *Origins* and in my introduction to Faulkner's *Vision in Spring* (Austin: University of Texas Press, 1984). Robert Storey notes that the stylized guise of Pierrot permitted the nineteenth-century French pantomimists to pursue an order of realism far in excess of the Naturalists themselves. He quotes Zola's review, "La Pantomime," where the author says he can imagine "with what an angry outcry a work of ours, of the Naturalistic novelists, would be received if we were to push so far the analysis of the human grimace, the satire of man in the grips of his passions" (*Pierrots on the Stage of Desire: Nineteenth-Century French Literary Artists and the Comic Pantomime* [Princeton: Princeton University Press, 1985], 186). Faulkner's drawings of Pierrot serve a similar autobiographical purpose: his fictional photographs permit his characters to release unspeakable emotions as well.

33. Estelle Oldham Faulkner, interview, *Charlottesville Daily Progress*, 26 January 1969, 3–C1. Maud Butler's realistic imaginative perception reveals itself in her paintings and her comments about her own and Faulkner's art. Speaking of her painting of Caroline Barr, "She used to come up here and sit with me to keep me company. In her old rocker, just like my picture" (Dahl, 1027). In a painting Maud Butler did of the inside of a black sharecropper's cabin, she has painted a photograph of Eleanor Roosevelt on the wall (Interview, *Memphis Press Scimitar*, 14 September 1954). Speaking of Faulkner's fiction, Maud Butler said, "Now, Jason, in *The Sound and the Fury*—he talks just like my husband did. My husband had a hardware store uptown at one time. His way of talking was just like

Jason's, same words and same style. All those 'you knows.' And of course Dilsey is Mammy Callie" (Dahl, 1028).

34. Estelle Oldham Faulkner, interview, *Richmond News Leader*, 3 November 1964, 11–12.

35. Estelle Oldham Faulkner, interview, *The Charlottesville Daily Progress*, 26 January 1969, 3–C1.

36. Blotner, Goffman, Grimwood, Sensibar (*Origins* and "'Drowsing Maidenhead'"), and Harvey Strauss, M.D., "A Discussion of J. L. Sensibar's 'William Faulkner, Poet to Novelist: An Imposter Becomes an Artist,'" *Psychoanalytic Studies of Biography*, ed. George Moraitis, M.D., and George H. Pollock, Ph.D., M.D. Monograph 4: Emotions and Behavior Monograph Series of the Chicago Institute for Psychoanalysis (Madison, Conn.: International UP, 1987). One photograph Faulkner sent to his mother from his RAF training camp in Canada showed him posing beside "his plane." During his brief service Faulkner never flew. Maud, the realist, did a painting of this trick photograph, which she and others believed (Dahl, 1027). In the '60s when she agreed to sell it, her own son forbade her to. It was "too personal." Faulkner wanted control of his trick photographs, it seems. At that point in his life, judging from his letters to Malcolm Cowley, he appears to have been embarrassed by this early imposture. See *Selected Letters of William Faulkner*, ed. Joseph Blotner (New York: Random House, 1974), and *The Faulkner-Cowley File: Letters and Memories, 1944–1962*, ed. Malcolm Cowley (New York: Viking Press, 1957).

37. Barthes, *Camera Lucida*, 13–14.

38. William Faulkner, *Absalom, Absalom!* (New York: Vintage Books, 1936, 1972), 14; subsequent citations to this edition are given in the text.

39. Minrose C. Gwin first questioned the judgment of the male gaze in *Absalom, Absalom!* and argued that Rosa "is the force which drives the past into the present, which insists on the telling of the tale, which must know why. . . . She is both artist and participant. It is she who insists not only that the story be told, but that it be *understood.*" See her *Black and White Women in the Old South: The Peculiar Sisterhood in American Literature* (Knoxville; University of Tennessee Press, 1985), 116. See also her brilliant reading of *Absalom, Absalom!* in her forthcoming *Faulkner and the Feminine* (Knoxville: University of Tennessee Press).

40. Other photographs or photographic images occur on 14, 75, 91, 101, 110, 128–29, 146–47, 150, 358–59, and 377.

41. John Berger, "Uses of Photography," *About Looking*, 51.

42. Slave narratives and Southern white women's journals and diaries contain numerous examples of the constant acting required of both subjects for maintaining a sense of self and for survival in a slave culture. This behavior extends into the present. As Southern fiction and cultural studies reveal, Southern society privileges the theatrical. For discussion of the importance of theater in Faulkner's life (particularly his marriage) and his art, see Sensibar, "'Drowsing Maidenhead.'"

43. Jones, 42.

44. This, of course, is an inside joke.

45. "[The artist] is completely amoral in that he will rob, borrow, beg, or steal from anybody and everybody to get work done. The writer's only responsibility is to his art. He will be completely ruthless if he is a good one. . . . If a writer has to rob his mother, he will not hesitate; the 'Ode on a Grecian Urn' is worth any number of old ladies." Faulkner, interview 1956. Reprinted in *Lion in the Garden: Interviews with William Faulkner*, ed. James B. Meriwether and Michael Millgate (Lincoln: University of Nebraska Press, 1980), 136–37.

46. Sontag, *On Photography*, 16.

47. In answer to a question about the Southern writer's audience, Faulkner said that for these writers "the publisher, and to an extent his readers, are Northerners. I think that most Southerners know that his home folks ain't going to like what he writes anyway. That he's not really writing to them, that they simply do not read books. . . . The non-writing

Southerner, the non-reading Southerner, he wants the sort of brochure that the Chamber of Commerce gets out. There are things in his country that he's not too proud of himself, but to him it's bad manners to show that in public." William Faulkner, interview 13 May 1957. Frederick Gwynn and Joseph L. Blotner, eds. *Faulkner in the University: Class Conferences at the University of Virginia, 1957–1958* (Charlottesville: University of Virginia, Press, 1959), 136–37.

48. Jones, 8, 12–13.

49. Berger, *Ways of Seeing*, 54–55.

50. Sontag, *On Photography*, 16

51. Faulkner here invokes Eliot for his own purposes. "Writhing" in *Sanctuary* is always associated with illicit sex. Tommy writhes watching Temple, Popeye writhes watching Temple and Red. Miss Reba describes Temple and Red as "nekkid as two snakes." Temple writhes against Red just before he is murdered.

52. In response to Faulkner's remarks about Southerners not caring to read his books, a questioner asked if that wasn't universal—that no region likes to be criticized. Faulkner answered, "but didn't the people of his own country have a fierce pride in people like Thoreau and Emerson? Or was that just the educated, intellectual New Englander felt that?. . . . I always thought that everybody—they might not have approved so much of all that Emerson or Thoreau said, but they had a fierce, almost provincial pride in—. . . Can a man write about ideas excepting in the provincial terms of his background?" Interview, 13 May 1957 in *Faulkner in the University*, 137.

53. A journalist interviewing Maud Butler in 1956 writes: "On the day of our visit, Miss Maud seemed disconsolate, for, as she expressed it, 'I've been unable to do a lick of work for two weeks.' Discussing her routine, Maud Butler Falkner explained that after breakfast, 'If I feel like painting, I leave the dishes and go at it. If the spirit is moving, I paint right on through dinner—but once I get tired, I just walk out and leave it.'" Asked whether she painted when her children were growing up, she said that the only painting she could remember "for a 35-year span consisted of a few pictures she worked on while standing at the living room mantle with her equipment safely above" her children's reach. Margaret T. Silver, "A Visit with Miss Maud" typescript for *McCall's* article (Oxford: University of Mississippi Library), 2.

54. Joseph Blotner, *Faulkner: A Biography* (New York: Random House, 1974), 57.

55. John Faulkner, *My Brother Bill* (New York: Trident Press, 1963), 123–24.

56. In 1941 Maud Butler had her only "formal" lessons with the exception of a two-week art class in college. "The instructor insisted her technique was all wrong, that she should sketch the whole portrait before painting. But Miss Maud said she would 'paint one eye and if that was right, I really went to town.' Finally, she was left to her own devices" (Silver, 2). For more discussion of Estelle Oldham, see Sensibar "'Drowsing Maidenhead.'"

57. Berger, *About Looking*, 64.

58. Ibid., 68.

NOTE: My research for this article was supported by an Arizona State University Women's Studies Faculty Summer Stipend (summer 1988) and an American Council of Learned Societies Fellowship (partially funded by NEH) 1988–89.

"The Kotex Age": Women, Popular Culture, and *The Wild Palms*

ANNE GOODWYN JONES

In a 1940 letter to Robert Haas, Faulkner described himself as an "artist . . . of the first class, who should be free even of his own economic responsibilities." Instead, he complained, he had become the "sole, principal and partial support—food, shelter, heat, clothes, medicine, kotex, school fees, toilet paper and picture shows—of my mother . . . [a] brother's widow and child, a wife of my own and two step children, [and] my own child." Not only that, he was responsible too for "my father's debts and his dependents."[1] The language—"sole, principal and partial support"—echoes the phrase he had put on his map of Yoknapatawpha County four years earlier: "William Faulkner, Sole Owner & Proprietor." When he used language in these ways, it is clear Faulkner was thinking of himself specifically as a man. In his time and place (and for the most part in his fiction), questions of ownership, proprietorship, and inheritance were men's concerns, not women's. The responsibility for supporting dependents came as a consequence of this division of power by gender; lacking ownership, wives and children lacked certain types of responsibility. Estelle's irresponsible spending and Faulkner's resentment of it during this period were made possible by this imbalance. Despite such experiences, a strong and persistent force in Faulkner clung to those conventional yet unrealistic definitions of masculine and feminine within which he and Estelle had been raised. This commitment to convention is particularly evident in Faulkner's relations to women, both personal

142

and fictional. Even his most intimate relationships with women were marked by his idealizations and disillusionments. Faulkner's ambivalence about women in his fiction has led some critics to see him mistakenly as either gynophobic or gynophiliac. For some, Faulkner is a living Joe Christmas, contemptuous of womanflesh, repelled and yet reluctantly drawn to womansmells and woman-tastes. For others, he is a champion of women, awestruck by their fecundity in a Lena or Eula, admiring their grit, in the Miss Jennys, or in love with his heart's darling, the girl-child Caddy Compson. Both positions are in fact correct, for Faulkner partici-pated fully in both sides of his culture's ambivalence toward women, that is, in its simultaneous exaltation and degradation of the sex it perceived as fundamentally different from the norm, men. Yet I will claim in this paper that in his persona as a writer and in his fiction, especially in *The Wild Palms*, Faulkner seems also to find a third position, a place to experiment with the pieties of gender he had inherited. In *The Wild Palms* he uses his am-bivalence to explore and contest the ontological certainty of the gender dichotomy itself, and he seeks the sources of that di-chotomy in the stories men tell out of their deepest fears.

In the first letter I cited, Faulkner claimed that an artist should have no economic responsibility; given the gender assumptions at play here, this would put the artist in the place of woman. Indeed, Faulkner entertained notions of himself as a woman writer else-where. For example, though he wrote his publisher in 1934 that he was working on "the story . . . of a *man* who wanted a *son* through pride" (my emphasis), he said he had not finished it because "I have not gone my nine months."[2] If he saw *Absalom, Absalom!* as pregnancy, he saw another form of writing as pros-titution: asking his publisher for money two years earlier, he had argued that "it's either this, or put the novel aside and go whoring again with short stories."[3]

With the metaphor of whoring, Faulkner introduces another dichotomy within that of gender: the opposition of art to popular fiction, of high culture to popular culture. Interestingly, although he codes both types of writing as female, only popular writing takes on the conventionally negative association. It is probably safe to say that pregnancy as generativity or fecundity frequently takes a hallowed place in Faulkner's fiction, and that whoring—if not formal prostitution—is treated at best with sadness, and at worst, contempt. When he thinks of himself as a woman writer, then, Faulkner the artist is a good woman, and Faulkner the hack is bad.

Like most mainstream modernists, Faulkner apparently believed in a radical dichotomy between art, which was original, individual, and good, and popular culture, which was slavishly imitative, mass-produced, and bad. More typically, modernists render the opposition between art and popular culture not as good versus bad woman but as man versus woman. Andreas Huyssen has argued that mass culture has "always been the hidden subtext of the modernist project."[4] He observes that the masses as well as mass culture were persistently described in terms of a feminine threat. Floods, swamps, ooze, the red whore at the barricades—such metaphors use fear of woman-as-other to articulate the dominant culture's fear of the masses. On the other hand, as Huyssen begins to suggest, the characteristics of the modernist aesthetic have masculine associations. Like "man," for instance, modernist "art" is thought to be autonomous, while mass culture, like "woman," is contingent upon larger forces (such as market research and ultimately profit). Like "man," art transcends everydayness; like "woman," mass culture is embedded in it. Faulkner is not so far off the modernist mark then in coding popular culture as a bad—that is, sexually promiscuous—woman. Certainly he was not unusual in joining the issues of gender and pop culture.

But does Faulkner contest the reality of this dichotomy between art and popular culture? In general, Faulkner's feelings about popular culture seem to have been less ambivalent and less exploratory than his feelings about gender. Even his persistent choice of words to describe his work in popular culture—"trash," "potboilers"—shows no sign of deviating from the conventions of the modernist hierarchy. Yet I will argue that *The Wild Palms* shows signs at least of stepping aside from this conventional dichotomy. The novel is thick with allusions to both high and popular culture. Written just after an extended stay in Hollywood, *The Wild Palms* differs from Faulkner's norms in its continual, almost obsessive references to artifacts of popular culture, from dance marathons to movies to pop fiction—romances, true confessions, westerns, and detective stories. Their effect is to raise questions about the *reasons* for the difference between pop and high culture, and still more to comment on the motivation and effects of stories of any kind. *The Wild Palms* is one of the few places in Faulkner's fiction where one can find not only popular culture but also an adult woman who is both actively and happily sexual and also appears to have intelligence, imagination, and a certain independence of spirit. Faulkner treats Charlotte Rittenmeyer with a respect (and here I depart from Thomas McHaney's view of her) that is absent from his treatments of other sexually active and assertive and intelligent women: Joanna Burden's unbelievable sexual games come to mind. For once, then, he seems to have broken through the conventions marking good from bad women on the basis of their sexual autonomy.

Faulkner wrote *The Wild Palms* at what seemed to him the painful end of a love affair with Meta Carpenter, a woman with whom he had been deeply involved both romantically and sexually and a relationship whose setting had been Hollywood, the Xanadu of pop culture. It seems likely that this was Faulkner's first sustained and intimate encounter with a woman who was both profoundly sexual and increasingly autonomous and his first encounter with an entire world constructed around mass culture. These encounters, I would speculate, stirred up very personal questions for him both about gender and about art. I think it is no coincidence that in the novel in which Faulkner comes closest to exposing the dichotomy between the genders as an artifact of patriarchal culture, a fiction that disables as much as it enables, he also comes closest to using the forms of popular fiction to expose the political motivation of all fictions. In fact, I will argue, *The Wild Palms* locates the interests served by these dichotomies of gender and culture, and finds those interests to be a patriarchal oxymoron: masculine fears.

Speaking of masculine fears, let me return for a moment to the Kotex Age. In describing his duties as a patriarch, as we saw earlier, Faulkner made the following list of what he must provide: "food, shelter, heat, clothes, medicine, kotex, school fees, toilet paper, and picture shows." It is interesting to observe that the conventionality of this list—food, shelter, clothing, and so forth—breaks down just after "medicine" at the word "kotex." Following it come school fees, toilet paper, and picture shows. It seems that when menstruation breaks into the orderly linguistic structure of the list, children, excretion, and popular culture—all a bit on the disorderly side—swarm in at the breach.

The tone of contempt that is muted here is explicit in another reference to Kotex. Writing to his agent in 1936 from Oxford, Faulkner said:

> Since last summer I seem to have got out of the habit of writing trash, but I will still try to cook up something for Cosmopolitan. Maybe I can get hold of one of the magazines and take a story that they will buy and change locale and names, etc. That's probably hard work too and requires skill, but I seem to be so out of touch with the Kotex Age here that I can't seem to think of anything myself.[5]

Is this contempt for formula writing? for mass marketing, whether of stories or of sanitary napkins? Is it contempt for women as readers? or for women as bleeders?

Two comments: First, the ancient taboos surrounding menstruation, taboos which persist today, suggest that menstruation has been used to represent woman's powerful difference from men, her cyclical intimacy with nature, her ability to bleed for days and survive, her ability to reproduce people. Although certain cultures express their awareness of this difference with signs of awe or respect, Judaeo-Christian culture has expressed it with signs of disgust and contempt, fearing what other cultures revere. Women in our culture still call it "the curse." The phrase "periodical filth" is used to describe menstrual blood in *The Sound and the Fury* and in *Light in August*. Secondly, women's power in literary culture has long been a source of anxiety for American writers. From the beginning of the novel, women have been its primary consumers and often its most financially successful producers. Women too have had a tendency to prefer readability and personal identification to experimentation and aesthetic distance. No wonder, then, the Kotex Age should strike fear into the heart of a "masculinist modernist."[6]

EXCURS(E)US ON KOTEX

If Kotex was a villain to men, it was a hero—or heroine—for women. Until 1921, when Kotex was first marketed, American women dealt with their periods by wearing diapers made of flannel which they washed and reused. "Imagine the effect," writes Janice Delaney, "this cumbersome and unhygienic garment must have had on the average woman's workday outside the home, whether in a factory or in an office, and you have some idea of why women probably did not venture out of the house when they menstruated." But during World War I, French nurses "discovered that the cellulose material used for bandaging wounds absorbed menstrual blood better than cloth diapers," and the disposable sanitary napkin was born. It came just at the time when American women were getting the vote, joining the work force, and moving towards more sexual freedom. But it took ten years for American magazines to overcome their reluctance to advertising sanitary pads. And ads in the 1930s that Faulkner would have seen, perhaps in the pages of *Cosmopolitan,* played on the familiar taboos, offering women "no revealing outlines" to let out their "guilty secret." In the thirties, too, the taboos against exercise during menstruation were in force; swimming, riding, dancing, or tennis would caused a prolapsed uterus, irregular menses, and difficult menopause.[7] This then was the world of menstrual meanings that Faulkner inhabited.

END OF EXCURS(E)US

When Faulkner met Meta Carpenter, she was working as Howard Hawks's secretary. Faulkner had just arrived in Hollywood to work on *The Road to Glory;* he felt lonely and displaced. Meta, a native of Tunica, Mississippi, spoke like people back home, and Faulkner's first words to her were, "You're from the South: I can tell by your voice." He reminded her constantly that they were "both from Mississippi and therefore different."[8] Faulkner's original title for *The Wild Palms* was "If I Forget Thee, Jerusalem," a line from Psalm 137 which is followed by "let my right hand forget her cunning." Psalm 137 is about the Babylonian captivity, and begins "By the rivers of Babylon, there we sat down, yea, we wept, when we remembered Zion." It is tempting to imagine Faulkner thinking of Meta as a kindred soul in a strange land, and of *The Wild Palms* as his answer to the question the psalm asks in verse 4: "How shall we sing the Lord's song in a strange land?" But what he told Meta about their first meeting comes out of an even more romantic plot: "When I stood in that door and saw you, I said to myself, 'There she is!'" Faulkner courted Meta in a manner similarly romantic, as she reports it. He asked her to dinner, repeatedly, and repeatedly she said no, unwilling to go out with a married man and afraid of his drinking. But the drinking seemed to stop, and at work he continued to look at her with a kind of "wonder and worship" in his eyes. Meta finally decided he was "no womanizer but a gentleman."[9] After she agreed to go out to eat with him, the two of them gradually became virtually inseparable friends, and finally passionate lovers.

At least by this report, Faulkner's relationship to Meta Carpenter took the form of the literary romance: the immediate, intuitive sense that she was "the one," the chivalric courtship. Later, Faulkner was to write poetry to Meta, place gardenias on

their bed, and lovingly name their genitals Mr. and Mrs. Bowen.
Meta's description of their relationship identifies it both as deeply
romantic and deeply sexual. Thomas McHaney, following
Cleanth Brooks, argues in his book on *The Wild Palms* that
Faulkner drew on the literary tradition of romantic love to invent
the story of Charlotte Rittenmeyer's and Harry Wilbourne's quest
to incarnate the dream of perfect love.[10] No doubt this is the case.
But it seems further to be the case that Faulkner also used that
tradition in his construction of his relationship with Meta Carpenter, and it seems likely that that experience added a particular
energy and personal stake to the plotting of this novel. Complicat-
ing matters still further, whereas romantic love may have had its
literary origins for Faulkner in works like *Romeo and Juliet*, and
from male protagonists like Don Juan and Tristan, for Meta
romantic love came from popular culture, and had a female protagonist. "Like every young woman in the 1930s," she wrote, "I
had been conditioned by romantic novels and fantasy movies."
Repeatedly during her memoir she sees herself through the lens
of a movie camera; when Faulkner leaves for Oxford, for instance,
she goes to work the next day refusing to be "Lillian Gish be-
trayed, Helen Hayes suffering quietly, Janet Gaynor wringing
expressive hands."[11] Thus for both, the affair was mediated by
cultural images and plots; it could be said, fancifully, that in their
affair they married high culture to popular culture.

Whatever might have been the case biographically, both used
the plots of romance in constructing their written versions of the
experience: Meta her memoir, which she wrote with Orin
Borsten, and Faulkner his novel, *The Wild Palms*. A comparison of
the plots they used will show how intimately gender affects the
romance, whether high culture or pop. And finally, such an
analysis will allow us to see "Old Man" to be pursuing the same
profoundly masculine concerns as "Wild Palms," albeit in a different system of representation.

Of the studies of popular romance fiction, I have found the most
interesting to be Janice Radway's book *Reading the Romance:*

Women, Patriarchy, and Popular Literature. Radway made an unusual move for a literary critic: in addition to analyzing the texts of romance fiction, she talked to the women—and it *is* almost exclusively women—who read them. Her critique of more traditional criticism has to do with what she sees as its hidden assumption that reading is a fixed, even a coercive event: that what is "in" the text is exactly what readers take away from it, if they read well. Radway sees reading as a process by which a person produces meaning out of a relationship with a text, that is, an engagement between the plots already within the reader and those within the text. As Radway says, her focus on reading as well as on texts is a way to remind us that the "essentially human practice of making meaning goes on even in a world increasingly dominated by things and by consumption."[12] Clearly, Radway expects and endorses multiple and diverse readings; nevertheless, her interest is in finding *patterns* both within her texts and among her readers.

For our purposes now, Radway's most useful discovery was the contrast between what her readers see as the good romance and the bad one. A good romance focuses its attention on one character, a woman, who triumphs in the end by finding a man who loves her for herself. In this way she accomplishes two apparently contradictory aims: freedom (or individuation or separation) and connectedness (or union or merger). She is free because he loves her just as she is; and she is connected in a marriage, a union with another person that is depicted as a type of symbiosis. The plot of the good romance must reach this happy conclusion after a period of alienation and distance, based on mistrust between the woman and her man. That mistrust always turns out to be based not on reality but on the woman's misunderstanding, that is, on a type of misreading of the man's character. Once the readings are corrected—once the man's gruffness or violence or downright hostility are seen correctly as his inarticulate love for the woman, once sex is seen as really love, once marriage is seen as not a social or economic arrangement but, again, as really love—the distance vanishes, and the two are free to love one another as they truly are. The focus of a good romance, then, is on the *process* of a relationship, the everydayness of it, and that process is seen as an exercise in hermeneutics, in coming up with the correct interpretation. Clearly such a plot is wishful—in real life, some hostility is hostility. But Radway argues that readers use these stories in at least two helpful ways: first to lay claim to some time alone—most of the romance readers spend most of their time responding to others' needs—and second to offer, if only temporarily, a compensation for the actual lack of nurturance from men that is the result of the patriarchal family structure. Yet because the consolation is temporary, because it fails to provoke any real change, Radway argues, women must read this plot over and over again, consuming popular fiction as they might any other drug.

Radway finds the root of the matter in Nancy Chodorow's analysis of patriarchal family structure. Briefly, Chodorow argues in *The Reproduction of Mothering* that mothers, as the primary parents, produce gender difference by the differing ways they respond to male and female infants. The key poles of this difference have to do with identification and separateness, or connection and freedom. A woman's mothering of her female child "tends to cement a daughter's identification with her mother, a state that later produces difficulties in the daughter's individuation." When a girl enters the oedipal period, she retains her connection to her mother and thus carries an "internal emotional triangle" into adulthood, including a desire to "reconstruct the lost intensity of the mother-daughter bond." Boys, on the other hand, need to differentiate themselves radically from their mothers in order to accomplish a sense of gender certainty. Thus the boy feels the need to "suppress his feelings of dependence and his sense of having been merged with [his mother]." This results in a "negative definition of masculinity as all that is *not* female."[13] The results of these sexually differentiated processes are, for the adult woman, an experience of the self that involves continuity with others, what Chodorow calls permeable ego boundaries, and an ongoing need for nurturance. For adult men, the result is an experience of the self as autonomous and independent from others, and a devaluation of women. But these solutions are inadequate for both sexes, clearly; grown women lack the capacity for autonomy or "freedom," and grown men the capacity for merging with others, or "connectedness." The woman's ideal romance plot, then, tries to solve the problem for grown women by offering a fantasy that combines freedom and union.

Radway's readers would no doubt love Meta Carpenter's love story; probably they would dislike William Faulkner's. A *Loving Gentleman* works precisely within the norms for the good romance. The focus is on Meta; she finds a man, Faulkner, who loves her for herself; and a large part of the plot has to do with the continuing uncertainty of her readings of his character and ultimately his love. This hermeneutic uncertainty is produced in several ways. Faulkner is reclusive; he does not tell her what he thinks and feels—until he leaves, when his letters are full of the words Meta longed to hear in person. What should she believe? If Faulkner loves her, then why does he not divorce Estelle? Is it really Jill that's the issue? Can Meta continue to live by reading the signs, guessing what he plans, or will she ask him directly? And if she does, how will she interpret his response? Such enigmas keep the plot going. As in any "good romance," their resolution is always the same: he loves her after all. Finally, Wilde chose as her epigraph this passage from Faulkner's *A Green Bough:* "A singing fire that spun/ The gusty tree of his desire/ Till tree and gale were one"; it is a perfect articulation of love as symbiosis, the merger of two persons in one.

But Meta Carpenter Wilde (and Orin Borsten) go further than the formula, apparently improvising on it in two ways. First, Wilde self-consciously plays with the conventions of the genre. For example, she sets up her fantasized picture of Faulkner in the style of the typical romantic hero: "I had imagined him to be tall, darkly handsome, with a scowling visage." But then she subverts it with reality: "and now he stood before me, an unimpressive, almost diminutive man, whose nose was curved and pointed over a neatly trimmed moustache and whose glowing brown eyes never left my face."[14] But such literary maneuvers offer only a pretense of subversion. It's not the appearance that counts, in romance; it's what lies beneath, in the heart. And it is the heart that the woman must learn to read correctly. Faulkner's eyes could be bright purple, but as long as they never leave her face, we are still in the "good romance."

Carpenter's second apparent improvisation on the genre has to do with introducing a counterplot, the development of the autonomy of the heroine. In a typical romance, the heroine begins as a rebel, willful and tomboyish, yet withal deeply "feminine." But at this point she is also presexual. The romance plot then offers her both sexuality and the freedom of being truly loved but takes as its price that "girlish" freedom of tomboyish defiance. In Wilde's variation, Meta grows more confident and independent, even defiant, *as* she gains more sexual experience. Once, while she is listening to an opera on the radio, Faulkner interrupts her; she waves him away. He is furious, but Meta sticks to her musical guns. And in a major shift from the good romance plot, Meta calls off the relationship once she is convinced Faulkner does not plan to marry her. At that point Meta takes over her own variant plot: writing Faulkner out of the part, she substitutes an attentive pianist, Wolfgang Rebner, and marries him instead. True to its title and to the "good romance," however, the focus of this love story remains the romance with Faulkner. Its continuity suffers somewhat from the aberrance of the marriage to Rebner, but not as much as one might assume; in fact, it provides only one more of those periods of alienation on which the romance plot depends. Wilde and Borsten thus manage to sustain the basic premises of the good romance while carrying out innovations and variations on the theme.

What about Faulkner's version of the romance, "Wild Palms"? Not only does it fail to do what the "good romance" must do, according to Radway's readers, but it actually bears the marks of the "bad romance." "Wild Palms" fails to meet the minimal

requirements of a good romance because it focuses on the consciousness not of a female but of a male protagonist: though
Charlotte Rittenmeyer is remarkably fully developed, we never
have access to her private thoughts and feelings. Instead, we see
things through the consciousness of the narrator, and, frequently,
of Harry Wilbourne. Secondly, the story does not take as its
project the subtleties of a developing relationship that finally
eventuates in mutual trust, respect, and love. On the contrary, it
assumes the condition of love from the outset. At their second
meeting, Charlotte

> crushed out the cigarette and rose and came to where he stood before
> the cold hearth and stopped, facing him. 'What to—Do they call you
> Harry? What to do about it, Harry?"
> "I don't know. I never was in love before."
> "I have been. But I don't know either."[15]

That's about it for a developing relationship of the kind the good
romance cherishes.

Not only does it fail to fulfill the requirements of the good
romance, "Wild Palms" actually meets most of the requirements
of the bad romance, as Radway's readers see it: physical torture, a
weak hero, and a sad ending.[16] Harry's bungled abortion satisfies
all three. All that's missing are rape and promiscuity.

Within the romance called "Wild Palms" there are actually two
subsidiary love plots spun out, one by Charlotte and one by Harry.
In Charlotte's plot love itself is an abstraction, a Platonic ideal.
Harry repeatedly comments that Charlotte loves the perfect idea
of love rather than an actual man (59, 83–84); elsewhere he sees
her idea of love as a bubble balanced above, not in, the world (92).
Charlotte's idea of romance thus has certain resemblances to the
modernist and masculinist view of art. It is separate from life,
superior to everydayness, and must remain pure—autonomous—or it will die. A child would ruin it. One is reminded of
Faulkner's use of the image of the Grecian urn. The test of love,
too, is rendered more abstractly than personally. In some myste-

rious way, the lovers either will or will not be worthy of the entity, love. Charlotte says, "It isn't love that dies, it's the man and the woman, something in the man and the woman that dies, doesn't deserve the chance any more to love" (218).

Harry, not Charlotte, is the pop artist, the "woman writer" in "Wild Palms." He writes true confessions from the woman's point of view for pulp magazines. But his stories are not like the good romances we have discussed; instead, they are repetitively concerned with the loss of literal sexual innocence. Such a loss constitutes, as Harry writes it, a "sad ending" and quite possibly "physical torture." Harry sees his stories as "moron's pap," "sexual gumdrops" (123), but like Miniver Cheevy, he keeps on writing.

Neither story is a "good romance," then, but Harry's is worse. According to Radway, a bad romance "refuses to maintain the illusion that an ideal relationship is a plausible and extended possibility in the real world."[17] Charlotte's project, however abstract, is to make the ideal possible; Harry's, as a pulp writer, is to deny it.

If these are, in a sense, "dueling plots," then which author wins? Which plot, if either, shapes the form of "Wild Palms"? Plainly, it is Harry's. For "Wild Palms" is itself the story of the loss of sexual innocence and its doleful consequences, and of the impossibility of sustaining an ideal relationship. Only because he has waited so long to lose his virginity is it possible, Harry believes, to live as long as he does in the dream of timeless love that Charlotte wills. And indeed, when Harry snaps out of the dream at the lake—using Charlotte's menstrual periods to re-enter time—the relationship starts on its downward path to Chicago, Utah, and Charlotte's pregnancy. The larger plot bears out in other ways as well this valorizing of the tragic story of lost sexual innocence over the hopefulness of Charlotte's dream of love. It is, like Hemingway's *A Farewell to Arms*, a tragedy of death as the result of sexuality; even more than *A Farewell to Arms*, however, *male* sexuality stands as the culprit, for Harry's knife is explicitly compared to his penis.

In fact, the story is riddled with metaphors connecting not life but death with sexual love. The lovers meet near a stagnant pool. When they first make love, Harry is convinced that they carry a smell of "unsanctity and disaster" (60). Chicago is compared to a corpse (96), the limousines to hearses (97), and in Wisconsin Harry fantasizes, like Quentin Compson, of a watery death as the future of the affair. The narrator, describing the cold of Utah, compares it to the "first sex experience or the experience of taking human life" (182), and Harry, looking at the dying body of his lover, her waist, thighs, belly, and "female hair," can think only that death is now cuckolding him. Sex and death: if ever a story was doomed by its metaphors, this one is. And those metaphors belong to Harry.

What kind of romance plot is this, then—neither the interpersonal story of Meta and women and popular culture, nor the Platonic art form of Charlotte's masculine "high" culture? I submit that this is a masculine popular romance plot, a plot written by men for men, a plot that derives specifically from male fears and that attempts to warn men away from the dangers it articulates. Further, I submit that it is exactly these dangers that the story "Old Man" represents, in its depiction of the tall convict, the pregnant woman, and particularly the flood.

What then are these terrors? They must be connected to the loss of sexual innocence, specifically to the male sexual act, for that is the keystone both to Harry's true confession stories and to the "Wild Palms" story itself. Indeed, we can find more direct clues in "Wild Palms" itself. Here is Harry's description of the loss of his virginity:

> . . . you are one single fluxive Yes out of the terror in which you surrender volition, hope, all—the darkness, the falling, the thunder of solitude, the shock, the death, the moment when, stopped physically by the ponderable clay, you yet feel all your life rush out of you into the pervading immemorial blind receptive matrix, the hot fluid blind foundation—grave-womb or womb-grave, it's all one. (138)

From a Chodorowian point of view, the terror Harry describes comes out of that point when the boy's sense of himself as different from his mother and therefore male is threatened by his memory of and desire to return to a blissful merger with her. Adult men reexperience these fears in the act of sex, particularly romantic sex; it can feel like a kind of engulfment, a loss of separate identity in a flood of identification, a rather sinister "little death." It is no wonder then that Harry sees it as both a sexual and an emotional victory to survive Charlotte. The thrice repeated masturbatory image that appears in the final scene when Harry is in prison—"it will stand to his hand" (324)—suggests that his identity as well as his sexuality have made it through the "matrix," the woman. In his relief, even grief feels better than nothing at all.

Klaus Theweleit's 1988 study of the German Freikorps—the men in volunteer armies after World War I who became the core of Hitler's SS—might seem to make an unlikely pair with "Old Man." Yet Theweleit's book, *Male Fantasies*, finds in the writings of these men patterns that are startlingly similar to those apparent in "Old Man." Chapter 1 is called "Men and Women"; chapter 2 is "Floods, Bodies, History." Bluntly, the Freikorpsmen "hated women's bodies and sexuality . . . their perpetual war against the rebellious German working classes was undertaken to escape women." Women (and their representations in nature) evoke such anxiety because they stir up desires in the men that men fear they cannot control. Specifically, says Theweleit, they stir up men's desire for merger and fear of total annihilation, by means of engulfment. For "women's bodies are the holes, swamps, pits of muck that can engulf." In the face of erotic femininity, then, the Freikorpsman struggles to "hold himself together as an entity, a body with 'fixed boundaries.'"[18] Thus images of towers, of dams, of standing tall are deployed against those of flowing or streaming.

Nor is it only women and nature that evoke these feelings. Communism, like individual women, is a "nameless force that seeks to engulf." The Freikorpsmen's art—for example, the monuments of the Third Reich—represents a "safety mechanism against the bewildering multiplicity of the living. The more lifeless, regimented, and monumental reality appears to be, the more secure these men feel." [19]

Still more interesting for our purposes are the metaphors that structure the psychic worlds of the Freikorpsmen. Because they flow and thus transgress boundaries, floods are a central metaphor; Communism, for instance, is the Red Flood. In the face of the Red Flood, the Freikorpsman "defends himself with a kind of sustained erection of his whole body." [20] Both the highest excitement and the highest fear come when the Red Wave hits a lone man. That moment of contact results in the death of the man; blood, rather than a "river of love," flows in this deathly orgasm. Women are associated with floods, tides, waves, dirt, slime, mires, morasses, and "shit"; men with whatever is firm, clean, solid, apart from and preferably above the flood.

The interpersonal effects of this way of thinking are predictably depressing. The Freikorpsmen cannot experience women except "through fear, deceit, mistrust, or domination." [21] Amazingly, to distract themselves from the appeal of women, one Freikorpsman remembers reading popular western fictions.

The tall convict surely would have been a prime recruit for the Freikorps. His fear of and hostility towards women never change; the quiet courage of the pregnant woman does not seem to make a dent in his rigid view, and he is happy only when he returns to the safety of the all-male prison. The last words of the novel are his— "Women shit!" (339). His battle against the flood is a struggle against yet another avatar of the female, the flowing streaming water that will uproot fixity and instigate change. Dozens of passages establish the connection between femininity and the flood; "Old Man," the Mississippi, is really a male impersonator, like Charlotte Rittenmeyer. The tall convict even reads westerns.

Only once in the story does the tall convict experience the possibility of generative change. That takes place when he is living at the Cajan's. Some of Faulkner's most effective language appears in the description of the convict's encounters with the alligator, encounters that revive in him a memory of the satisfactions of work and a sense of his personal worth. It's interesting, then, that these killings are described—like the operation on Charlotte—as sexual engagements:

> But the knife was home, he knew that even on his back in the mud, the weight of the thrashing beast longwise upon him, its ridged back clutched to his stomach, his arm about its throat, the hissing head clamped against his jaw, the furious tail lashing and flailing, the knife in his other hand probing for the life and finding it, the hot fierce gush. (258–59)

Once again, death is associated with male sexual experience. Like the Freikorpsman facing the Red Wave alone, the highest excitement comes with the moment of bloody death. Why? The experience of fighting a man or an alligator allows the excitement of sexual stimulation without the threat of engulfment by a watery, slippery other; on the contrary, the boundaries of the self are mobilized in defense against a clearly defined other: the enemy. Thus violent sexuality, or sexualized violence, enables the tall convict, the Freikorpsman, even Harry Wilbourne, to circumvent the anxieties stirred up by women without relinquishing the excitement of sexuality. Yet the tall convict's experiment with growth comes to an end, and he returns to prison. There he is safely surrounded by men to whom he can tell his story, narrating from a foetal position and inflecting the story with sexual gestures using his cigar—all the benefits of a regressive merging with a woman but without an actual, contemptible female to deal with.

Of course, Faulkner problematizes the tall convict's solution in a number of ways. I will comment on only one, and hope with this discussion to bring us back to the topic of popular culture and to conclude.

As you remember, the tall convict did not imagine himself when he was nineteen as a dutiful proto-Nazi but as an outlaw. From reading the popular fiction stories of Diamond Dick and Jesse James, he conceived an idea of heroism that turned on a radical resistance to authority, on taking the law into his own hands, on acting as an individual against the law. The failure of that plot landed him in prison. This had not been only an idea of heroism, however; it was a method of seduction as well. We learn, only at the end of "Old Man"—seeing only there the source of the bitterness that has motivated the narration all along—that the convict's girlfriend first encouraged him to act out his plot and then, when his stories failed him, deserted him for another man. The tall convict's struggle for sexual manhood and his struggle for individuality, then, were intimately connected in the outlaw plot, and both collapsed at once. Why? Ironically, the convict *read* popular fiction in a manner that subverted his desire for individuation. For he read dutifully and absolutely literally, seeing the language of the text as simple and referential, suppressing any possibility of a multivalent or metaphoric reading, and avoiding any sense of the political motivation of language—even though he obviously knew the lantern he used was part of a moneymaking project in which he himself had participated. Like Janice Radway's women reading their romances, the tall convict reads in a manner that contradicts the very freedom he seeks in the book's content.

Faulkner underscores this point about reading popular fiction with a little story about how stories are politically motivated and hence unreliable. I am thinking of the scene in which the deputy warden, the governor's emissary, and the warden negotiate their variant stories to come up with an expedient narrative to save face and keep the convict in jail. This story about stories makes the tall convict's capacity to misread even more sadly evident. For, after all we now know of the fictive quality of the law—"tell him it's a jury," they say; "Just call it a new train robbery" (328)—the convict still says about his extra ten years, "All right. If that's the rule" (331). Just as he read the Diamond Dicks as a set of rules, so does he now read his unfair and fabricated prison sentence. As a (mis)reader, he has been sentenced indeed.

So if Harry "wrote" "Wild Palms," who "wrote" "Old Man"? Not the tall convict, for whom it would tell only of an escape from the horrors of women and into the safety of the law. Rather, the story belongs to the narrator, whose voice sounds to me a lot like Faulkner's own. And in the reflexivity of this last move—making a fiction of the law—Faulkner suggests that Harry's story in "Wild Palms" too may be a lie, and, in fact—as he enters the infinite regress—so may be even his own.

Perhaps Faulkner's final comment on the certainties of gender and the credibility of fictions, popular or not, can be located in the structure he chose for the novel as a whole. Each story has its internal coherence, but they were written and they stand border to border in relation, in counterpoint, in an interpenetrating marriage of sorts that defines each by its position in relation to the other. A doublevoiced discourse of gender and gendered fictions, *The Wild Palms* thus presents an alternative to the loneliness and the anxieties of the men in it who fear not only women but, more important, their own deepest feelings, their living itself, and who end up, both, high above any flood in Parched Man prison.

NOTES

1. Joseph Blotner, ed., *Selected Letters of William Faulkner* (New York: Vintage, 1978), 122.

2. Ibid., 84.

3. Ibid., 59.

4. Andreas Huyssen, "Mass Culture as Woman: Modernism's Other," in *Studies in Entertainment: Critical Approaches to Mass Culture*, ed. Tania Modleski (Bloomington: Indiana University Press, 1986), 191.

5. Blotner, *Letters*, 95–96.

6. The term comes from Sandra Gilbert and Susan Gubar, *No Man's Land: The Place of the Woman Writer in Twentieth-Century Literature. Volume 1: The War of the Words* (New Haven: Yale University Press, 1988).

7. Janice Delaney, Mary Jane Lupton, and Emily Toth, *The Curse: A Cultural History of Menstruation*, rev. ed. (Urbana: University of Illinois Press, 1988), 58, 139, 130, 108.

8. Meta Carpenter Wilde and Orin Borsten, *A Loving Gentleman: The Love Story of William Faulkner and Meta Carpenter* (New York: Simon and Schuster, 1976), 16, 27.

9. Ibid., 22, 30.

10. Thomas L. McHaney, *William Faulkner's "The Wild Palms": A Study* (Jackson: University Press of Mississippi, 1975), 52.

11. Wilde and Borsten, *Loving Gentleman*, 28, 94.

12. Janice Radway, *Reading the Romance: Women, Patriarchy, and Popular Literature* (Chapel Hill: University of North Carolina Press, 1984), 221.

13. Ibid., 135, 136, 137.

14. Wilde and Borsten, *A Loving Gentleman*, 16.

15. William Faulkner, *The Wild Palms* (New York: Vintage, 1939), 43. Subsequent references to this novel will be cited parenthetically in the text.

16. Radway, *Reading the Romance*, 73.

17. Ibid., 176.

18. Klaus Theweleit, *Male Fantasies, Volume I: Women, Floods, Bodies, History* (Minneapolis: University of Minnesota Press, 1988), xiii, 244.

19. Ibid., xv, 218.

20. Ibid., 241.

21. Ibid., 373.

Harrison Smith: The Man Who Took a Chance on *The Sound and the Fury*

TOM DARDIS

Harrison or "Hal" Smith, Faulkner's chief editor and publisher from 1928 through 1936, has been a rather vague, shadowy figure lurking behind the various imprints under which he launched the first publication of *The Sound and the Fury, As I Lay Dying, Sanctuary, These Thirteen, Light in August, Pylon,* and, as a Random House partner, *Absalom, Absalom!* If you recognize his name at all, it is probably because he was the man to whom Faulkner dedicated *As I Lay Dying.* The working relationship between Faulkner and Smith is of considerable interest, because Faulkner might well have simply stopped writing his experimental novels that never succeeded in selling more than a few thousand copies—books that appeared to have no place in the publishing world of the late '20s and early '30s—had not Smith encouraged him to continue writing them by supplying him with advances that kept Faulkner going from one book to the next.[1] When it appeared that no one in New York would undertake the publication of *Flags in the Dust,* Faulkner claimed that he wrote *The Sound and the Fury* purely for his own pleasure, without thinking of a publisher. When Smith agreed to take on *Flags* (published as *Sartoris*) he became, in effect, the principal audience for the books that followed. From the beginning, Smith displayed an unshakeable conviction about Faulkner's importance as a writer. It was this amazing personal faith in him that once prompted Faulkner to say of Smith: "My friend in the North, one man I like."[2]

163

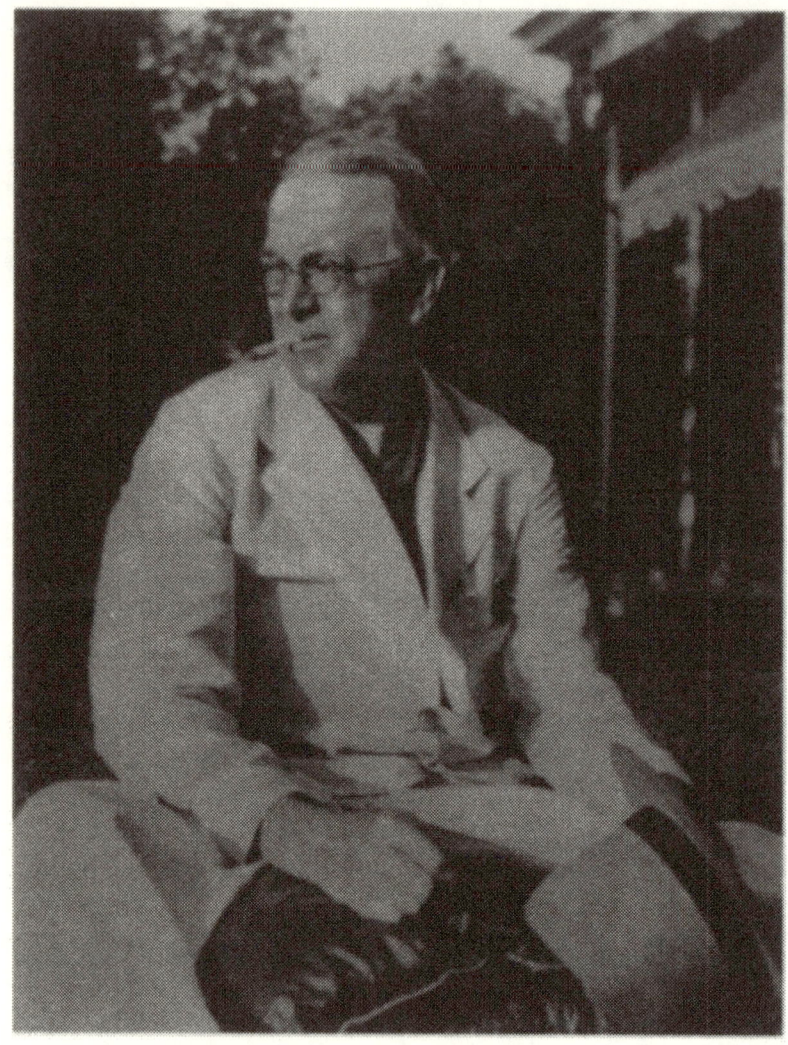

Harrison Smith in 1933, Farmington, Connecticut. Credit: C. Bran-
dendurg and Edith Haggard. Courtesy: Tom Dardis.

Faulkner dedicated *As I Lay Dying* to Smith at least partly because he might never have written the book had he not needed to borrow $500 from Smith in order to marry Estelle Franklin. His letter requesting the money shows how much Faulkner was willing to confide in his publisher at a particularly agonizing moment of his life:

20 June, 1929

Hal, I want $500.00. I am going to be married. Both want to and have to. THIS PART IS CONFIDENTIAL, UTTERLY. For my honor and the sanity—I believe life—of a woman. This is not bunk; neither am I being sucked in. We grew up together and I dont think she could fool me in this way; that is, make me believe that her mental condition, her nerves, are this far gone. And no question of pregnancy [*sic*]: that would hardly move me: no one can face his own bastard with more equanimity than I, having had some practice. Neither is it a matter of a promise on my part; we have known one another long enough to pay no attention to our promises. It's a situation which I engendered and permitted to ripen which has become unbearable, and I am tired of running from the devilment I bring about. This sounds a little insane, but I'm not in any shape to write letters now. I'll explain it better when I see you.

If you will let me have $500.00, I'll give you a note with ten percent interest or whatever you wish, due the first of next March, with the reversion of all accruing royalty on the two novels of mine you have in case I die, and I will promise in writing to deliver to you a third novel before that date; if it fails to please you, the note and interest to be paid on the above date.

I need not say this is confidential—the reasons, I mean—and urgent. I believe it will be the last time I'll bother you for money before time, because from now on I'll have to work. And I work well under pressure—and a wife will be pressure enough for me. Will you wire me Yes or No collect? If No, of course I'll understand.

/s/ Bill Faulkner
/t/   Faulkner

Oxford, Mississippi[3]

The story of how Smith managed to continue publishing Faulkner's books in the early years of the Great Depression when many New York publishing firms were operating at a loss and close to bankruptcy is a testimonial to his superb taste and personal courage in not only going on with Faulkner but also such other new writers as William March, Kay Boyle, Robert Graves, Evelyn Waugh, Raymond Radiguet, André Malraux, and Antoine de Saint-Exupéry. Faulkner never forgot the importance of Smith to him in his early days as a writer, once telling the literary agent Edith Haggard, Smith's long-time companion, who had apparently said something slighting to him about Smith's business judgment, that "Hal Smith published all my *best* books, Edith, and don't you ever forget it!"[4] Perhaps this remark will serve to remind us that Harrison Smith's financial and editorial support was attached to nearly *all* the major Faulkner novels while the much more widely known Saxe Commins coped largely with the later, far inferior works. It is time that Smith received his due as a major figure in Faulkner's early career.

There are several reasons for Smith's relative obscurity among those who played significant roles in Faulkner's writing career; we are much more familiar with people of lesser consequence in his life. Although Smith died only as recently as 1971 at the age of eighty-two, he suffered for many years from what then was diagnosed as a circulatory problem involving the flow of blood to the brain, causing the near total erosion of his memory. It is more than likely that he was a victim of Alzheimer's disease. His illness made it impossible to interview him in his final years.

Although I had only one conversation with Hal Smith—in 1960, just before the onset of his illness—I have never forgotten the intensity of his reply to my question about his willingness to publish as uncommercial a novel as *The Sound and the Fury:* "When I first saw a section of that manuscript of *The Sound and the Fury* and confronted that tiny, tiny script of his, line after line of it, I thought immediately that this is a man who believes absolutely in the importance of what he is doing—it's just *got* to be published!"[5]

Besides his literary acumen, Smith possessed a high degree of personal charm that nearly everyone who ever knew him attests to. It was this aspect of Smith along with his unbusinesslike approach to the business of book publishing that endeared him to Faulkner. He was decidedly eccentric. One example of Smith's unconventional approach to running his firm was the occasion when he submitted his wife's, Claire Spencer's, novel *Gallow's Orchard* to the Literary Guild. He had recently submitted Maxim Gorki's new book *Bystander* to the Book-of-the-Month Club; both books were rejected. By chance the books were returned to his desk by the messenger service at the same time. Smith studied them for a long moment before deciding to reverse the submissions: now each book was sent to the club which had turned the other book down. His intuition proved uncannily accurate; both books became full book club selections in the same month, an extraordinarily rare achievement for a publishing house.

Smith was famous in New York literary circles for his acute absentmindedness; he had a habit of turning up at dinner parties at either the wrong house or on the wrong night or perhaps not at all. He was also famous for mislaying manuscripts, a trait that later exasperated his three partners at Random House. Smith's notorious absentmindedness was just one of the factors that has caused confusion about the circumstances surrounding the publication by him of *The Sound and the Fury* in 1929.

The central problem is concerned with time, with most accounts of what happened assuming incorrectly that Smith only decided to publish the book sometime *after* January 1929 when he officially opened his own firm, Cape and Smith, for business. But Smith had clearly decided to publish *The Sound and the Fury* during Faulkner's New York visit of September through early December of 1928, during which time he completed the book. Smith's publishing plans for his new firm had appeared in *Publishers Weekly* in early October of 1928. What has caused the confusion is the fact of the retention of the manuscript of *The Sound and the Fury* in the Harcourt, Brace safe as late as the middle of February 1929, as well as Alfred Harcourt's "rejection letter" about the manuscript in February of that year.

It was Faulkner's Greenville, Mississippi, friend, Ben Wasson,

who served as the agent who sold *Flags in the Dust* (published in
January 1929 as *Sartoris*) in 1928 to Hal Smith when he was the
chief editor at Harcourt, Brace. Wasson's memoir of Faulkner,
Count No 'Count, is not very reliable and is marred by Wasson's
vagueness concerning events that had occurred nearly half a
century before he wrote his account. In addition, Wasson told
contradictory versions of these events during the course of the
various interviews he gave. Wasson's description of the circumstances attending his giving the manuscript of *The Sound and the
Fury* to Smith in the fall of 1928 is a particularly unreal one, to say
the least. Wasson tells us tersely, with no further explanation, that
"Hal ordered that it be placed in a safe."[6] Now a safe is scarcely
the place to keep a manuscript which is under active editorial
consideration by a publishing house. But by the 1970s Wasson had
forgotten that the reason for Smith's having the manuscript locked
away on the Harcourt premises was *that he knew he was going to
publish it himself.* The mysterious $200 that Faulkner received at
the end of his New York visit in December 1928[7] was doubtless
Hal Smith's advance for *The Sound and the Fury,* the exact
amount called for in the contract signed the following February.
(It was not unusual for Smith to pay advances *before* the signing of
a formal contract or, as in the case of *As I Lay Dying,* to sign the
contract many months *after* the book's publication.[8])

In the summer of 1978, Mrs. Louise Williams, who was known
professionally as Louise Bonino, explained to me some of the
confusion about the facts concerning her departure from Harcourt at the end of 1928 to follow Harrison Smith in his new
venture. She made it clear that Alfred Harcourt's reputed anger
over Smith's departure from his firm was absolutely untrue; Harcourt had, in fact, turned down Jonathan Cape's offer to use
Harcourt as the basis for an American branch and had given
Cape's proposal to Smith, knowing perfectly well that he had
wished for some time to start his own firm. It was, rather, Louise
Bonino's departure that stirred Harcourt's "wrath." He had been
having an affair with her for several years and the fact of losing her

and her professional services as a top administrator was hard to bear. As for the manuscript of *The Sound and the Fury*, Mrs. Williams told me that Harcourt's "rejection letter" was merely a formality to get it on the record that Faulkner's manuscript had been turned over to Smith; she doubted very much if anyone else at that firm ever read a word of it.[9] If anyone there had read it, it is quite unlikely that the firm would have undertaken publication; only a venturesome soul like Smith would have dared to take it on.

Smith's famous absentmindedness enters the picture in February 1929, when the Faulkner manuscript was scheduled to enter the Cape & Smith production process. But where, indeed, *was* that manuscript? Smith had quite literally forgotten that he had left it behind him in Harcourt's safe. Once Wasson, who was now working for Smith as an editor, reminded him of its whereabouts, he was quickly dispatched to Harcourt to retrieve it. The mission also produced Harcourt's letter to Faulkner, who replied accurately that he had never considered his book to be a Harcourt submission.

The foregoing set of circumstances may serve to clear up some of the mysteries concerned with the book's publication, among them the hitherto peculiar fact that the Cape & Smith contract for the book was signed *in the very same week* that Faulkner received his "rejection letter" from Harcourt. It should also explain what Faulkner meant by referring to "our book" when writing to Smith after its publication: he was including Smith in the tiny elect of these two who had dared the lightning by publishing such an affront to literary convention.

Oliver Harrison Smith entered book publishing as a salesman and was later an editor for the old Century Company shortly after his graduation from Yale in 1911. Besides his B.A., Smith also acquired an M.A. in English, a rare achievement at the time for a man interested in book publishing. After a short stint as a journalist for the New York *Herald-Tribune*, Smith managed to get himself assigned to Russia just in time to witness and report the

October Revolution in St. Petersburg. He later liked to tell his friends that he was the only American journalist in Russia who had not written and *would not* write a book about the events of 1917–18. It was in 1919 that he began working at Harcourt, Brace, in the very first year of the firm's existence. Harcourt quickly established itself as a major American house through publishing in two major areas: the contemporary English writers now known as the Bloomsbury Group and which included the economic theories of Maynard Keynes, Lytton Strachey's biographical studies, the novels of Virginia Woolf, as well as the political writings of her husband, Leonard. The major American writer published by the firm was Sinclair Lewis, who, after the smashing success of *Main Street*, remained with Harcourt through *Dodsworth* of 1929. Smith wore two big hats at Harcourt: he was the advertising manager as well as the chief acquisitions editor; it was mainly through his efforts that the firm became Virginia Woolf's publisher for all her books. He once recalled his first meeting with Virginia Woolf, in the early 1920s: "I thought of her as a stricken deer, about to jump out of her skin."[10]

As Sinclair Lewis's editor, Smith was doing extremely well professionally by 1928, but he was eager to strike out on his own. It was in response to overtures from Jonathan Cape in England that he got his chance. By switching his role from editor to publisher, Smith exposed himself to a difficult challenge: although he had an extraordinary eye for literary talent, he was relatively indifferent to the financial side of book publishing, a dangerous weakness for a new publisher.

It was the success of T. E. Lawrence's *Revolt in the Desert* that made Jonathan Cape decide to invest some of his huge profits in an American branch to be located in New York. He first approached Alfred Harcourt with his proposal. Harcourt turned him down, knowing perfectly well that he could never be an equal partner with such an imperious man as Cape, who always insisted on his own dominance in any business venture. But Harcourt turned over the proposal to Harrison Smith, who believed he saw the chance to set up a major firm in partnership with England's most prestigious name in postwar publishing. Cape was impressed by Smith's enthusiasm, as well as by the range of his friends in the American book trade. Cape & Smith was set up with 20,000 pounds of Cape's money and 10,000 of Smith's, making Cape the final decision maker in London, The books on the firm's first list, including *The Sound and the Fury*, appeared in the late summer of 1929, just a few months short of the 1929 stock market debacle that inaugurated the greatest depression in the history of the United States. This was a time that proved to be disastrous for many New York firms. Smith had told Faulkner that the sales on "our book" would be small: he was right, for only about a thousand copies were sold in the book's first season out of the 1,793 that Smith printed; in the first thirteen years the book was in print, a total of under 3,000 copies were sold.

The firm of Cape & Smith predictably lost money from the start; new ones nearly always do, but in 1930 and 1931 it was virtually guaranteed. The company's losses mounted month by month in the first two years of Cape & Smith; no best sellers emerged to bail the firm out. (Contrary to popular belief, *Sanctuary* sold only about 12,000 copies.) Despite all his efforts, Smith was unable to persuade his old friend Sinclair Lewis to leave Doubleday for Cape & Smith. If he had been successful, the fate of his firm might have been very different. Cape insisted that Smith take on a number of British books that were totally unsuitable for the American market; at the same time he disliked many of the American titles his younger partner was bringing out in New York. These included all the books of William Faulkner. Cape turned down *The Sound and the Fury* for his London imprint, which meant that it and all the following Faulkner titles went to Chatto & Windus. There is a tale of a single meeting between Cape and his Mississippi author, in New York. As the story goes, Cape became infuriated by his chance examination of a set of uncorrected galleys of *As I Lay Dying*. He found much of the book's punctuation alien and demanded of staff member Robert

Ballou why the "bizarre errors" had not been corrected. When Cape discovered that Smith's custom was to print Faulkner's books pretty much the way he wrote them, he was upset, even more so the following day when he met Faulkner for the first and last time. Upon being asked by Cape what a certain passage in the galleys meant, Faulkner told him that he didn't know and that "I was pretty co'ned up when I wrote that."[11] There are apocryphal elements in a narrative relating these events, written by the son of Cape's London partner, Michael Howard. Faulkner, for example, was not *in* New York in the summer of 1930. One thing, however, is certain: Cape did not like Faulkner's books. In later years, Faulkner returned the compliment by referring to Cape as "that Limey with the false teeth."[12]

By the fall of 1931 Smith had decided to break away from Cape and the stream of titles that his English partner kept insisting he publish; Smith had hopes of raising enough new American capital to buy Cape out and unwisely told Cape of his intentions. Cape retaliated by essentially firing Smith, cutting off funds from London, and forcing the firm into bankruptcy with one sole aim: to make worthless the shares in the company held by Smith. If Smith had dared to offend both Cape's purse and his taste by publishing these bizarre books, it was only fair that he should pay for his crimes. The American book trade was so outraged by Cape's treatment of Smith that Cape did not dare show his face in New York until the end of the '30s. The bankruptcy cost Faulkner the three or four thousand dollars earned by *Sanctuary* and left Smith in the position of starting all over again at the beginning of 1932. His second imprint bore his name alone. This arrangement was only of a few months duration, for Smith was suddenly able to obtain the financial backing of Robert Haas, who had been associated with the founding of the Book-of-the-Month Club. In the next three years the tiny firm of Smith & Haas on East 49th Street, with never more than six or seven people on the payroll, published, in addition to Faulkner's, a number of books that have endured as classics of modern literature: *Man's Fate* by André

Malraux, *I, Caudius* by Robert Graves, *Seven Gothic Tales* by Isak Dinesen, and *Fontamara* by Ignazio Silone. These titles, along with all the *Babar the Elephant* juveniles, placed the firm on what appeared to be a firm basis for survival.

In addition to the two partners, Smith & Haas was staffed mainly by bright young women. Smith was an early advocate of what became the women's movement in the 1960s, believing as he did that intelligent women were fully capable of holding down jobs normally held by men. For this reason his chief of design and production was Evelyn Harter, and Louise Bonino was the advertising and publicity director. Both women have recalled for me their delight in being given responsible positions that also included reading and commenting on nearly everything the firm considered publishing. As Evelyn Harter remembers the occasion, it was Louise Bonino's initial reaction to *Sanctuary* that caused Smith to begin worrying about the wisdom of publishing the book. When Smith decided to publish a limited signed edition of *Light in August*, Evelyn Harter talked him out of the idea by drawing his attention to the disapproval of the booksellers for still another limited Faulkner edition coming so soon after *These Thirteen* and just before the forthcoming *A Green Bough*. Smith read her memorandum and cancelled his plans for the limited *Light in August*. Although she had alerted Smith to the legal dangers of publishing *Sanctuary* in its original version, Louise Bonino, as publicity director, arranged for the $500 payment made to Alexander Woolcott as a condition for his reviewing the book on The Town Crier radio program. The review was a factor which contributed much to the book's modest success.[13]

Both Evelyn Harter and Louise Bonino feared for Smith's life when he proposed flying down to Mississippi with Faulkner in his new Waco plane in 1933. They made every effort to talk their employer out of the trip, drawing his attention to the fact that nearly all of Faulkner's trips to New York involved large amounts of alcohol: the two women were convinced that Smith would be insane to go up in the air with him, but Smith told them patiently that he had to demonstrate to their star author that he had as much faith in him as a flyer as he had in his writing ability. The 1933 flight, from Washington, D.C., to Memphis, proved uneventful.

Smith's basic editorial policy with Faulkner was to print his manuscripts very close to the way he received them; except for minor alterations for house styling, Faulkner's work was not subjected to editorial interference on the part of Smith or any of his staff. In effect, a basically "hands off" policy prevailed. Two notable exceptions to this policy were Smith's reluctance to publish *Sanctuary* as submitted originally and Faulkner's subsequent decision to revise the book in galleys. The second exception concerns *Absalom, Absalom!*, the first book Faulkner submitted to Smith in his new role as one of the four partners at Random House in 1936.[14]

We must all be thankful that Noel Polk has tidied up some of the dust that has accumulated on the Faulkner texts over the years. Having said that, however, I must express dismay over at least one of these "restorations," to the text of the very last book that Smith worked on with Faulkner. A huge scandal has been provoked by the so-called corrected text of *Ulysses* based on the textual work performed by Herr Gabler and his two associates in Munich. There are some unfortunate analogies between the "restoration" of the Joyce text and the recently issued "corrected" texts of Faulkner's work. As Joseph Blotner pointed out in a lengthy note in the second volume of his 1974 biography, Faulkner agreed to Hal Smith's cutting several passages from the manuscript of *Absalom, Absalom!* which he found to be either unnecessarily obscure or repetitious.[15] I have only enough time to tell you about one of these, the one that I have come to call the "onerous carks" passage.

Quite far along in an especially long sentence dealing with Miss Rosa Coldfield's decision to come to live with her sister Ellen at Sutpen's Hundred, the original manuscript (and the published book) read this way:

—it's not this, not this that she is depending on to keep body and soul together: it is as though she were living on the actual blood itself, like a vampire, not with insatiability, certainly not with voracity, but with that serene and idle splendor of flowers abrogating to herself, because it fills her veins also, nourishment from the old blood that crossed uncharted seas and continents and battled wilderness hardships and lurking circumstances and fatalities.[16]

The original sentence continued on, however, for another thirty-seven words, as follows:

with tranquil disregard of whatever onerous carks to leisure and even peace which the preservation of it incurs upon what might be called the contemporary transmutable fountainhead who contrives to keep the crass foodbearing corpuscles sufficiently numberous and healthy in the stream.[17]

Hal Smith indicated his feeling about this final portion of the sentence by writing the words "TOO MUCH!" in the margin. He suggested that Faulkner drop the last part, and it did not appear in the published book. At no time between the book's original publication in 1936 and Faulkner's death in 1962 did he ever indicate that he was unhappy over the removal. It has, however, been "restored" in Noel Polk's 1986 text. This editorial decision goes against the grain of Faulkner's amicable editorial relationship with Smith, the basic character of which was that Faulkner nearly always agreed with Smith's suggestions but had no compunction in telling him when he didn't. For example, Smith proposed that Miss Rosa Coldfield's fifty-page monologue be set in roman type rather than in the italic specified by Faulkner; the author's choice of type was carried out to his satisfaction.

I will add here parenthetically that the most probable reason for Hal Smith's need to question Faulkner's occasional carelessness in preparing the manuscript of *Absalom, Absalom!* for publication arose from the ever-increasing effect of Faulkner's alcoholism, a subject that I deal with at some length in my book *The Thirsty Muse*.

Although a number of the Smith & Haas titles were relatively

successful, Haas felt they would have been far more so if they had
been launched by a firm with considerably more funds available
for advertising and promotion, precisely the thing that Bennett
Cerf of Random House offered him when he proposed a merger of
the two small firms at the end of 1935. Again contrary to widely
held views, Smith & Haas was not close to bankruptcy at the time
of the merger: it was simply undercapitalized. Haas was only too
glad to oblige Cerf, and Smith & Haas became a part of Random
House at the beginning of 1936. Cerf had a genius for publicity, as
well as having more working capital to invest in the enlarged firm,
most of it derived from the Modern Library series of reprints that
he had purchased from Horace Liveright in 1925. Within just one
year after the merger, Smith found himself voted out of the
company: his three partners, Haas, Cerf, and Donald Klopfer,
had found Smith's eccentric ways of doing business too much of a
burden. They objected to his habit of taking naps in the middle of
the business day after a night spent talking with Faulkner or
Sinclair Lewis. His famous absentmindedness about manuscripts
was not getting any better; the partners felt that Smith belonged
to a bygone era in book publishing and was really out of place at
Random House. His farewell letter to Faulkner as his publisher is
an affecting one:

> . . . I do not have to tell you what publishing your books has meant to
> me through all these years since the time of "Sartoris" and Harcourt,
> Brace, or how important for the future and for literature your work
> has always seemed to me.

> I will write again when I have decided just what I intend to do.
>
> HS[18]

Smith spent the next two years working at Doubleday as a trade
editor, to follow that by assuming the editorship in 1938 of the
moribund *Saturday Review of Literature*, a relationship that
lasted into the 1960s at the time of his final illness. Smith was able
to increase the circulation of the *Saturday Review* beyond 40,000
copies a week to past the 650,000 mark by the beginning of World

War II. During these last years, Smith started a number of extremely small-scale publishing houses bearing his name: Harrison-Hilton Books and Smith & Durrell, both of which had very short lives.

Harrison Smith's publishing record in the '20s and '30s has certainly earned him an honorable place among such other major publishers of the period as Thomas Seltzer, Alfred A. Knopf, Horace Liveright, and Ben Huebsch of the Viking Press. His friendship with Faulkner never wavered. When Faulkner came to New York in the summer of 1940 to break away from Random House and perhaps join the Viking Press list of Harold Ginzberg, Faulkner spent a long weekend on Smith's yacht which he kept moored on City Island. The two old friends discussed the pros and cons of the proposed move, which very nearly took place. In later years, Faulkner was often Smith's house guest at his East Side apartment on 63rd Street. He remained as eccentric as ever in his later years, especially about trying out new food products. Joan Williams was a dinner guest there on several occasions in the early 1950s with Faulkner when Smith's butler served them the recently marketed Stouffer's frozen chicken pot pies—on Wedgewood china. Smith never regretted his decision to be swayed by the tiny script which contained the words, "Through the curling flower spaces, I could see them hitting."

NOTES

1. Southern Studies Program, *The Making of William Faulkner's Books, 1929–1937: An Interview with Evelyn Harter Glick* (Columbia: University of South Carolina, 1979), 6.
2. *New York World Telegram*, 14 November 1931, 27.
3. Henry and Albert A. Berg Collection of English and American Literature, New York Public Library, Astor, Lenox, and Tilden Foundations.
4. Interview with Edith Haggard, New York City, September 1974.
5. Interview with Harrison Smith, New York City, July 1960.
6. Ben Wasson, *Count No 'Count: Flashbacks to Faulkner* (Jackson: University Press of Mississippi, 1983), 90.
7. Joseph Blotner, *Faulkner: A Biography*, 2 vols. (New York: Random House, 1974), 1:87.
8. The contract for *As I Lay Dying* is dated 3 April 1931, or about five months after publication.

9. Interviews with Louise Williams, August 1978, and Evelyn Harter Glick, June 1982.

10. Letter, Harrison Smith to Betty Gram Swing, 20 April 1954.

11. Blotner, 1:729. Another version of this story can be found in Michael Howard, *Jonathan Cape, Publisher* (London: Jonathan Cape, 1971), 120–21.

12. Blotner, 2:1073.

13. Interviews with Louise Williams, August 1978, and Evelyn Harter Glick, June 1982.

14. Deletions were made in *Pylon*. Four-letter words could not be printed legally in the United States in 1935; Faulkner replaced Smith's deletions with dots—one dot for each letter in the word.

15. Blotner, 2:437.

16. William Faulkner, *Absalom, Absalom!* (New York: Random House, 1936), 86.

17. Typescript, *Absalom, Absalom!*, Alderman Library, University of Virginia.

18. Letter, Harrison Smith to William Faulkner, 21 December 1936.

Dismantling the *Saturday Evening Post* Reader: *The Unvanquished* and Changing "Horizons of Expectations"

SUSAN V. DONALDSON

Ever since *The Unvanquished* was published in 1938, critics have been quick to characterize this collection of stories drawn mostly from contributions to the *Saturday Evening Post* as "Faulkner of the magazine stories rather than the Faulkner of the most powerful books," in the words of one contemporary reviewer.[1] Indeed, the original publication of the stories in the country's most famous family magazine has seemed reason enough for a good many readers to dismiss the book as a series of slight tales designed expressly for mass consumption. "We perceive in their narrative verve and lack of serious moral complication," Michael Millgate charged in his 1966 study, "the mark of stories skillfully and professionally created for the particular market offered by *The Saturday Evening Post*, and we are not surprised that the book was purchased by Hollywood—according to Faulkner's own story, as a potential rival to *Gone with the Wind*."[2] From this perspective, the tales, reflecting the demands and expectations of *Post* readers, seem too slick and romanticized, too narrowly conceived and tightly unified, not to be damned as a "readerly" text in the most derogatory sense ever meant by Roland Barthes.

A far more elusive and difficult text emerges, however, if one examines the intertext—that is, the tissue of connection, repetition, change, and addition—lying between the original *Saturday Evening Post* stories and the revised text of *The Unvanquished*,

179

which includes two stories in addition to the five original *Post* stories.[3] Reading text and intertext suggests that *The Unvanquished* first arouses and then frustrates and subverts expectations associated with those *Saturday Evening Post* readers Faulkner supposedly accommodates. Indeed, the last story, "An Odor of Verbena," and the passages added to the preceding stories in *The Unvanquished* imply that reader expectations attuned to tales of adventure and glory can be misleading and even dangerously blind to the rigid codification of storybook legends. For a writer who enjoyed setting "traps" for his readers—a trait noted by scholars ranging from Granville Hicks to Joseph Blotner—nothing could have served as a more suitable strategy.[4] In tales about revenge during the Civil War and Reconstruction, Faulkner managed to wreak his own special brand of vengeance on the *Saturday Evening Post,* a magazine that rejected far more of his stories than it ever published.[5]

Faulkner's revenge says something both about the writer's ambitions and about the monumentality of the *Saturday Evening Post* itself. By the second decade of the twentieth century, the *Post* was already an American institution. Its prominence had a good deal to do, no doubt, with the thirty-seven-year reign of its legendary editor, George Horace Lorimer, and his uncanny ability for gauging the opinions, demands, and reactions of his readership—an ability that made the *Post* at one time the country's most popular magazine.[6] As Wesley Stout, who succeeded Lorimer as editor in the late thirties, noted astutely, "He set out to interpret America to itself, always readably, but constructively."[7] Buoyed by fervent patriotism and boundless optimism, Lorimer once remarked in a famous interview, "What this country needs is more professional Pollyannas"; and in a sense, he set out to create those Pollyannas in the pages of the *Saturday Evening Post,* molding the reader in his own image.[8] In business and finance articles, biographies, autobiographies, anti–New Deal crusades, romances, adventures, and advertisements extolling products for the magazine's hard-working audience (in particular, accurate alarm clocks for early office days and cleansers for dutiful black servants), a unified image of the *Post* reader emerged defined by conservatism, appreciation of business, hard work, celebrations of the past—and a largely white Anglo-Saxon Protestant heritage.

At times this portrait of the reader and the reader's expectations, created by advertisements, tales, and business articles, came into sharp focus. For a while in the early thirties the *Post* included a book review section by Donald Gordon titled, not insignificantly, "The Literary Lowbrow: Book-Market Flashes." Featured prominently in its columns were romances, mysteries, and westerns, all proper fare for business-minded readers interested in recreation. Occasionally, a stray book by Ernest Hemingway would appear in "The Literary Lowbrow"—nothing to be excited about, Gordon reassured readers suspicious of "high" art—and he added, somewhat equivocally, "If you are a person of literary pretensions, it is safe to rave about Hemingway."[9] Literature, in short, was there to entertain and to reassure, not to unsettle and to question.

The *Post*, of course, was careful to portray itself as a periodical decidedly without pretensions or disturbing questions in order to ensure a broad middle-class audience, for Lorimer was an editor who took pains to cater to people who bought the magazine. He seemed to understand intuitively the outer limits of expectations, prejudices, and stereotypes characterizing the reading habits of a set community of readers—limits that *Rezeptionästhetik* critic Hans Robert Jauss would define as "horizons of expectations" in the late 1960s and early 1970s. In particular Lorimer was shrewdly aware of the public's power in defining the perimeters of "acceptable" and "unacceptable" literature, and no doubt he would have agreed with Jauss that "in the triangle of author, work, and public the last is no passive part, no chain of mere reactions, but rather itself an energy formative of history."[10] Long before the advent of reception theory, Lorimer was already shrewdly sensitive to the way a literary work could make use of certain narrative strategies, from characterization to set endings, to arouse a particular response from readers and to construct a certain "horizon of expectations"—in the case of the *Saturday Evening Post*, a penchant for romance, fast-paced adventure, resolution, unity, and reassurance about the goodness of American life.[11] As one associate editor noted, the *Post*'s publishing policies "consistently and continuously stood for law enforcement, for cleaner living and sounder thinking, and for raising the moral and material standard for all classes and all peoples."[12]

Reflecting those publishing policies—and Lorimer's tutelage as well—was the work of hugely popular writers who came to be known as members of "the *Post* school of fiction"—Edna Ferber, Fannie Hurst, Charles Francis Coe, John P. Marquand, Norman Reilly Raine, Mary Roberts Rinehart, P. G. Wodehouse, Kenneth Roberts, and Booth Tarkington. Over the years the *Post* had also published writers like Willa Cather, Joseph Conrad, Owen Wister, Edith Wharton, O. Henry, Ellen Glasgow, Theodore Dreiser, Stephen Crane, and James Branch Cabell, but it was "the inner circle" of authors closely associated with Lorimer—those appealing to the widest popular audience—who set the pattern for *Post* short stories. These were the writers who attracted the most mail from readers and who generally commanded the highest prices. In her heyday Mary Roberts Rinehart earned more than $4,000 for a single story, and $60,000 for a serial.[13]

A good many of the stories published by the *Post* in the mid-thirties concentrated on society life and the travails of the well-to-do, although Octavus Roy Cohen managed to attract a sizeable following with his Amos-and-Andy stories of black life in Birmingham and Harlem.[14] Civil War stories, however, were also fairly popular in a decade fairly glutted with fiction about the conflict. In 1934 alone the *Post* welcomed contributions from Elsie Singmaster, Joseph Hergesheimer, and J. P. Marquand, along with three stories by Faulkner that eventually turned up in *The Unvanquished*. Early on in the next year, the *Post* published

"No Enemy," by MacKinley Kantor, whose following was large enough to attract comparisons with Faulkner in early reviews of *The Unvanquished*.[15]

More often than not, these Civil War tales followed a fairly stock narrative pattern set two generations before by Thomas Nelson Page in *In Ole Virginia*. Both Hergesheimer and Kantor contributed tales in which potential opponents divided by war or by class are united in the happy ending of romance. Hergesheimer's story recounted the growing attachment of a languid Charleston belle and an impoverished Confederate soldier from the North Carolina mountains while Kantor's piece traced the inevitable romance between a Union officer and the daughter of a Confederate raider. It was a romantic pattern that attracted J. P. Marquand as well in his popular Civil War series following the adventures of Union secret agent Bill Price. After stopping a treaty offering French recognition of the Confederacy and confronting Jefferson Davis himself, Price wins the hand of a resistant Charleston lady and escapes to the safety of Bermuda.

It was this sort of stock narrative pattern, with its penchant for derring-do, adventure, and happy, resolved endings, that drew the scorn of a good many writers in the twenties and thirties who deplored the *Post*'s cultivation of mass readership. Faulkner himself apparently had much the same attitude toward the stories he wrote for the *Post*. They were, he told correspondents in the thirties—specifically his publisher Robert Haas and literary agent Morton Goldman—"pot boilers," "mechanical stories in which I had no faith," "big check stuff," and tales that were simply "knock[ed] out."[16]

Like other writers of the twenties and thirties, though, Faulkner was attracted by the *Post*'s generous fees for stories, and beginning in the mid-twenties, Blotner reports, he started sending the *Post* stories, all of which were rejected until 1930 with the publication of a World War I story called "Thrift."[17] By the time of his death in 1962, the magazine had published eighteen stories and novel excerpts, "far more," James B. Meriwether notes, "than any other magazine." It was, nonetheless, a strained relationship at best between America's most popular periodical and a writer who had already proved himself with the publication of several novels. In the early thirties the *Post* was far more likely to reject than accept a Faulkner story. According to Meriwether, only five out of thirty-two stories sent to the magazine by Faulkner in the lean years of 1930, 1931, and 1932 were accepted.[18]

Not surprisingly, then, Faulkner's letters to the *Post* tended to be marked by a certain veiled hostility. In 1927 the young novelist informed the magazine's editors that he had two or three stories in the works that might interest them. "If they do not please you," he remarked with what must have been forced jocularity, "the Post does not know its own children." And he closed his letter by declaring: "And hark in your ear: I am a coming man, so take warning."[19]

Thomas B. Costain, then literary editor of the *Post* and a popular historical novelist in his own right, appears to have responded with amusement to Faulkner's barbed humor and even urged Faulkner to visit the magazine's Philadelphia offices for a discussion of his writing. But like Lorimer and other *Post* editors, Costain had no qualms about making the Mississippian's work conform to the *Post* notion of a story. Those stories by Faulkner that the magazine did accept quite often had to be revised to meet *Post* requirements—to provide "clearer motivation," the editors told Faulkner, and most important of all, to increase "the number of appreciative readers."[20]

The Civil War stories that would eventually end up in *The Unvanquished* proved to be no exception. By autumn of 1934 the *Post* had already published three tales about the adventures of Bayard Sartoris, his playmate Ringo, and "Granny" Millard— "Ambuscade," "Retreat," and "Raid"—complete with illustrations by F. R. Gruger and preview notices praising "Raid" in particular as "one of the author's most vivid and amusing stories of Civil War days."[21] No doubt encouraged by this unexpected success, Faulkner sent the *Post* two more stories in the series,

"The Unvanquished" (later "Riposte in Tertio" in *The Unvan-quished*) and "Vendée." The *Post* expressed interest but insisted that "Vendée" needed to be clarified and tightened.[22] Hard-pressed for money, Faulkner agreed as usual to do the requested revisions, but it would be two more years before the last two stories would be published in the magazine.

Writing "pot boilers," it seemed, could be draining, frustrating, and not particularly profitable. The *Post* had shown no interest in meeting Faulkner's original price of $10,000 for six Civil War stories, and the tales themselves had taken precious time and energy away from the writing of the work that really concernd him—*Absalom, Absalom!*[23] A good deal of Faulkner's anger and frustration spilled over into passages of *The Wild Palms* recounting Harry Wilbourne's difficulties writing for pulp magazines and into letters. Even more explicit were Faulkner's complaints to Morton Goldman in 1936:

> Since last summer I seem to have got out of the habit of writing trash but I will try to cook up something for Cosmopolitan. Maybe I can get hold of one of the magazines and take a story that they will buy and change locale and names, etc. That's probably hard work too and requires skill, but I seem to be so out of touch with the Kotex Age here that I cant seem to think of anything myself.[24]

It was, however, those very pot boilers from the *Post* that attracted contemporary reviewers when the revised stories, cou-pled with "Skirmish at Sartoris" and "An Odor of Verbena," were issued under the title of *The Unvanquished* in early 1938. Louis Kronenberger of *The Nation* was not alone in declaring that the book "gains from having been partly published in the *Saturday Evening Post.*"[25] For some reviewers, like Herschel Brickell of the *New York Post* and Dale Mullen of the *Oxford Eagle*, the book's origin in the *Post* was bound to come as a relief to readers frequently intimidated by Faulkner's "difficult" language and ba-roque concerns. "The simple fact that the greater part of this book appeared originally in the *Saturday Evening Post,*" Mullen observed, "should be sufficient evidence of the [stories'] intelligibility and morality."[26]

A sizeable number of reviewers, in fact, considered *The Unvanquished* Faulkner's best work so far and predicted that the book would earn Faulkner a large new audience of appreciative readers, especially in the South. What is noteworthy about those contemporary reviews, though, is not so much their strongly favorable tone as the strikingly unified pattern of reading that links so many of them. An impressive number of the book's positive reviews focused attention on those stories drawn from the *Post*, stories that seemed, according to this perspective, to reveal little significant revision of the original magazine yarns.

Curiously enough, reviews following this pattern of reading generally made little or no mention at all of the book's last story, "An Odor of Verbena," the only one in the collection not previously published in a magazine. Those notices that did take time to discuss the story remarked, a bit uneasily, on the "incongruous," "different," or "question-marked" nature of "An Odor of Verbena."[27] It was a tale that quite simply did not seem to "fit"—a characterization that has been echoed by more recent critics also inclined to stress the overall unity of *The Unvanquished*.[28] The tension created by "An Odor of Verbena" and the rest of the stories seemed somehow "disturbing," in Michael Millgate's words, and the story itself appeared, as Joseph Reed noted, "set apart," a section "somewhat out of sequence."[29]

Part of the sense of discontinuity created by this last story no doubt has to do with the much later date of its composition. Written to "finish" the collection of stories as a book (and summarily rejected by the *Post*), "An Odor of Verbena," along with fairly lengthy passages added to several of the preceding tales, was composed three years after the five *Post* stories were written.[30] But the break in narrative that "An Odor of Verbena" has suggested to a good many reviewers and critics also tells us a good deal about reading strategies inscribed in the story itself. If "An Odor of Verbena" signals an end to the adventures of Bayard and

Ringo, it also casts a disturbing new light on the preceding tales. Coupled with passages added to the revised stories, this last tale raises serious questions about the earlier stories, about the way to read the adventures of Ringo, Bayard, and Granny Millard and the stern Sartoris code of honor, glory, and vengeance underlying all the tales.

Above all, what those questions focus on is the reading strategy associated from the very beginning with Bayard and Ringo, both of whom are dazzled by dreams and fragmentary tales of war and glory much the same way, one suspects, that *Saturday Evening Post* readers found vicarious satisfaction in Civil War yarns by John P. Marquand and MacKinley Kantor. When John Sartoris makes one of his infrequent visits home from the battlefields in "Ambuscade," Bayard and Ringo wait breathlessly for the stories he tells in the evening. "Then," declares Bayard, who is, not incidentally, the first-person narrator in all these accounts, "we listened. We heard: The names—Chickamauga and Lookout Mountain—the words, names like Gap and Run that we didn't have in this country; but mostly the cannon and the flags and the charges and the yelling."[31] In the story's revised form this starry-eyed mode of listening appears not quite so straightforward or self-evident. After John Sartoris's stories have emerged in fragments of names and places, Bayard notes, "But we were just twelve; we didn't listen to that. What Ringo and I heard was the cannon and the flags and the anonymous yelling. That's what we intended to hear tonight."[32] For lying between the telling of the tale and listening to it are the romantically charged expectations of the two boys.

So strong are those expectations that Bayard and Ringo barely hear the specific details in the stories Sartoris tells. Instead, the lengthy addition to this particular story implies, they listen with ears already attuned to the adventure and romance provided by the books in the Sartoris office, which included not just a volume of Napoleon's Maxims and an odd history of werewolf men in Britain but complete sets of Walter Scott, Fenimore Cooper, and Dumas, "save for the volume," Bayard notes, "which Father lost from his pocket at Manassas" (18). Indeed, the two boys can hardly see John Sartoris himself without resorting to familiar tales of battle and glory since they have already transformed him into a story himself, much as, for that matter, John Sartoris's neighbors, like Uncle Buck McCaslin, have done. For all of them, Sartoris is a hero marked, Bayard observes in retrospect, by "that odor in his clothes and beard and flesh too which I believe was the smell of powder and glory, the elected victorious but know better now: know now to have been only the will to endure, a sardonic and even humorous declining of self-delusion" (11).

To a certain extent, this gap between the way twelve-year-old Bayard "reads" and the way the older Bayard "reads" in retrospect is implicit here and there in several of the original *Post* stories, especially the darker and grimmer "The Unvanquished." But it is in the passages added to these stories in *The Unvanquished* and in "An Odor of Verbena" that we learn just how far apart these two readings are. For while young Bayard's reading elicits a text bearing a rather uncomfortable resemblance to the blood-and-thunder tales in which the *Saturday Evening Post* excelled, a text, moreover, that is unified, celebratory, and even a trifle smug, the retrospective Bayard—particularly the Bayard of "An Odor of Verbena"—offers a reading that is skeptical, discontinuous, and fragmented. No wonder, then, that both contemporary and more recent critics have expressed a certain uneasiness about "An Odor of Verbena." It is a story, coupled with the revisions, that deliberately addresses storybook expectations—the kind associated with *Saturday Evening Post* readers—"only," as Jauss says, "in order to destroy [them] step by step."[33] Even more so than the original *Post* stories, "An Odor of Verbena" makes reference to all those stock traditions comfortably familiar to the magazine's readers— former cavalry officers still legendary in their stature, stalwart Southern ladies dressed in yellow ball gowns, columned mansions adorned with chandeliers, adventurous deeds, and easily resolved endings—in this case, Bayard's anticipated shooting of Redmond, the man who has killed John Sartoris. It is an expected denouement of revenge, moreover, that symmetrically "fits" with the two "satisfactory" endings in the preceding stories—with the killing by Bayard and Ringo of the guerilla fighter responsible for Granny Millard's death in "Vendée" and with the triumphant appropriation of electoral proceedings by John Sartoris and Drusilla in "Skirmish at Sartoris," published in *Scribner's* in 1935. But if "An Odor of Verbena" evokes the sort of "horizon of expectations" associated with *Post* stories, it also seeks to shift that horizon by casting stock traditions and the expectations they arouse in a suspect light. Essentially, what this final story does is offer not one but two ways of reading those stock traditions, one that is defined by those original expectations and one that resists and disrupts them.

The first reading, associated with all those who readily expect Bayard to avenge John Sartoris's death at the hands of his former partner, is defined by the same strong sense of anticipation characterizing twelve-year-old Bayard and Ringo as they impatiently await John Sartoris's stories of war and glory in "Ambuscade." Indeed, one perceives in the waiting attitude of Drusilla Sartoris, now wed to John Sartoris, and George Wyatt, a former trooper under Sartoris's command, an unspoken demand for a denouement that has already been written in countless revenge tragedies. They have no doubt that Bayard will avenge his father just as Bayard and Ringo avenged the death of Rosa Millard.

Hence Bayard's return home has all the earmarks of a drama enacted a thousand times before. On the road to Jefferson the young man already knows what awaits him—the body of John Sartoris dressed "in his regimentals (sabre too)" and Drusilla "beneath all the festive glitter of the chandeliers, in the yellow ball gown and the sprig of verbena in her hair, holding the two loaded pistols" (252). Greeting Bayard upon his arrival are all the assembled players in the drama. "With that curious vulture-like formality which Southern men assume in such situations" (267), the old trooper George Wyatt offers help in meeting the obligations of the Sartoris code of honor "as if he had already rehearsed all this, his speech and mine, and knew what I would say" (268). Equally well rehearsed is the entrance of Drusilla, "standing at the top of the front steps, in the light from the open door and the windows like a theatre scene"—just as Bayard anticipates (269).

In this stately and ritualized scene Bayard feels curiously doubled, an outsider standing apart from the well-worn drama, and in the distance he provides, a second reading of the scene evolves. "Then, although I had dismounted and someone had taken the mare," he says, "I seemed to be still in the saddle and to watch myself enter that scene which she had postulated like another actor while in the background for chorus Wyatt and the others stood with the unctuous formality which the Southern man shows in the presence of death" (269). Allowing himself to be led to the room where the body of John Sartoris—dressed in Confederate gray—lies in state, Bayard is presented by Drusilla the weapons he is to use for vengeance, the dueling pistols that his father used so often during a violent life—pistols signifying all the weight of the expectations now codified and hardened into ritual. But because he does feel that doubleness and detachment, he is able to resist the momentum of those expectations; and indeed, Drusilla suddenly intuits in the midst of that scene that Bayard has no intention of following his assigned role in the drama. Quite simply, Bayard resists the pressures of his "audience" by declining to read his lines according to the preordained cues and by disregarding the role that has been assigned to him in the storybook drama.

He eventually faces down Redmond, his father's killer, but the confrontation is on his own terms—unarmed—and not on those of his expectant audience, "the avid eyes like caught breaths" that watch him from windows and from the Holston House as he slowly walks to Redmond's office (284). Bayard has, in a sense, broken the momentum of the storybook drama that has marked his father's life from the beginning, and in doing so, he disrupts and dissolves the audience that has followed the Sartoris legend and helped in part to create it. By the time he leaves Redmond's office, the watchers at the Holston House have disappeared,

Drusilla has prepared to leave Sartoris, and George Wyatt has conceded—with a certain puzzlement, "Maybe you're right, maybe there has been enough killing in your family" (289).

By posing an alternative reading and an alternative ending, Bayard also strips the Sartoris legends of their self-evident and "natural" aura. Such storybook tales may have helped John Sartoris survive in war and build a railroad through sheer nerve and daring, but by the time of "An Odor of Verbena" these legends have also settled into a set code of expectations and formulae seemingly independent of the man they extol and of the community that admires and fears him. Those who greet Bayard upon his return home with theatrical formality are puppets in a stilted drama written by time-worn expectations, just as John Sartoris himself, who bears in his last years, Bayard says, "that spurious forensic air of lawyers," is finally more the creation of the storybook tales than their instigator (265). In a sense, then, Bayard reveals in "An Odor of Verbena" that those expectations and narrative patterns have undergone what Marxist critics might recognize as reification and commodification.[34] Time and unthinking acceptance have rendered the Sartoris legacy of gallantry and heroism autonomous and self-perpetuating. Having once served John Sartoris's uses in the marketplace of the postbellum South, those stories are now themselves no more than commodities, specialized forms of labor cut off from those who helped create the legend. It is a judgment, finally, that offers a telling comment indeed on the *Saturday Evening Post*'s own shrewd manipulation of stories marketed to a mass audience.

But if this last story reveals that readers can be trapped by their own expectations, it also suggests that the horizons or boundaries defining those expectations can be changed and expanded. Initially resistant, both George Wyatt and Drusilla finally acknowledge Bayard's right to step outside the familiar drama. George remarks upon Bayard's behavior with wonder and reluctant admiration, and Drusilla, who abruptly leaves the Sartoris home, nonetheless leaves on Bayard's pillow a parting gift of verbena, the only scent, she says, "you could smell above the smell of horses and courage" (253).

From Jauss's perspective, their admission implies that the disruption in pattern represented by Bayard's actions and model of reading "can break through the expectations of . . . readers and at the same time confront them with a question, the solution to which remains lacking for them in the religiously or officially sanctioned morals."[35] For ultimately *The Unvanquished* is a text whose stories pose questions for its readers rather than ready answers already given long before in the *Saturday Evening Post.* They are questions, Faulkner suggests in the revised texts of "Retreat" and "Raid," that can create new and broader realities for readers.

In "Retreat," after all, we learn that Uncle Buck and Uncle Buddy McCaslin have devised a system of emancipation for their slaves so new and unfamiliar for Mississippi that "maybe fifty years after they were both dead people would have a name for" it (54). Equally startling is the story of the two racing locomotives, one Union and one Confederate, that Drusilla tells Bayard and Ringo in "Raid"—a story so vivid and compelling, Bayard says, that all three are struck by the same question: *"Where could we have been at that moment? What could we have been doing, even a hundred miles away, not to have sensed, felt this, paused to look at one another, aghast and uplifted, while it was happening?"* (106). But most moving of all are the crowds of slaves in "Raid" who march night after night seeking the freedom they have heard in fragmented stories of Jordan. More than anything else in *The Unvanquished,* that haunting march serves as testimony to the power of stories to liberate and to question as well as to confirm and imprison. For the great crowds on the road are impelled, Bayard tells us, by "one of those impulses inexplicable yet invincible which appear among races of people at intervals and drive them to pick up and leave all security and familiarity of earth and home and start out, they don't know where, empty-handed, blind to everything but a hope and a doom" (92).

Such passages tend to unsettle and disrupt, to undermine the easy assumptions and unified reading habits usually underlying the sort of Civil War fiction appearing in the *Saturday Evening Post*, and the unease these revisions evoke marks even the harshest critical assessments of *The Unvanquished*. Michael Mill-gate, for one, might dismiss the series of short stories as so much pulp fiction, but he does note in somewhat puzzled tones that the last tale "presents us with certain difficulties." Bayard's character, in particular, seems to have changed markedly since the earlier stories, and Drusilla's "overwrought" speeches to Bayard, Mill-gate adds, very nearly parody the Sartoris code "as a means of exorcising it, of breaking its hold."[36] Similarly, even those early readers of *The Unvanquished* who voiced enthusiastic support could not deny that *The Unvanquished* offered a curious sort of resistance to easy categorization. It was a book, fervent Agrarian Donald Davidson argued in the *Dallas Times Herald*, that seemed "to challenge us to think of where we are at present in comparison with where we were a decade or more ago."[37]

Above all, it is a book that ultimately refuses to comply with a "safe" and easy reading. Taken together, "An Odor of Verbena" and Faulkner's final revisions underscore the limitations of such a response, and the text's tendency to disrupt and disturb unified interpretations is reflected in the hesitations and qualifications we find more often than not in critical reactions and commentaries. Accordingly, those additions and changes serve as a fitting rebuke to the *Saturday Evening Post*, whose pages were generally marked by what Roland Barthes would call "a *comfortable* prac-tice of reading," elicited from a text "that comes from culture and does not break with it."[38] In issues including advertisements of white men in black face and of black domestic servants deferring to white employers, there was little room for alternative pos-sibilities and realities, just as there was scant space for the sort of questioning that defines the difference between *The Unvan-quished* and the original *Post* yarns. Forcing the reader to con-front the restrictions and dangers implicit in this sort of "comfortable" reading is the great accomplishment of *The Unvan-quished*. For if Faulkner found it necessary in his hard-pressed years to "reduce" stories in order to meet the *Saturday Evening Post*'s expectations, his revisions in *The Unvanquished* enabled him to expose the circumscribed nature of those expectations. Rewriting he might have done to sell stories to the *Post*, but in the end he "rewrote" the magazine's readers as well.

NOTES

1. Untitled Review, Boston (Mass.) *Herald*, n.d., n.p., William Faulkner Collection (#6271-ay), Manuscripts Division, Special Collections Department, University of Virginia Library (hereafter cited as Faulkner Coll.). I would like to thank the Manuscripts Division at the University of Virginia Library for permitting me to quote from materials in the Faulkner Collection. I should also note here my indebtedness to my colleague Colleen Kennedy for reading and commenting on an earlier version of this essay.

2. Michael Millgate, *The Achievement of William Faulkner* (New York: Random, 1966), 170.

3. For information on revisions made after the publication of the stories in the *Saturday Evening Post*, see notes to *Uncollected Stories of William Faulkner*, ed. Joseph Blotner (New York: Random House, Vintage Books, 1979), 681–84. See also James B. Carothers, *William Faulkner's Short Stories* (Ann Arbor, Mich.: UMI Research Press, 1985), 84–87; Joanne V. Creighton, *William Faulkner's Craft of Revision: The Snopes Trilogy, "The Unvanquished," and "Go Down, Moses"* (Detroit, Mich.: Wayne State University Press, 1977), 73–84; and John Pilkington, *The Heart of Yoknapatawpha* (Jackson: University Press of Mississippi, 1981), 194.

4. Joseph Blotner, *Faulkner: A Biography*, rev. one-vol. ed. (New York: Random House, 1984), 284 and 380.

5. For a short description of Faulkner's relationship with the *Saturday Evening Post*, see James B. Meriwether, "Faulkner's Correspondence with *The Saturday Evening Post*," *Mississippi Quarterly*, 30 (Summer 1977), 461.

6. For the early years of Lorimer's career, see John Tebbel, *George Horace Lorimer and "The Saturday Evening Post"* (Garden City, N.Y.: Doubleday, 1948), 16–40.

7. Qtd in Tebel, 25.

8. Qtd in Tebbel, 113.

9. Donald Gordon, "The Literary Lowbrow: Book-Market Flashes," *Saturday Evening Post*, 20 January 1934, 48.

10. Hans Robert Jauss, "Literary History as a Challenge to Literary Theory," *Toward an Aesthetic of Reception*, trans. Timothy Bahti, introd. Paul de Man, Theory and History of Literature, 2 (Minneapolis: University of Minneapolis Press, 1982), 19 and 23. Tebbel notes that Lorimer's first and foremost criterion for accepting articles and stories was the likes and dislikes of the *Post* audience (Tebbel, 42).

11. For instance, two stories by F. Scott Fitzgerald, "May Day" and "The Rich Boy," were turned down by the *Saturday Evening Post* for being "too realistic" (qtd in Thomas A. Gullason, "The 'Lesser' Renaissance: The American Short Story in the 1920s," *The American Short Story, 1900–1945*, ed. Philip Stevick [Boston: Twayne, 1984], 80).

12. Qtd in Tebbel, 48.

13. Tebbel, 45–46, 44, and 59.

14. See, for example, Octavus Roy Cohen, "Fast Blacks," *Saturday Evening Post*, 10 November 1934, 26, 28, 59.

15. Elsie Singmaster, "The Raid," *Saturday Evening Post*, 2 June 1934, 11, 29–30; Joseph Hergesheimer, "The Crystal Chandelier," *Saturday Evening Post*, 14 July 1934, 12–13, 53, 55, 58, 61; for an example of Marquand's 1934 Civil War series, see "Take the Man Away," *Saturday Evening Post*, 12 May 1934, 12–13, 42, 44, 46, 48, 50, 52; and MacKinley Kantor, "No Enemy," *Saturday Evening Post*, 22 February 1935, 12–13, 72, 74, 75, 76. Faulkner's stories—"Ambuscade," "Retreat," and "Raid"—appeared September 29, October 31, and November 3 in 1934.

16. William Faulkner to Robert K. Haas, Sunday [28 April 1940], *Selected Letters of William Faulkner*, ed. Joseph Blotner (New York: Random House, Vintage books, 1977), 121; Faulkner to Robert K. Haas, Monday [received 7 December 1939], *Selected Letters*, 116; Faulkner to Morton Goldman, [probably late July 1935], *Selected Letters*, 92; and Faulkner to Morton Goldman, [probably April 1935], *Selected Letters*, 91.

17. Blotner (1984), 124 and 256.

18. Meriwether, 461.

19. William Faulkner to *Saturday Evening Post*, 21 December 1927, in Meriwether, 465.

20. *Saturday Evening Post* to William Faulkner, 9 October 1930, in Meriwether, 469 and 468; qtd in Joseph Blotner, *Faulkner: A Biography*, 2 vols. (New York: Random House, 1974), 1:431–32.

21. "Next Week," *Saturday Evening Post*, 27 October 1934, 96.

22. Blotner (1974), 1:859.

23. Faulkner to Morton Goldman, [probably late Spring 1934], *Selected Letters*, 80; Faulkner to Morton Goldman, 29 July [1934], in *Selected Letters*, 83; Hans Skei, *William Faulkner: The Short Story Career* (Oslo: Universtetsforlaget, 1981), 84.

24. Faulkner to Morton Goldman, [probably June 1936], *Selected Letters*, 95–96.

25. Louis Kronenberger, "Faulkner's Dismal Swamp," *Critical Essays on William Faulkner: The Sartoris Family*, ed. Arthur F. Kinney (Boston: G. K. Hall, 1985), 132.

26. Dale Mullen, "[Our People]," in Kinney, 128. See also Herschel Brickell, "Book on Our Table," *New York Post*, 18 February 1938, n.p., Faulkner Coll.

27. Russell Smith, "Mr. Faulkner Enters a New Phase," *Washington Post*, 20 February 1938, n.p., Faulkner Coll.; and Katherine M'Clure Anderson, "Today's Book." Macon [Ga.] *Telegraph*, 2 March 1938, n.p., Faulkner Coll.; and Kronenberger, 131.

28. James B. Carothers has noted in his recent study of Faulkner's short fiction that the changes Faulkner made in revising the magazine stories for publication in *The Unvanquished* served generally to "unify the material of the stories" (86).

29. Millgate, 169; and Joseph Reed, *Faulkner's Narrative* (New Haven: Yale University Press, 1973), 185.

30. Faulkner to Morton Goldman, 24 July [1937], in *Selected Letters*, 100; Blotner (1984), 381.

31. William Faulkner, "Ambuscade," *Saturday Evening Post*, 29 September 1934, 12.

32. William Faulkner, *The Unvanquished* (New York: Random House, Vintage Books, 1965), 17. Hereafter quotations are cited parenthetically within the text.

33. Jauss, 24.

34. See, for example, Ross Chambers, *Story and Situation: Narrative Seduction and the Power of Fiction*, Theory and History of Literature, 12 (Minneapolis: University of Minnesota Press, 1984), 3–17.

35. Jauss, 44.

36. Millgate, 169.

37. Qtd in O. B. Emerson, *Faulkner's Early Literary Reputation in America* (Ann Arbor, Mich.: UMI Research Press, 1984), 283.

38. Roland Barthes, *The Pleasure of the Text*, trans. Richard Miller (New York: Hill and Wang, 1975), 14.

Sharecropping in the Golden Land

Bruce Kawin

If the modernists' key insights were that the conventionally known world—the world before Cézanne, Freud, Einstein, and mustard gas—had ceased to exist, both in itself and for the purposes of art; that its false notions of order confirmed themselves in the structures of false art; that the world not only lay busted into exciting fragments but was also inherently and almost unanalyzably multiple, so that the look might well become many looks as attention passed through the prism of consciousness, emerging multicolored and multivectored to fan open space and time; and that disturbingly powerful and beautiful works of classic import could be constructed not just out of fragments but as systems of fragments—then their key determination was to ensure that those systems of fragments were themselves coherent, projecting an underlying unity and declaring their own completeness. When they called a halt, they did so with an authorial imperiousness that was itself refreshing, like Joyce's "Yes" or Stein's "This is it." The modernist ending might be open or closed, but it was never ajar. *Absalom, Absalom!* builds to the most intense unresolution in American fiction and stops on a dime.

The majority of modernist works foreground their complexities and leave their syntheses to silence, to the reader's intuition, and to the integrity of the completed work. *Ulysses*, rigorously fragmented, declares its seamless plenitude throughout; *The Cantos* projects an epic wholeness and particularly a voice that eclipse its so-called failure to cohere. The modernist synthesis may be implicit in the work, made manifest by the nature of the work,

196

projected beyond the work as an ineffable paradox, or constructed as a frustration. It is the unnamable silent partner of the text.

The modernist synthesis, whether textual or metatextual, is often the hard-won product of a jutty montage: in some cases the systematic opposition of what is present and what is missing, in some the parallel treatment of opposites, but most often the dynamic interaction of unreconciled fragments. The integrity of the fragment—each chapter in *The Sound and the Fury*, each shot in *Battleship Potemkin*, each letter in *Patterson*—is respected and in fact counted upon to have its full effect when it is juxtaposed smack up against a conflicting element in the generation of a metaphorical synthesis, even if that might be only one in a series, with the ultimate synthesis necessarily hovering outside the work like the aura around the sailor's tale in Conrad. Eisenstein called this dialectical montage, Hegel called it history, Proust called it the structure of metaphor, and Faulkner called it nailing a henhouse together in a hurricane.

The modernist work projects a viable unity, a focused parallax, that is grounded in an often idiosyncratic system of artistic and moral values. Pound looked back and ahead to a time in which the worth of money and words and actions had integrity; Eliot looked for a healing, transcendent order and found it in religion, although that didn't stop him from composing his greatest devotional poem as a system of *Four Quartets* rather than one; Proust found freedom from death as well as from pettiness and failure in the transcendent experience of the timeless self, and a figure for personal and cultural integration in the joining of the Méséglise and Guermantes ways.

When I speak of the completeness Faulkner envisioned, I'm referring not to the fact that Yoknapatawpha County is as fully realized in detail and scope as Joyce's Dublin, but to the way he calls our attention to the gaps in his work, to what is missing, to what is felt to be needed to complete or to heal the imagined world. Something he still believes in and whose value persists.

Sanctuary appeals beyond itself for honor, grace, a hiding place;

it includes no unviolated temples. The completeness of *The Sound and the Fury* is projected beyond, and by means of, the multiplicity of its points of view, the irony of its false-order ending, and the gap at its center that is Caddy's silence, the absent point of view of the one character everyone else is trying to define and control—like the absence from Stoker's *Dracula* of any journal by Dracula. To fill such a gap—as in *As I Lay Dying*, where Addie's point of view commands a chapter—is not to settle an old mystery but to detect a fresh one. A gap like this is not, say, the missing piece of a puzzle or a pizza, but the hole that creates the donut. Thus the Faulknerian structure comprises fragments, embraces unresolution, and houses gaps, all in the interest of the hurricane, but the henhouse stands—for all its drafty gaping holes, and, since this is a Faulkner henhouse, because of them.

It was part of the modernist paradox to see the live tradition as a presence in the wasteland, to see the absent Hamlet in the absentminded Dedalus. And it is often the absent, which may well be the lost or foregone, that is at the heart of a Faulkner work.

What Faulkner discovered when his Romantic, heroic, idealistic ambitions were frustrated and turned bitter, when he was rejected in love and war, and as his heart continued to break and harden until it cracked into wisdom and declared its form, is what Crazy Jane told the Bishop: that "nothing can be sole or whole / that has not been rent." While he never stopped being bitter and ironic, and his heart never unbroke, he found in himself and in a few folks and writers he admired the drive and strength to endure, not just to survive but to do something worth doing. If Proust concluded that the only true paradise is one that has been lost, what Faulkner learned is that nothing can endure that has not been crushed. Hence in his work it is the defeated South that has a chance to win, the foregone chivalric values that are insisted upon, the frozen moment that moves, and the mule that rules.

Thanks to Joe Blotner, we know that one draft of Faulkner's Nobel Prize acceptance speech summed up his Hollywood experience in terms of a conflict of values, not of aesthetics. One might have expected him to denounce the movies as he often did in his fiction, or praise the source of income that allowed him to write much of that fiction, or compare on a well-informed level the formal structures of cinema and literature from the point of view of one who had worked hard in both arts. But what he wrote was this:

> A few years ago I was taken on as a script writer at a Hollywood studio. At once I began to hear the man in charge talking of "angles," "story angles," and then I realized that they were not even interested in truth, the old universal truths of the human heart without which any story is ephemeral—the universal truths of love and honor and pride and pity and compassion and sacrifice.[1]

What appears to have bothered him most about the film industry, then, was not its insistence on chronological and apparently seamless narrative structures but its dumbfounding alienation from what Faulkner, both as an artist and as a moral being, considered universal truths and values. His response might sound platitudinous, the ravings of a Southerner as out of step with the studio system as Pound was with the Roosevelt administration, until you realize how truly irrelevant these values often are to "the man in charge" unless they happen to coincide with current popular concerns and may therefore be capitalized upon. What Faulkner says here about "story angles" is real; it is precisely the way that stories are "rethought" and "developed" in Hollywood, and what remains upsetting is that all this off-the-wall tinkering, this plethora of little brainstorms and twists, is launched at the work from outside, without much respect for nor any intimate engagement with the developing organic integrity struggling in the work, from which it has its only chance to grow to something true. What Faulkner was complaining about was in fact at stake: there are storymakers in the world who don't know the first thing about stories or what they're good for. The man was in culture shock, and so was the modernist.

From the evidence of the story "Golden Land," written just after *Pylon*, it appears that Los Angeles struck him much the same way: an imitation world without foundation, indifferent not just to the old truths but to truth itself.

The main character, Ira Ewing, is a misogynist alcoholic realtor who visits his mother daily but does not and never really did understand her Nebraska pioneer values ("something about fortitude," he tries to remember, "the will to endure"). His son, aptly named Voyd, is a bitch. His daughter—whom, perhaps as part of his lip-service commitment to the values of the old family farm he had fled as a child, he had named Samantha after his mother—has adopted the professional name of April Lalear (with an "a," as in that king with the rotten daughters, as if she were rubbing it in, rather than an "e" as in the masculine leer she wants to attract and manipulate) and is everything a chaste, honest, and respectful daughter is not. Compared to a tragic, ambivalent, doomed heroine like Caddy, the morally indifferent April/Samantha is a bug; she wouldn't even make it into the same Hell.

Ira's wife is a closed door, one that she closed to him and that he closed on her. His mistress is honest and unpretentious, and he allows himself to be relatively intimate with her. But we find out soon enough that Ira Ewing is lower than a snail's trail and twice as slimy, that he worships publicity just as much as his would-be starlet of a daughter and is delighted to advance both their careers by exploiting the news coverage of a sex scandal—April Lalear surprised naked on the casting couch—by making sure that his daughter's real name, his own picture, and the name of his business are featured in that coverage. He just doesn't want his mother to find out.

The light fits the place. The sun has to strain through a haze that makes everything nebulous (and values appear equivocal); then it shines "with a kind of treacherous unbrightness."[2] In the "bright soft vague hazy sunlight"—this being twenty years Before Smog—the city looks "rootless," ungrounded, a scatter "of houses bright beautiful and gay, without basements or foundations, lightly attached to a few inches of light penetrable earth." Anyone who's spent time in L.A. knows that is no metaphor. The film

industry, too, has a shallow foundation: "a few spools of a substance whose value is computed in billions and which may be
completely destroyed in that second's instant of a careless
match"[3]—in other words, the explosively flammable nitrate stock
on which movies were shot and printed.

The place is ungrounded physically and morally. It's so corrupt
that if it were a barn full of rats, Ira's father would burn it down to
clean it out. Ira's mother, the original Samantha Ewing, has been
saving her pennies for years in her determination to buy a train
ticket back to Nebraska, the harsh real world where everything
isn't so easy that it means nothing and where parents know
enough to teach their kids not to steal. But it doesn't look as if
she's leaving soon; she's dollars and years away, if she lives that
long, and in the meantime she is trapped in an Elysian paradise
where nobody dies and it can't snow:

> The sun was high; she could see the water from the sprinkler flashing
> and glinting in it as she went to the window. It was still high, still
> afternoon; the mountains stood serene and drab against it; the city,
> the land, lay sprawled and myriad beneath it—the land, the earth
> which spawned a thousand new faiths, nostrums and cures each year
> but no disease to even disprove them on—beneath the golden days
> unmarred by rain or weather, the changeless monotonous beautiful
> days without end countless out of the halcyon past and endless into
> the halcyon future.
> "I will stay here and live forever," she said to herself.[4]

What we expect her to say is something more like "I'll get out of
here if it kills me." But that is dynamic unresolution at work.

Even if there were some fairy-dust in the Los Angeles ozone
that bleached out the conscience and could beach Moby-Dick,
this woman is not giving up. She may not get to die in Nebraska,
but her refusal to quit trying and her sticking to what she and her
husband "had learned through hardship and endurance of honor
and courage and pride" are a big chunk of what Faulkner meant by
"endurance."

And how endurance posed itself to the momentarily baffled

screenwriter—who today would be staggered by the charmingly ruthless power babies who run the studios in the age of "plot points" and "complications"—was in the form of doing the best work he could as a writer. He did his job without abandoning his sense of what made a good story or motivated significant emotional conflict. He packed his scripts with "love and honor and pride and pity and compassion and sacrifice," notably in such early works as *Turn About* and *War Birds*, but also in such later works as *The Road to Glory* (written about the same time as "Golden Land") and, if you think he had anything important to do with it, *The Southerner.*

Not that every one of his heroic sacrificial romantic brilliant scenes made it to the screen, of course. Some of them never made it past rewrite.

Feature filmmaking is not a solo act. It is of course true that a movie can be made by a single person—a film artist like Stan Brakhage, for instance—who is free to work with the autonomy, and the budget, of a novelist. But in the Hollywood where Faulkner worked, it took about a hundred professionals to make a movie, and creative collaboration was a fact of the business. The cinematographer is in charge of the cinematography just as much as the writer is in charge of the words; the production requires a designer, the footage an editor, the system a star, the budget a producer, and so on—a host of creative professionals expertly performing fulltime jobs.

In by far the majority of cases, the producer delegates full creative authority and responsibility to the director, whose job and creative opportunity is to make the best use of the expert personnel and expensive materials provided. All this is said, usually by lawyers, to be in the interest of realizing the script, that is, turning the movie-as-written into an actual and releasable film. But the cruel facts are that the writer creates the movie and then the director creates *the* movie. What is realized may follow the script, diverge now and then from it, or toss it; directors and actors revise dialogue during production, and a film editor can cut out a sentence just as neatly as a copy editor. But by the time most of that happens, the writer has gone on to other things. Where the writer and the director collaborate or collide most often is before production, when the script is being written and revised.

There is no need to run through all the ways a story can happen to make it to the scripting stage; the point is that when it does, whether the screenwriter is adapting a novel or expanding an original treatment or trying to give the director an immediately usable scene five hours ago, that material is *then* written for the screen by *that* writer. A director may make explicit or vague suggestions over the phone or in an office, and there's no question that that constitutes creative collaboration, but the writer makes it up and gets it down, the writer incorporates or distorts the suggested element so that it works or has a chance to make sense, the writer polishes it, the writer changes it, the writer *finishes* it. And then, regardless of whether the writer or somebody else happens to have rewritten it in the meantime, the script is inevitably reconceived in the creative working consciousness of the director who makes what he or she sees in it.

Let's say you're Faulkner and you're writing a script based on your story "Turn About." You and the director, Hawks, got drunk and talked all night about how to do it, or anyway how it could be done. You end the script with the same ending as the story, because it's just as terrific as it ever was, and it creates exactly the right tone for the ending even when you're writing the *second* draft and they've told you to put "a girl" in the picture. You have Bogard and Ann, after the raid and their marriage, standing in a chapel and facing a window inscribed in memory of Ronnie and Claude, and you have them say:

ANN: But you did. You went. When you flew down at that chateau and knew that you wouldn't get home again.

BOGARD: Yes. God, God. If they had only all been there: generals, the admirals[,] the presidents, and the kings—theirs, ours, all of them!

ANN: Hush. (Draws his head down to her breast, holding it there) Hush—hush.[5]

In the movie, however, they just stand there silently in the chapel. This is the movie *Today We Live,* made from your script from your story. This is your favorite joke without the punch line. This blows the whole thing.

But it is not YOUR *Today We Live.* Let the auteurists wrangle over whether it was Hawks's personal creation; the fact is that MGM owned it—or did then, anyway. Faulkner had sold Hawks and MGM the right to adapt "Turn About" any way they chose. In cases where he was not adapting his own work (like the novel *Dreadful Hollow,* which turns out to have been written by H. M. E. Clamp, alias Irina Karlova, in 1942), he fully understood that by accepting a paycheck he was selling what he wrote and that anything could be done to it or in spite of it. Either way, the property (that is, the feature in development) on which he worked was somebody else's literal *property.*

Faulkner wrote his books the way he wanted to, and he wasn't happy when another fellow's idea of what would sell turned *Flags in the Dust* into *Sartoris.*

It must have been hard for him to rewrite scripts the way he was told, to change endings and cut off scenes and revise characters. The waste of all that good writing, all those fully realized scenes that would never be shot, those lines that could never work so well in anything else. . . And beyond that, the affront to the dignity and good sense of the solitary writer, not to mention the master modernist. Because when you've done your work and you know it's done, there is no way it isn't going to hurt when some jerk sends it back for rewrite, whether they pay you every Saturday or not.

But Faulkner could contemplate and even watch *Today We Live* and the other pictures without blowing a gasket. Since he would not let anyone treat his novels or his stories this way, since he tolerated no rewriting but his own, how could he of all people have adapted to the demands of creative collaboration? That certainly must have been as difficult for him as to negotiate the angles and values of a script conference.

To do his job, to write well and hard enough to provide something at least as good as what was asked for, was to endure and prevail in a way that would satisfy his personal and cultural values, allying himself with the mother, Samantha, to save himself from the corruptions of Ira. But it is my guess that the artist in him would still have gone privately nuts if he had not gone on to solve the screenwriter's key problem: authorial control. It had to be his writing, or he could not write it; but it could not be his, since he had sold the right to say whether it was good or when it was complete. Hoisted on the horns of this dialectic, and still striving to reconcile modernist and commercial values as well as Southern and Southern California values, what synthesis between author and not-author could he discover?

The resolving metaphor might have occurred to him as sharecropping, an honorable occupation in which to practice the moral discipline and suffer the indignities of Faulknerian endurance. Like a sharecropper he worked on somebody else's property, not his own. He raised the best crop he could because he was a good farmer, and he got to keep enough of it to keep going.

Since he never took the easy out of writing as less than himself, the only way I can see that he could have insulated himself from collaboration's burden of rejection and disappointment, waste and loss—so that he *could* write well for the studios, live up to his own sense of values, and care enough about the popular culture he was affecting to structure his best scripts around the truths he respected—was to have reminded himself, as often as necessary, that he worked as a sharecropper in the golden land. But when he drew his own map,[6] he signed it "Sole Owner & Proprietor."

NOTES

1. Joseph Blotner, *Faulkner: A Biography* (New York: Random House, 1974), 1357.
2. "Golden Land," *Collected Stories of William Faulkner* (New York: Random House, 1950), 706.
3. Ibid., 719.
4. Ibid., 725–26.

5. Conclusion of the second draft; see *Faulkner's MGM Screenplays*, ed. Bruce F. Kawin (Knoxville: University of Tennessee Press, 1982), 101–127, 255.

6. Of "Jefferson, Yoknapatawpha County, Mississippi" for *Absalom, Absalom!*, published the year after "Golden Land."

Faulkner/Reforestation

LEON FORREST

Reinvention is a primary attribute of intelligence, identity, and endurance in the character make-up of many memorable black figures in William Faulkner's *The Sound and the Fury:* Dilsey, Deacon, Louis Hatcher, and Reverend Shegog.

I believe that this major Afro-American cultural attribute—reinvention—was also used by Faulkner as a salient and ironic instrument of structural linkage to reveal the discontinuities and the failures of Quentin Compson, Jason Compson IV, and the decline of the South.

The idea of reinvention suggests a broad spectrum of personal invention, when we turn to such divergent characters as the artful Dilsey, or the highly adaptable, ever reappropriating Deacon. They appear to stand in sharp opposition to each other on the character spectrum, yet they are connected around this thematic pattern of reinvention out of chaos, or disorder, as *the* condition of this old world.

Let me simply point out here the idea of Deacon as trickster, who reinvents his situation and his identity out of an array of materials and clothing. Reinventing himself out of chaos, Deacon's identity ironically enough is of a cloth, although his attire remains chaotic in appearance, and Faulkner weaves a cunning suit of social satire through Deacon's inventive apparel, concerning our American rage for upward mobility. For the white audience of incoming students he plays up to, Deacon must ever appear to be the butt of jokes played on him by society and history, not the captain of the chaos he so masterly manipulates.

Recalling those Negro stage performers of the nineteenth and early twentieth century who had to blacken up to get on the stage, play the "darkie-role," and somehow through it all place their stamp of individualism upon their art, to transcend the grease-paint as it were, Deacon blackens up enough to save his act (and endure at Harvard); but he also satirizes his assigned task, by becoming an individual and even a power in the consciousness of the white students, precisely by mocking several American institutions and identities, while appearing to honor them so much on the surface. Quentin also observes this about Deacon: "They said he hadn't missed a train at the beginning of school in forty years, and that he could pick out a Southerner with one glance. He never missed, and once he had heard you speak, he could name your state."[1]

One of the central problems for Quentin—the white Southerner, whom we see confronting Deacon in essentially comic stage scenes—is that of identity. The hypersensitive, highly intellectual Quentin is mastered by the smear of fantasy and reality, about his inner and outer worlds. Deacon is at home with chaos, fantasy, reality, and he manipulates identities for his advantage at Harvard. Ultimately Deacon's presence in the novel forces us to reflect upon another trickster, Jason. But Jason is an example of the trickster-as-demon, as we view the cruel intentions of his staged, evil designs and deeds. The cruel pranks Jason plays almost always backfire on him. We are intrigued by his perverse angle of comic vision; but his failures at reinvention make him again and again the butt of his own racial and chauvinistic jokes.

From all appearances, jokes seem to be on Deacon all of the time, and he courts some of these jokes, to appear as simply the traditional minstrel show "darkie" buffoon. Deacon can be seen as constantly dressing up, or reinventing the properties of his act into a comic wholeness. As presented to us through the eyes of Quentin, Deacon is a combination of trickster, wise fool, confidence man, confidante, shape-changing proteus, psychologist, "darkie" buffoon, and old plantation master.

Deacon has set up his own school of parody on the white South's imposed role of servitude for the Negro (at the railroad station, in Harvard's very back yard, as it were) by pressing into constant service a white boy to *caddy* the bags for newly arriving students. We can see and hear Deacon manipulate the masks of his act (while he instructs the white boy, as *red cap*) and shape-change from "darkie" buffoon, then trickster parodist, now commanding ole master, himself, through the listening and observant Quentin:

> "Yes, suh. Right dis way, young marster, hyer we is," taking your bags. "Hyer, boy, come hyer and git dese grips." Whereupon a moving mountain of luggage would edge up, revealing a white boy of about fifteen, and the Deacon would hang another bag on him somewhere and drive him off.[2]

I do not want to make too much of Deacon's powers for reinvention here, by extracting him from the sociology of his condition. He can't transcend the racist terrain of current thinking, nor the roles assigned his people; but he can and does artfully manipulate a slew of stereotypes, and, as we see elsewhere, patterns of Americana. Deacon is willing to demean himself—play the "darkie"—because he knows that's the final word the whites want to hear, South or North. For as he drives the white boy—as lackey—off, with the luggage, we hear Deacon embrace the "darkie"-lackey role, when he says: "Now, den, dont you drap hit. Yes, suh, young marster, jes give de old nigger yo room number, and hit'll be done got cold dar when you arrives."[3]

Yet Quentin must leave his clothing to Deacon as an overshadowing legacy of master-servant relations. Using the scenes between Quentin and Deacon as a kind of metaphor for the overarching power and shadow of the Negro upon Quentin's soul and the soul of the South, Faulkner deploys a wonderful kind of parody on the "Me and My Shadow" routine of the American dance theatre, in which a white dancer did a soft-shoe dance upon a semidarkened stage, with only a spotlight upon him, while in the background, a Negro dancer danced in the white man's shadow, imitating the Caucasian's footfall. But in point of fact, as often as not, the actual steps the white dancer was performing were culled from patterns and routines he had either stolen or simply incorporated from black dancers he had observed or learned from—his *masters* in other words.

Something similar is happening here in the novel as Quentin is shadowed by the presence of the Negro, along with his other obsessions. In leaving these clothes to Deacon, as *the* Negro—who reminds him of Roskus—Quentin attempts to order chaos, personal and private, back to the order of the Old South, in which the blacks were given the handed-down effects of historical interpretation, and clothing, by the white man, playing out the role of the Great White Father, Patriarch, and The Man. This joke of history is now on Quentin; his fantasy of recreating the old order, or reinventing it, is as dead as flat-irons attached to a drowning man's shoes.

Dilsey of course was Faulkner's most beloved character, personally. We are intrigued by her innovative qualities and her ultimate needs for spiritual transformation and renewal, even as she successfully manipulates, through reinvention, the virtual chaos of the Compson household, and its dying light condition.

We mainly see her in the famous Dilsey/Faulkner section; her quest at this point is to put the household together and coordinate the morning breakfast. Soon we come to see that spiritual transformation is Dilsey's deeper quest (beneath the many layers of clothing apparel, as she dresses and redresses); and that her soul motive is quite similar to what her preacher sees as his flock's need, when a minister from St. Louis, the Reverend Shegog, is called to resurrect the spirit of the congregation, by reinventing the Easter story through the resurrection sermon. Faulkner was wrong when he said that Reverend Shegog at first sounded like a white man. What Faulkner meant, or was trying to get at here, I believe, was the manner in which a black folk preacher will start off his sermon in a very serious, proper diction, even stately intonation and pronunciation, before he goes into the idiomatic-folk voice.

From her Negro perspective, the secular side of Dilsey accepts

the idea of trouble and chaos as the condition of constant initia-
tion, and perhaps I should say, constant reinitiation into the world
as the perpetual agony of humankind. Trouble and confusion is
the state of this world, and of existence, but out of this you re-
create life around you. Experience is your talisman, reinvention
your discipline. This means that personality is ever in process,
nothing is ever static, in this secular truth of existence; therefore
reinvention is the order of everyday. (The furor and excitement
over this secular perception of the world was best revealed, I
think, when Southern blacks often sang—"Hurry Sun Down, see
what tomorrow brings.")

Although much of Dilsey's life could provide seasoning for a
blues lyric, she is not a blues woman; she needs spiritual renewal.
She may be able to bring a semblance of order to Compson-chaos,
through reinvention, but she cannot reinvent herself spiritually;
and this is what she needs on that fateful Sunday; and she needs a
revelation of meaning that her life with the white folks surely
cannot provide. Dilsey Gibson needs spiritual nourishment for
her considerable intelligence about the meaning of the Fall of the
house of Compson, the South, and the imminence of death in life,
reinvention of the Resurrection for her, and in her own time,
before her spiritual identity can be rested. Quentin thinks he can
reinvent himself through suicide. His fantasy is that of cleaning
out Hell for himself and Caddy, as a final dwelling place-kingdom-
come. His *reality?* Handing down his clothing to the Negro,
Deacon, who as it turns out, has found his heaven at Harvard.
(But it's important here to remember that Deacon is not an-
enslaved-to-tradition Southern black, in another way; he may be
tied to Brer Rabbit; but he's a new kind of reinventive, black
Yankee stage trickster that Quentin's static notion of the Negro has
not prepared him for.)

Reverend Shegog and Dilsey may be bound for the kingdom on
the character spectrum around the theme of spiritual reinvention;
but the practical Dilsey was always aware of the dialectical relationship between the need for reinvention and private chaos; and

how private chaos connected up to social disrepair and imminent familial doom. And as she ushers Benjy into the carriage, at one point we hear:

> "Git in, now, and set still until your maw come." Dilsey said. She shoved me into the carriage. T. P. held the reins. Clare I don't see how come Jason won't get a new surrey." Dilsey said. "This thing going to fall to pieces under you all some day. Look at them wheels." [4]

One of the constants of Afro-American culture is the reinvention of life—or, the cultural attribute of black Americans is to take what is left over or, conversely, given to them (either something tossed from the white man's table . . . or, let us say, at the other end of the spectrum, the Constitution or basketball) and make it work for them, as a source of personal or group survival, and then to place a stamp of elegance and élan upon the reinvented mode; to emboss, upon the basic form revised, a highly individualistic style, always spun of grace, and fabulous rhythms . . . a kind of magical realism. The improvisational genius of jazz is the epitome of what I am getting at here. This is central to the art of Ellington, Armstrong, Lady Day, Sarah Vaughan, Ray Charles, Muddy Waters, Alberta Hunter; I could of course go on. Or in athletics Doctor J., Jackie Robinson, Willie Mays, Michael Jordan, to name but a scant few.

And from my earliest reading of the best in William Faulkner, I have continually been impressed with, and deeply influenced by, his respect for the significance of black folklore; his willingness to explore some of the ranges of racism, as this poison circulated within the tormented souls of his characters of mixed blood; his willingness to confront the racial agony of the South, and to eloquently lift this travail to stage center, as the ever constant moral issue at the very heart and soul of this Republic; by the brilliant way he, on occasion, seized upon the genius of the race in terms of reinvention and celebrated it. And I am thinking not only here of the great Dilsey/Faulkner section in *The Sound and the*

Fury; but the jazzlike motifs in the passages with Uncle Louis and the lamp, in the Quentin section. And there are many others; but for me as a black novelist, Faulkner reached his greatest heights in celebrating and exploring this attribute of reinvention with the character of Rider, in "Pantaloon in Black." His descriptions of Rider handling the logger's tasks, with fabulous rhythms, grace, and elan, might serve as a primer for any writer, black or white, attempting to describe, say, Michael Jordan's reinvention of the game of basketball, as he does some of his unbelievable moves on the court each night. And Faulkner's experimental approach to the very form of the novel certainly has influenced my sense of artistic possibility. Conversely, I believe that the powerful presence of the black agony, in his vaulting imagination, provided Faulkner with the *essential* materiality for his greatest novels and the towering and tragic vision, so central to the Faulkner canon: *The Sound and the Fury, Light in August, Absalom, Absalom!, Go Down, Moses* (and sections of *Intruder in the Dust*). To strip these works from Yoknapatawpha would be like excluding the black presence from the body and soul of this, *our* American culture.

NOTES

1. William Faulkner, *The Sound and the Fury* (New York: Vintage Books, 1956), 119.
2. Ibid., 120.
3. Ibid.
4. Ibid., 9.

Neon Light in August: Electric Signs in Faulkner's Fiction

WILLIAM BREVDA

I don't know if William Faulkner had an epiphany when he beheld neon light in August 1925 illuminating the Eiffel Tower, but he wrote to his mother:

> Lots of the trees are dying here, the elms about the Place d'Etoile and some of the old chestnut trees in the Luxembourg. American papers blame it on the Eiffel tower where there is a big wireless station and where they advertise automobiles by electric signs.[1]

Faulkner saw the word CITROEN spelled out in giant neon letters on the sides of the Tower. The French government, needing money, had allowed its most famous symbol to be appropriated by an auto maker and transformed into the world's largest advertisement. The event was associated with the International Exhibition of Decorative and Industrial Arts that first popularized Art Deco, the new look that was designed to evoke the image and spirit of the machine. The Eiffel Tower as neon sign can be interpreted as symbolizing the new age of the dynamo and the dynamic, the twentieth-century world of mechanization, urbanization, and speed. The new medium of neon was itself a message, a sign of the "new," as "neon" means in Greek, a revelation of progress.[2] Not everyone was enamoured of such progress. Faulkner would later liken the "glittering ephemerae of progress and alteration" to the "wash and glare of the neon sign." The neonized Eiffel Tower also heralded an age of commercialism, artificiality, mass culture, illusion, and the nighttime id. On that

214

un-Mississippi-like August night in Paris, 1925, Faulkner may
have harkened to an ill wind that "blows Nay on good," as James
Joyce once punned.[3]

In his 1927 novel *Mosquitoes*, Faulkner included a scene in
which an electric sign serves as a signifier of the American Dream,
or rather, of the corruption of that Dream. The first and second
generation Ginotta family are an American "success " story. They
have built up their small neighborhood Italian restaurant into a
swank club with an electric sign that announces their new prosperity, their new "American" identities, and their Gatsby-like
fulfillment of the American Dream:

> that electric sign with the family name on it had marked a climacteric:
> the phoenix-like rise of the family fortunes from the dun ashes of
> respectability and a small restaurant catering to Italian working peo-
> ple, to the final and ultimate Americanization of the family, since this
> fortune, like most American ones, was built on the flouting of a
> statutory impediment.[4]

Historically, Americans have always advertised their membership in God's or society's "elect" through certain external
"signs" of social and material success. When the Ginotta family
modernize their restaurant, their fancy new electric sign is only
the very latest in such "signs" of secular American grace. Thus
when Joe Ginotta proudly surveys his restaurant, it is the electric
sign that summarizes the family's highest achievement:

> With the quiet joy of ownership his gaze . . . passed on to . . . that
> electric sign, that ultimate accolade of Americanization, flashing his
> name in golden letters in rain or mist or against the remote insane
> stars themselves. (249)

For Faulkner, however, the electric sign of material and social
success also points to spiritual loss. Before the modern fixtures,
the Ginotta restaurant served good cheap food to neighborhood
people in a dingy but happy atmosphere. The change from mom
and pop family restaurant to slick, sophisticated, overpriced
lounge kills pop, destroys the family, and chases away the neigh-

borhood Italian clientele. To Faulkner, then, the electric sign, "that ultimate accolade of Americanization," connotes a present that threatens to sunder the moral, regional, ethnic, and family ties of the past. Faulkner's electric signs also imply the externalization of life, the *Great Gatsby*ish theme of character as gesture and facade in an age of advertising. The Ginottas have been re-created as an American success story, but their new identity is only a flashing sign and the Ginottas themselves are lost.

Ironically, in 1927, when *Mosquitoes* was published, the Ginottas would soon need a new success sign, for in the late 1920s neon signs began to replace electric bulb signs, a historical transition captured in James M. Cain's 1934 novel *The Postman Always Rings Twice*:

> Nobody has bulb signs any more. They got Neon signs. They show up better, and they don't burn as much juice.
> . . . Why don't you get a new sign?
> . . . it's important. A place is no better than its sign, is it?

Like the Ginottas, Cain's Papadakis might have had a happier ending had he not been blinded by his "red, white, and blue Neon" American Dream sign.[5]

For Faulkner, that epitome of the modern, the electric advertising sign (whether electric bulb or neon), symbolizes a selling of the soul to the commercial god—"And the people bowed and prayed/To the neon god they made," as Paul Simon would later intone. In the *Sound and the Fury* (1929), soulless Jason Compson pursues Quentin and her lover to a town called Mottson that has erected its own sign of "progress":

> He led Jason on around the corner of the station, to the empty platform where an express truck stood, where grass grew rigidly in a plot bordered with rigid flowers and a sign in electric lights: Keep your 🔲 on Mottson, the gap filled by a human eye with an electric pupil.[6]

Mottson has heeded the modern axiom that "a place is no better than its sign." The sign's intended booster message to the world would seem to be "watch Mottson modernize into the new age of electricity, steel, glass, automobiles and neon." But to the reader, the sign's message is ironic. The passage's context links the sign to cold-hearted Jason Compson, who personifies the evils of modern commercialism and whose pursuit of Quentin (the reason Jason has his eye on Mottson) symbolizes modern man's furious and meaningless pursuit of money and social appearances. The citizens of Mottson, Mississippi, would have been proud of their electric slogan sign, but the electric pupil in Faulkner's literary sign implies Jason's and modern man's blindness to the values Faulkner venerates, the "truths of the heart": love, honor, pity, pride, compassion, sacrifice, courage, hope.[7] Faulkner further undermines the sign's intended message by locating the sign in a place "where grass grew rigidly in a plot bordered with rigid flowers." This juxtaposition of an optimistic sign advertising progress against a "rigid" natural landscape also signals irony.

There is more and less than meets the eye in Mottson's electric-eye sign. Like a latter-day Roland Barthes, Faulkner exposes the mythologies or ideologies latent in cultural signs.[8] Mottson intends its electric sign to denote Mottson, Mississippi, and to connote Mottson's modernity since electric signs held such a cultural significance in 1929. That such modernity constitutes true progress is the myth Faulkner perceived electric signs elaborating. To Faulkner, progress, both in the physical form of an electric advertising sign and as symbolized by an electric sign, was no progress at all if it left only a dead ("rigid") world to be inherited by dead people like Jason Compson. Faulkner's literary electric signs have meaning; they signify the myth of progress-through-modernity. This signification emerges through the realization that society's electric signs advertise a lie. Full of sound and fury, they signify nothing.

Like the unseeing billboard eyes of Doctor T. J. Eckleburg in *The Great Gatsby*, Faulkner's Mottson sign is situated in a wasteland. In general, Faulkner's electric and neon signs evoke the wasteland metaphor of T. S. Eliot, which avows that life in the twentieth century is deracinated and spiritually sterile. This meaning is evident throughout Faulkner's Eliot-influenced *Pylon* (1935) in which the characters move back and forth between two symbolic landscapes. The Vieux Carré in New Valois (New Orleans) is an "unreal City" of decadent Mardi Gras partying that is illuminated by glaring neon signs. Feinman Airport, the other domain, is a Futuristic landscape that is also characterized by electric sign illumination.

Surely the writing of *Pylon* owes as much to the movement known as Futurism, in reaction against it, as it does to T. S. Eliot and James Joyce. In Paris, Faulkner had attended a Futurist exhibition, describing it as a "very very modernist exhibition" in a letter to his mother written twelve days before his "the trees are dying" letter.[9] Futurism celebrated "the complete renewal of human sensibility brought about by the great discoveries of science." Mechanization, urbanization, electricity, and speed were hailed by the Futurists in their numerous manifestos. Futurists waxed ecstatic over racing cars, airplanes, and electric signs. Indeed, Futurist leader F. T. Marinetti called for "great cities to blaze with electric signs," and in this same manifesto he gave specifications for an electric eye sign.[10] "The Founding Manifesto of Futurism 1909" affirmed the birth of "a new beauty: the beauty of speed." "We want no part of . . . the past," Marinetti insisted, "we the young and strong Futurists." *Pylon* is Faulkner's statement that he wanted no part of this Futurist future.[11]

Machines in *Pylon* portend a dangerous evolution of man into machine and machine into man. The reporter's mother is compared to a locomotive with an old engine that has been modernized to look like a new one:

> it is a new engine on the outside only, because everyone is glad and proud that inside it is still the old fast one of nineteen-two or-ten. The same number is on the tender and the old fine, sound, timeproved workingparts, only the cab and the boiler are painted robin'segg blue and the rods and the bell look more like gold than gold does and even

the supercharger dont look so very noticeable except in a hard light, and the number is in neon now: the first number in the world to be in neon?[12]

Here, as always, Faulkner locates neon at the cutting edge of change, but hints at two different kinds of change. On the one hand, neon is associated with the mechanization of life, a real change. Faulkner also associates neon with the illusion of change in that the neon numbers help to create only an image of newness by making this old engine look like a modern one. Progress is also an illusion since the old engine was better than the new one this engine has been packaged to suggest.

During the 1930s erecting a neon sign was in fact the easiest way for a business to create an image of itself as modern. The Futurists had proclaimed the new beauty of speed. This once avant-garde aesthetic became the prevailing fashion. In the late 1920s the Art Deco machine-made look was an attempt to capture the spirit of the machine age. Streamline Moderne design, lasting from the early 1930s until after World War II, drew its inspiration from cars, airplanes, and speedy movement in general. Glassy gleaming walls with rounded corners and flowing lines suggested motion. Along with the porcelain enamel and glass brick of Streamline Moderne went neon, for neon, to quote Rudi Stern, "echoed the 30's demand for the smooth, the swift, the streamlined and the spectacular," and "echoed a reverence for speed and technology."[13]

Streamline Moderne also echoed a new reverence for image over reality. Worried about their sales during the Depression, businessmen and manufacturers paid increasing attention to the appearance of their product or business. A new profession of industrial designers took up this challenge "to develop a visual idiom capable of telegraphing such positive thoughts as 'up-to-date,' 'technologically advanced,' 'the shape of things to come.'"[14] Designers sold Streamline Moderne as this new idiom and merchandized "modern" as desirable. Soon the word "streamlining" entered the language as a synonym for "making modern." Since neon was positively associated with the "modern," it enjoyed enormous popularity during the 1930s. In a decade when "Modernize Main Street" became a slogan, modernizing could mean as little as installing a neon sign. Neon did much to telegraph the message, quoting Chester H. Liebs, "I'm modern, the latest scientifically designed object—buy me."[15]

To Faulkner, however, who had a semiologist's ability to discern not merely what signs mean but also how they mean, neon telegraphed the message "I've been merchandized to look modern, the latest industrial designer object—buy me." Faulkner understood how in a sign the relationship between signifier (image) and signified (meaning) is an artificial one fabricated by people. Neon signs in Faulkner's works, then, imply not only the marketing of modernity but also the commercialization of life in a designer age that fashions signs to create whatever reality is supposed to be in fashion. Since the new ethic was "a place [or person, one might add] is no better than its sign," "the truths of the heart" become less important than the truths of rhetoric. Faulkner wouldn't buy this neon ethic.[16]

Nor would Faulkner pay homage to the new worship of speed as it was manifested in the fluid architecture and morality of modern life. Futurist architect Antono Sant' Elia characterized "the antithesis between the modern world and the old," writing: "we have lost our predilection for the monumental, the heavy, the static, and we have enriched our sensibility with a taste for the light, the practical, the ephemeral and the swift."[17] Neon signs are literally and metaphorically indicative of contemporary man's lost "predilection for the monumental" past and his new predilection for "the ephemeral and the swift." Neon is designed to capture the attention of people on the move, a light for people too restless to alight for very long, a sign of and for the fast life and the age of hype. In an interview, Faulkner described his rootless fliers in *Pylon* as "ephemeral as the butterfly," and in the novel Faulkner characterized modern man as a "moral and spiritual waif."[18] Great cities ablaze with neon help to convey this theme in both *Pylon* and *The Wild Palms* (1939). Writing in a decade when Futurist visions were becoming streamlined realities, Faulkner saw the world of tomorrow proliferating in neon and repeated over and over again in his novels, "Tomorrow and tomorrow and tomorrow."[19]

The protagonists of the "Wild Palms" are moral and spiritual waifs who uproot themselves from their past in the name of love and flee to Chicago. Harry Wilbourne and Charlotte Rittenmeyer are determined to find a place for love in the modern wasteland. In these Chicago scenes, Faulkner uses symbolism of neon to imply that his doomed lovers cannot "escape from the world" because they embody it.[20] Thus neon light in August on a hot, Chicago night spotlights Harry and Charlotte glowing in the dark along with all the other urban corpses:

> It was evening, the hot August, the neon flashed and glared, alternately corpse-and-hell-glowing the faces in the street and their own too as they walked.[21]
> The neon flashed and glared, the traffic lights blinked from green to red and back to green again above the squawking cabs and hearse-like limousines. (97)

This is wasteland imagery—the Dantesque Unreal City of Eliot—but Faulkner supplies the infernal light of neon, as if to say "I had not thought neon had undone so many." Neon is one of the many ways throughout the novel that Faulkner distances himself from the actions and attitudes of his convention-defying lovers.

At one point in the novel, Harry and Charlotte meet in a bar every night for dinner. Here Wilbourne waits for the stores to empty and the people to "erupt into the tender icy glare of neon" (123). Neon's glare is icy in its highlighting of a Chicago winter, but icy also in its evocation of urban coldness, impersonality, artificiality and what Lewis Mumford called "the fake exhilaration of the commercial city."[22] The oxymoronic "tender icy" is as near as Faulkner ever came to investing neon with anything but a purely negative meaning. The figure offers an indirect hint of Faulkner's mixed feelings towards his new age, neon lovers and also captures a quality of their passive/aggressive relationship. Charlotte especially can be cold and hard but also tender.

There is no such ambiguity in the novel's next neon image. Fearing their love is endangered by routine and bourgeois respectability, Harry and Charlotte decide to move to an isolated Utah mining camp. The drive to the train station takes them into the nocturnal streets: "They had McCord's car; they went out to it in a mild glitter of minor silver, the final neon and clash and clang of changing lights" (129). Like an earlier description of "days dying in neon" (119), "the final neon and clash and clang of changing lights" has an apocalyptic ring, as if when Faulkner thought of the end, he saw neon, or when he saw neon, he thought of the end. The synesthesia of lights that clash and clang ties two elements of modern discord into one image. Since the wild palms are also described as making a "clashing" sound, Faulkner links the neon of the Unreal City with the novel's controlling wasteland metaphor of "the wild dry clashing of the palms" (291).

There is no escaping the Unreal City, Faulkner suggests, for even America's "little lost towns" have modernized their main streets with neon. After Harry and the now pregnant Charlotte leave the Utah mining camp, they head South across an America fast becoming one vast neon glow. On the bus, Harry looks at Charlotte's "head tilted back against the machine-made doily, her face in profile against the dark fleeing snow-free countryside and the little lost towns, the neon, the lunch rooms with broad strong Western girls got up out of Hollywood magazines (Hollywood which is no longer in Hollywood but is stippled by a billion feet of burning colored gas across the face of the American earth) to resemble Joan Crawford, asleep or not he could not tell" (209). Charlotte's face profiles an America undone by illusion; neon symbolizes this undoing.

Faulkner conveys the idea of the Hollywooding of America through his neon image of an America "stippled by a billion feet of burning colored gas." Here Faulkner also strips away neon's shimmering, nighttime illusion. Neon is a seductive invitation to glamour, romance, and fantasy, but enter into its mirage and find only tubes of burning gas. Analogously, given the numerous antiheroic quirks, confusions, and hypocrisies that Faulkner dramatizes in his doomed lovers, Charlotte and Harry expose the reality beneath neon's Hollywood/Broadway illusion that love can be "all honeymoon, always" (83).

Neon's illusion didn't bother everyone as much as it did Faulkner. In a 1927 travel book called *New York Nights*, Stephen Graham observed that the "whiteness of The Great White Way is not reality, it is transfiguration": "But it is not real," adds Graham, with no great concern, "The philosopher spurns its actuality. . . . It is not real. What is it? It is theatrical. The theatres have disgorged their gazers and listeners, and these have crossed the footlights and have all become actors themselves." [23] Faulkner was one of those "philosophers" who spurned the actuality of neon's Broadway and Hollywood light. What Graham applauded Faulkner deplored, the potential of such light to transform the world into a stage and people (like Wilbourne and Rittenmeyer) into parts.

As in many American places, neon probably first came to Faulkner's own "little lost town" of Oxford, Mississippi, via the marquee of the local movie theater. Since 1915, when citizens of Oxford had wanted to go to the picture show, they strolled to the Lyric Theatre. Like Chick Mallison in *Intruder in the Dust*, Faulkner must have "crossed the Square to the courthouse yard and sat down on a bench in the dark cool empty solitude among the bitten shadows the restless unwindy vernal leaves against the starry smore of heaven where he could watch the lighted marquee in front of the picture show." [24]

Although the dazzle of the Lyric's marquee was modest compared to such wonders as the Roxy, the Rialto, Grauman's Chinese Theatre, or the many other movie "palaces" of the 1920s and '30s, the principle of "architectural escapism" was the same. "The show begins on the sidewalk," explained architect S. Charles Lee. [25]

During the 1930s an America darkened by Depression found cheering contrast in neon's colorfully theatrical lights.

Not everyone was cheered by swirling neon marquees that projected Hollywood illusion onto the sidewalks and into the hearts of the disillusioned. Faulkner warned of the dangers of escape into fantasy. With Chick Mallison, Faulkner watched as "the first of the crowd dribbled then flowed beneath the marquee blinking into the light and even fumbling a little for a second or even a minute or two yet, bringing back into the shabby earth a fading remnant of the heart's celluloid and derring dream" (34). In "Golden Land" (1935) Faulkner warned of the dangers of Hollywood itself and the myth of California as a golden land. In this Hollywood-as-Babylon story, a red electric cemetery sign advertises Faulkner's theme that California is a hell not a heaven.[26]

Neon may have represented the dangers of escapism to a William Faulkner, but there was no escaping neon in the 1930s, neon's most creative decade. Restaurants, hamburger chains, movie theaters, movie sets, drive-ins, service stations, diners, motels, auto showrooms, supermarkets, churches—all were adorned with neon. In Times Square, America's great theater of signs, the curtain rose on the many famous neon sign "spectaculars." Most Americans regarded neon as a distinct improvement on the "shabby earth," and throughout the 1930s neon was identified with glamour, taste, prosperity, and progress. Expositions such as the New York World's Fair of 1939 did much to make neon synonymous with what the New York Fair called the World of Tomorrow.[27] A measure of Faulkner's alienation from the mainstream of American society is his negative attitude toward neon in a decade when the connotations of neon signs were positive to most people. In the 1930s neon had not yet come to be widely associated with tawdry low life; the neon jungle, a powerful Naturalistic metaphor in the fiction of Nelson Algren, had not yet overgrown into the public consciousness of neon. Yet as early as 1931, in Sanctuary, Faulkner used the glittering electric lights of Memphis to help display his whorehouse vision of the world. In this novel Faulkner anticipates film noir of the 1940s when he describes rooms illuminated by street signs from outside the window, as if to say: No boundaries exist between street and room. No sanctuary.

Faulkner's 1941 story "The Tall Men" offers further evidence that while most Americans looked at neon and saw signs of a bright future, Faulkner saw only a dying past. The story's theme is the cheapening of life. The "truths of the heart" and the Faulknerian verities of family, home, region, tradition, work, freedom, individualism, and the right to privacy are no longer valued. The story pivots on the contrast Faulkner draws between North Mississippi hill country people like the McCallums and the old marshal, who embody these verities, and the rest of the country. Faulkner's central image and metaphor to distinguish "the rest of the world" is neon:

> these here curious folks living off here to themselves, with the rest of the world all full of pretty neon lights burning night and day both, and easy, quick money scattering itself around everywhere for any man with a shiny new automobile already wore out and throwed away and the new one delivered before the first one was even paid for, and everywhere a fine loud grabble and snatch of AAA and WPA and a dozen other three-letter reasons for a man not to work.[28]

Neon is artificial sun and moon to a modern world of around-the-clock commercialism and hedonism. When neon's lights find the little lost towns of America, big government and mass culture threaten to reduce the individual "to one more identityless integer in that identityless anonymous unprivacied mass which seems to be our goal," to quote from Faulkner's essay "On Privacy."[29]

An America "full of pretty neon lights" is an America that has dedicated itself to, in the words of F. Scott Fitzgerald, "a vast, vulgar, and meretricious beauty." Faulkner had a keen sense of neon's meretriciousness but no appreciation for the beauty of neon's meretriciousness, no feel for the poetry of its vulgarity. Theodore Dreiser saw a certain beauty in how the yellow light of New York's blazing fire signs (as preneon electric signs were then

called) "beautifully reflected in the wet sidewalks and gray cob-
blestones shiny with water," thereby positing what might be the
archetypal recurring image of an electric sign's romantic evo-
cativeness. Unlike Dreiser or Fitzgerald, Faulkner had little
feeling for how the "mystery and promise" of a city is beheld in its
lights, though in *Sanctuary* Faulkner did evoke the "threat [not
mystery] and promise" of Memphis through the "colored coiling
shapes of its lights" (203). No doubt because city life never held
much personal temptation for Faulkner, he lacked Dreiser's,
Fitzgerald's, or Jack Kerouac's desire to render the allure of city
lights and the magic, or in Fitzgerald's and Kerouac's case the
sweet sadness, of their illusion. Nor did Faulkner understand the
kind of exhilaration in philistine vulgarity that enabled Nabokov
in *Lolita* to lyricise the perverse beauty of the American roadside
vernacular in such lines as "our neon-blue cottage in the stunned,
starry night" (202). Aesthetically speaking, Faulkner identified
neon with bad taste, pure and simple, though bad taste, he
argued in "On Privacy," was an American problem of wide ranging implication.[30]

Neon in "Delta Autumn" (1942) adumbrates a more serious
theme, the destruction of nature by man in the name of progress.
The wilderness has retreated before the encroachment of civilization. Isaac McCaslin has been witness to this change, the woods
become farms and plantations, the deer and bear paths become
roads and highways, the new towns arisen along these highways,
and the neon, the inevitable, inexorable, execrable neon:

> Now a man drove two hundred miles from Jefferson before he found
> wilderness to hunt in. Now the land lay open from the cradling hills
> on the East to the rampart of levee on the West, standing horseman-
> tall with cotton for the world's looms . . . the land in which neon
> flashed past them from the little countless towns and countless
> shining this-year's automobiles sped past them on the broad plumb-
> ruled highways.[31]

Faulkner measures the rapidity of America's destruction of its
natural landscape by the change from "the little lost towns" of

neon in *Pylon* to "the little countless towns" of neon in "Delta Autumn." Because Faulkner's neon is both metaphorical and literal, neon at once effects this destruction and is its effect. Man's destruction of the wilderness is at once his crime and his punishment: "The woods and fields he ravages and the game he devastates will be the consequence and signature of his crime and guilt, and his punishment" (349). This signature, Faulkner implies, is signed in neon.[32]

Isaac McCaslin's meditation on change occurs in a speeding car on the way to the wilderness. Appropriately, a car window frames Isaac's perception of a neon wilderness, for the automobile itself was the vehicle of this change. Living in Los Angeles in the early 1930s, Faulkner must have driven down Wilshire Boulevard, prototype of the American strip, prophecy of the paving of America's woods and fields. Gazing out the car window, Faulkner would have seen a landscape of signs. Thoreau was perhaps the first to warn of the dangers of this kind of commercialized signscape. In "The Village" chapter of *Walden*, Thoreau describes his excursions from nature into Concord, where he must run a gauntlet of signs. Whereas nature's signs, its leaves and ponds and animals, speak to the spirit or intellect and direct us to essential reality (natural facts being signs of spiritual facts as Emerson said), society's signs pander to the appetite or the fancy and lead us astray.[33]

Unfortunately, because Isaac McCaslin mystically believes in a primal wilderness dimension beyond space and time from whence he came at birth and to hence he will go at death, Isaac has given up his land, which would have enabled him to "arrest at least that much of what people called progress" (354). When he dies, Isaac will move "again among the shades of tall unaxed trees . . . where the wild strong immortal game ran forever" (354). Although there is no neon to kill the trees in Isaac's happy hunting grounds, back in the material world the trees were really dying. Faulkner's own conservation methods for preserving the forests of the past were more down-to-earth than Isaac's. Neither Isaac

McCaslin nor William Faulkner wished to go with the Futurist flow, but Faulkner realized that the closest thing to "a dimension free of both time and space" (354) that he had some control over was a book.

If words preserve the past, words don't always preserve the present from becoming the past. ("I would think how words go straight up in a thin line, quick and harmless, and how terribly doing goes along the earth.")[34] Faulkner saw a terrible doing crawling along the earth toward the old regional South, an invasion like the one on August 22, 1864, by the invading army of the United States that burned Oxford to the ground, but this new threat carried red, white, and blue neon battle flags and marched to the beat of a cash register bell. In a letter to the *Oxford Eagle* on March 13, 1947, Faulkner sounded a call to arms to join another lost cause. Sarcastically, Faulkner suggested tearing down the courthouse and replacing it with a neon sign of surrender to the enemy forces of Americanization:

> Bravo your piece about the preservation of the court-house. I am afraid your cause is already lost though. We have gotten rid of the shade trees which once circled the courthouse yard and bordered the Square itself, along with the second floor galleries which once formed awnings for the sidewalk; all we have left now to distinguish an old southern town from any one of ten thousand towns built yesterday from Kansas to California are the Confederate monument, the courthouse and the jail. Let us tear them down too and put up something covered with neon and radio amplifiers.[35]

Faulkner's letter to the editor of the *Oxford Eagle* anticipates his concerns in *Requiem for a Nun* (1950), a novel of fear and loathing in Oxford. From Paris to New Orleans, Chicago and Hollywood, to Mottson, Mississippi, and the other little lost towns in the American hinterland, Faulkner had traced the progress of progress. In *Requiem for a Nun* Faulkner tells how progress finally came to Jefferson, Mississippi: "there was neon in the town and A.A.A. and C.C.C. in the county, and W.P.A. ('and XYZ and etc.,' as 'Uncle Pete' Gombault . . . put it)."[36] No place to run, no place to hide for William Faulkner when the noise and neon of modern life have even come to Oxford, Mississippi, threatening the silence and slow time of Jefferson, Yoknapatawpha itself.

In "The Courthouse," "The Golden Dome," and "The Jail" sections of *Requiem for a Nun*, Faulkner contrasts America's past and present (via microcosmic Jefferson's past and present) and criticizes "progress," using architecture to advance his themes. Faulkner narrates the history of Jefferson from "frontier, pioneer times, when personal liberty and freedom were almost a physical condition like fire or flood" (6) to "a new time, a new age" (241) of neon. When Sutpen's architect designed Jefferson's square, "the courthouse in its grove the center . . . school and church and tavern and bank and jail each in its ordered place" (39), he had warned: "In fifty years you will be trying to change it in the name of what you will call progress. But you will fail; but you will never be able to get away from it" (39). Sure enough, Jeffersonians have violated the old order by modernizing pioneer settler Alexander Holston's original log tavern: "Alexander Holston became the settlement's first publican, establishing the tavern still known as the Holston House, the original log walls and puncheon floors and hand-morticed joints of which are still buried somewhere beneath the modern pressed glass and brick veneer and neon tubes" (8). Obviously, by these architectural differences Faulkner means to imply that modern America has forsaken and forgotten the virtues and values of its pioneer past (though Faulkner seems not to have appreciated that most neon signs were actually hand crafted). Yet this log cabin past remains "buried" within the neon present, thus confirming the architect's prediction that Jefferson's citizens will fail in their attempts to sever themselves from their heritage, that they "will never be able to get away from it," thus affirming Gavin Stevens's and the novel's major statement that "the past is never dead. It's not even past" (92).

In this novel about the importance of remembering, about the need to connect the past to the present, neon is a sign that this connection is broken. Most Jeffersonians don't remember the founders of their community. Only the courthouse remains untouched as a visual and symbolic reminder of "continuity" amidst change:

> the courthouse centennial and serene above the town most of whose people now no longer even knew who Doctor Habersham and old Alec Holston and Louis Grenier were, had been; centennial and serene above the change: the electricity and gasoline, the neon and the crowded cacophonous air. (47)

Continuity creates a sense of community. Awareness of continuity between past and present also fosters love, honor, compassion, and the other "truths of the heart" since an incentive to morally responsible actions is the realization that "you . . . may have to pay for your past; that past is something like a promissory note . . . which . . . can foreclose on you without warning" (162). Thus "the change," fueled by electricity and gasoline, guided by neon signs of forgetting, strikes at the very heart of the human community. Continuity gives life meaning. Without continuity with the past there is only tomorrow. "Tomorrow and tomorrow and tomorrow."

Jefferson's old jail is another symbol of continuity and community. The jail houses the prisoners "who would sleep there every night beneath the thin ruby checker-barred wash and fade of the hotel [neon] sign" (251). Faulkner describes this sign as reflecting on the solid old walls of the jail until disappearing in the light of dawn, neon's liquid wash and fade that represents all things ephemeral and vain.

The old jail, still known to the "old irreconcilables" (252) of the town, is Faulkner's key architectural symbol of "the town's composite heritage of remembering" (255). Like Dilsey, it "endured" (247, 248). Faulkner's key metaphor for the kind of progress that threatens to obliterate the town's heritage of remembering is neon. In a novel notable for its metaphors of false progress, the following passage's metaphor of progress as the image from a neon sign is climactic:

So only the old citizens knew the jail any more . . . men and women old not in years but in the constancy of the town, or against that constancy, concordant . . . with that thin durable continuity born a hundred and twenty-five years ago . . . that steadfast and durable and unhurryable continuity against or across which the vain and glittering ephemerae of progress and alteration washed in substanceless repetitive evanescent scarless waves, like the wash and glare of the neon sign on what was still known as the Holston House diagonally opposite, which would fade with each dawn from the old brick walls of the jail and leave no trace. (250–51)

Climactic too is the above passage in the electric sign system of Faulkner's fiction, for here the blinking neon sign is not just a metonymy but a metaphor of modernity, perhaps the most interesting single image of modernity in Faulkner's works. Modernity, celebrated by the Futurists in the 1910s, inculcated in the years that followed, finally came to reactionary Oxford, Mississippi, and was hailed even there as the neon wave of the future. But not hailed by "old irreconcilables" like William Faulkner who reckoned the modern fast life was motion without meaning, money without morals, a Lethean flow, a forsaking of the past. To Faulkner, progress is an enticing illusion without substance; those changes in the name of progress are as ephemeral as the reflected image from a neon sign that fades in the natural light of day and in the clear seeing of an enlightened mind, leaving no trace on the walls of reality. If all cultural "signs" are manmade meanings rather than meanings inherent in the natural order, though they sometimes pose as natural, Faulkner reminds us that progress is a sign not a reality, an advertisement not a fact.

Ironically, when *Requiem for a Nun* was published in 1950 neon had already begun its post–World War II decline that saw it rapidly change from a sign of the modern to a sign of the old-fashioned. Plastic signs were the new look, sounding a requiem for neon. Faulkner was living in the past. Once a sign of the good life, neon came to connote the low life of bars and strip shows.[37]

Neon's decline continued through the 1960s. The public began to see progress the way Faulkner had viewed it for years. Futuristic World-of-Tomorrow utopias were difficult to believe in after the horror of World War II. People also began to take notice of the effects of progress on the environment. Ike McCaslin would have approved of such books as *God's Own Junkyard* (1964) or of Lady Bird Johnson's plea to clean up the American roadside's "endless corridors walled in by neon, junk, and ruined landscape." These antineon trends continued through the 1970s, when the energy crisis darkened still more of America's neon signs. Yet in the late 1980s neon is reappearing on chic storefronts as a sign of trendyness, and urban planners are envisioning a revitalized Times Square that will return it to the bygone days of its neon glory. Some now regard neon signs as having been a form of American folk art. The final irony is that neon has come full circle. Once a sign of the future, neon is now a sign of nostalgia.[38]

One must remember, however, that Faulkner's literary neon signs play off the popular connotations of electric signs as they were most widely perceived in the years before the Second World War. Thus in *The Mansion* (1959) Faulkner anachronistically uses neon signs to capture the historical metamorphosis from the sleepy days of rural hamlet to the modern era of the giant, "unsleeping" metropolis, "the dark earth" in these years having become "spangled with the neon he [Mink Snopes, who had been in prison for thirty-eight years] had never seen before."[39]

Cars and neon. "Road signs and filling stations." This recurring phrase in "The Jail" section of *Requiem for a Nun* represents the domain of the modern America that Faulkner feels is rushing away from its heritage (252, 255, 261). Emerging from out "the road signs and filling stations" a stranger visits Jefferson "to try to learn, comprehend, understand . . . not specifically Jefferson, but such as here, such as Jefferson" (252). Thanks to the "old irreconcilables" and a certain ghost from Jefferson's past, when the stranger leaves "to unfumble among the road signs and filling stations" (261), he has learned the lesson of continuity and remembering "that there is no time: no space: no distance" (261).

Related to this lesson is Faulkner's use of the wheel figure in

The Mansion and other works. The wheel is an ancient symbol
found in both Eastern and Western cultural traditions. As explained by J. E. Cirlot, the symbol alludes "to the mystery of the
rotational tendency of all cyclic processes. . . . the splitting up of
the world-order into two essentially different factors: rotary movement and immobility—or the perimeter of the wheel and its still
centre, an image of the Aristotelian 'unmoved mover' . . . the
contrast between the volatile (moving and therefore transitory)
and the fixed. . . . It illustrates the way of escape from the illusory
world (of rotation) and from illusions, and the way towards the
'centre.'"[40] Faulkner was fond of the wheel figure. In *Requiem for
a Nun* Jefferson's courthouse is "the hub: sitting looming in the
center of the county's circumference" (40), the still center, the
unmoved mover, around which rotate the transitory generations
that traffic the Square (literally a square but figuratively a circle).
Faulkner believes the modern generations have gotten so caught
up in the whirl of modernity that they follow the wrong signs.
Instead of looking for signs that show "the way towards the 'centre,'" the motorized generations let themselves be guided by
neon signs that are emblematic of "the illusory world (of rotation)
and . . . illusions."

   In *The Town* Jefferson is described as the fixed hub: "beyond it,
enclosing it, spreads the County, tied by the diverging roads to
that center as is the rim to the hub by its spokes." In this famous
twilight passage, an old Gavin Stevens climbs a hill and "looking
back and down," sees "all Yoknapatawpha in the dying last of day."
Stevens becomes "detached as God Himself for this moment
above . . . the record and chronicle of your native land proffered
for your perusal in ring by concentric ring." He presides "unang-
uished and immune above this miniature of man's passions and
hopes and disasters." Stevens here is like the sage "who has
attained the central point of the wheel," thereby throwing off "the
bonds of things transitory" and entering into "the state of repose"
(Cirlot 352). Of course, Stevens in this passage is also Faulkner in
the twilight of his own life looking back at his Yoknapatawpha

novels, the God of his own creation, the sage "invisible at the centre of the wheel, [who] moves it without himself participating in the movement" (Cirlot 352). In the dying light of day come intimations of mortality but also come such moments of illumination in which are sensed the changeless change and motionless movement of the natural cycle and of literary creation.

At the heart of this sort of wisdom is a comparison that is being drawn between man and nature. A day in the life of the earth is analogous to the morning, noon, and night of a human lifetime. Thus the wheel in the wheel figure was anciently represented as the sun. As the source of natural light, the sun naturally symbolized intellectual and spiritual illumination. Since Faulkner always views man in the light of nature, natural light in Faulkner's fiction has a positive meaning. Nature's light is enlightening. It reveals to man his relation to the abiding earth. Man's artificial light, on the other hand, especially his neon, is not a source of true understanding. It casts the world in a false light.

This contrast between the artificial and the natural is brought out if the wheel figure in *The Mansion*, which is a car wheel, is compared to yet another wheel figure in *The Hamlet*. *The Hamlet*'s figure is more like the solar wheel of antiquity with the sun (not the car) as the driving force, wheeling the earth through the unhurryable cycle of a day:

> the soaring trunks which are the sun-geared ratchet-spokes which wheel the axled earth, powerful and without haste, up out of the caverns of darkness, through dawn and morning and mid-morning, and on toward and at last into the slowing neap of noon.[42]

In *The Mansion*'s figure, the driving force of the wheel is the machine, wheeling the earth at too hurried a pace not through morning, noon, and night, but into an unsleeping city of artificial light.[43] This suggests the rhythms of modern life have become mechanical and unnatural. Dazzled by neon, the "vain and glittering ephemerae of progress," people lose sight of nature, the ultimate "steadfast and durable and unhurryable continuity" (*Requiem* 250), within they are rooted and wherein they are bound.

Faulkner's scorn for neon, then, has a lot to do with his love of natural light. Natural light, he feels, is not only beautiful but also meaningful in its revelation of the natural order, the oldest of orders that modern man has turned away from. In the Ike-and-the-cow section of *The Hamlet*, Faulkner celebrates natural light in lyrical passages that emphasize the harmony between light and the earth. Light illuminates the cycle of a day in the life of the earth, from sunrise to sunset to sunrise. To underscore this harmony, Faulkner describes the light of sunrise as arising from the earth rather than descending from the sky:

> Now he watches the recurrence of that which he discovered for the first time three days ago: that dawn, light, is not decanted onto earth from the sky, but instead is from the earth itself suspired. (181)

Magnificently, the light of dawn seeps upward through the roots and leaves of nature itself:

> it wakes, up-seeping . . . first, root; then frond by frond, from whose escaping tips like gas it rises and disseminates and stains the sleep-fast earth with drowsy insect-murmur; then, still upward-seeking, creeps the knitted bark of trunk and limb where, suddenly louder leaf by leaf and dispersive in diffusive sudden speed, melodious with the winged and jeweled throats, it upward bursts and fills night's globed negation with jonquil thunder. (181)

Such music in a dawn's early light is difficult to discern amid "the neon and the crowded cacophonous air" of modernity (*Requiem* 47).

The rapport of natural light and earth is again reinforced in Faulkner's description of sunset's light as returning to the earth, reversing the process of sunrise:

> Then ebb's afternoon, until at last the morning; noon, and afternoon flow back, drain the sky and creep leaf by voiceless leaf and twig and branch and trunk, descending, gathering frond by frond among the grass, still creeping downward in drowsy insect murmurs. (186)

Again in *The Town*, when Faulkner describes a sunset, light doesn't return to the sky but to the earth:

> Yet it is as though light were not being subtracted from the earth,
> drained from earth backward and upward into that cooling green, but
> rather had gathered, pooling for an unmoving moment yet, among
> the low places of the ground so that ground, earth itself is luminous
> and only the dense clumps of trees are dark, standing darkly and
> immobile out of it. (315)

Who can see or know this "unmoving moment" of earth's luminosity in the glare of the artificial neons? In the age of neon, who
can know "the mystery of the rotational tendency of all cyclic
processes" (Cirlot 351) or see the most fragile moment of a twilight's beauty as described in the following passage?

> Because look how, even though the last of west is no longer green and
> all of firmament is now one unlidded studded slow-wheeling arc [a
> wheel figure] and the last of earth-pooled visibility has drained away,
> there still remains one faint diffusion, since everywhere you look
> about the dark panorama you still see them, faint as whispers: the
> faint and shapeless lambence of blooming dogwood returning loaned
> light to light as the phantoms of candles would. (317)

Appropriately, these twilight passages in *The Town* occur in the
scene where Gavin Stevens and William Faulkner, feeling old,
look back on "all Yoknapatawpha in the dying last of day" (315).
There is a logic in this for just as Faulkner describes light returning to the earth at sunset, so too he describes man returning to the
earth at death: "In fact, the ground itself never let a man forget it
was there waiting, pulling gently and without no hurry at him
between every step, saying, Come on, lay down; I aint going to
hurt you. Jest lay down" (434). Thus Faulkner establishes not only
a sympathetic relation between natural light and earth but also a
harmony between natural light and human life, a mutual rhythm
of earth to earth. Nature's light illuminates nature's cycle to which
everything earthly is bound. To grasp this meaning is to see the
light. Out, out, brief neon candle.[44]

In Faulkner's eyes, natural light presides over the creation of
meaning and order: the order of natural life; the order of community; even the order of literature. The dawn's yellow light "fills

night's globed negation with jonquil thunder," creating a new day in the life of man and earth (*Hamlet* 181). So, too, when Faulkner narrates the birth of Jefferson, his paradigm of community, as it is first shaped from the wilderness, he describes this same nature-colored, jonquil-yellow light: For an awkward moment the settlers look "unfamiliar even to one another in the new jonquil-colored light" (*Requiem* 32). "In that first yellow light," Jefferson is born when one settler, speaking the thoughts of all, utters the words "By God. Jefferson" (32). Since in another sense, the God who created Jefferson is Faulkner, we can say that in this same natural light came the dawning of Faulkner's literary creation, his world of Yoknapatawpha in which Jefferson is the hub.

"Let there be light," then, is an old ordering principle that Faulkner appreciated.[45] Faulkner saw disorder in the counterfeit yellow light of mechanistic, urban, electric signs that proclaimed the myth of modernity. In 1913 Futurist leader Marinetti had written: "penetration of an electric sign into the house across the street yellow slaps for that gouty, dozy bibliophile."[46] One imagines William Faulkner as this bibliophile. Though certainly not gouty, Faulkner did feel the slap of the sign's artificial yellow light and instantly awakened to its implications. One also imagines this awakening came to Faulkner on a Paris night in August 1925 when he saw the Eiffel Tower transformed into a neon sign advertising automobiles and speculated that this was killing the trees. Faulkner rejected this Futuristic spectacle as unnatural. He refused to see the world in this new light, this neon light. Faulkner beat a strategic retreat back to Mississippi, a place where he could still behold the world in an old light and thereby sustain his vision. Especially in August in Mississippi, Faulkner once explained, "there's a few days somewhere about the middle of the month when . . . there's a lambence, a luminous quality to the light, as though it came not from just today but from back in the old classic times. . . . a luminosity older than our Christian civilization. . . . an older light than ours."[47]

NOTES

1. William Faulkner to Mrs. M. C. Faulkner, [30 August] 1925, in Joseph Blotner, ed., *Selected Letters of William Faulkner* (New York: Random House, Vintage Books, 1978), 16.

2. Chester H. Liebs, *Main Street to Miracle Mile: American Roadside Architecture* (Boston: Little, Brown and Company, 1985), 54; Charles L. H. Wagner, *The Story of Signs* (Boston: Arthur MacGibbon, 1954), 42.

3. William Faulkner, *Requiem for a Nun* (New York: Random House, 1950), 251. For discussion of the neonized Eiffel Tower, see William Wiser, *The Crazy Years: Paris in the Twenties* (New York: Atheneum, 1983), 143–44. Sally Henderson and Robert Landan, *Billboard Art* (San Francisco: Chronicle Books, n.d.), 27; Rudi Stern, *Let There Be Neon* (New York: Harry N. Abrams, 1979), 121. On the Joyce pun, see Clive Hart, *A Concordance to Finnegans Wake* (Minneapolis: University of Minnesota Press, 1963), 492; Roland McHugh, *Annotations to Finnegans Wake* (Baltimore: Johns Hopkins University Press, 1980), 20. For a discussion of how the Eiffel Tower is always being interpreted as symbolizing various meanings, see Roland Barthes, "The Eiffel Tower," in *The Eiffel Tower and Other Mythologies* (New York: Hill and Wang, 1979), 3–17. Barthes writes: "the Tower attracts meaning, the way a lightening rod attracts thunderbolts. . . . it [will] always be something other and something much more than the Eiffel Tower" (5).

4. William Faulkner, *Mosquitoes* (New York: Boni & Liveright, Washington Square Press, 1985), 247; hereafter cited parenthetically in the text.

5. James M. Cain, *The Postman Always Rings Twice* (New York: Knopf, Vintage Books, 1978), 7, 10.

6. Paul Simon, "The Sounds of Silence," *Simon and Garfunkel: Sounds of Silence* (Columbia, CL 2469, 1965); William Faulkner, *The Sound and the Fury* (New York: Random House, Vintage Books, 1954), 388. That the eye is a traditional symbol of deity reinforces the idea of Mottson's eye sign as a "neon god" of commercialism.

7. William Faulkner, "Address upon Receiving the Nobel Prize for Literature," in James B. Meriwether, ed., *Essays, Speeches, and Public Letters by William Faulkner* (London: Chatto and Windus, 1967), 120. Electric slogan signs to boost communities were popular in these years. See "An Electric Slogan Sign Will Boost Your City," *Signs of the Times*, March 1919, 26.

8. See Roland Barthes, "Myth Today," in *Mythologies* (New York: Hill and Wang, 1957), 109–59.

9. William Faulkner to Mrs. M. C. Faulkner, 18 August 1925, in Blotner, *Selected Letters*, 13.

10. F. T. Marinetti, "Destruction of Syntax-Imagination without Strings-Words-in-Freedom 1913," in Umbro Apollonio, ed., *Futurist Manifestos* (New York: The Viking Press, 1973), 96; the electric-eye sign description is in Marinetti, "The Variety Theatre 1913," in Apollonio, 131. In addition to electric-eye signs, another possible source for Faulkner's  on Mottson is the Pinkerton detective agency logo (Jason playing private eye):

11. F. T. Marinetti, "The Founding and Manifesto of Futurism 1909," in Apollonio, 21, 23. In this paper, I make much of Faulkner's quarrel with Futurism. Although Faulkner did attend a Futurist exhibition, I cannot prove that Faulkner ever read any of the many Futurist manifestos. Such proof is irrelevant, however, because the important point to note is that Faulkner's quarrel was with the implications of Futurism, which Faulkner would have been familiar with since Futurist philosophy prefigured many features of the modern age.

12. William Faulkner, *Pylon* (New York: Random House, 1935), 11.

13. Stern, 31, 125; see Liebs, 54–57.

14. Liebs, 56.

15. David Gebhard, *Tulsa Art Deco: An Architectural Era 1925–1942* (Tulsa, Oklahoma: The Junior League of Tulsa, Inc., 1980), 139; Hans Wirz and Richard Striner, *Washington Deco: Art Deco Design in the Nation's Capital* (Washington, D.C.: Smithsonian Institution Press, 1984), 71–72; Liebs, 57.

16. See Liebs, 56–57; Gebhard, *Tulsa Art Deco*, 139; Wirz, 71–72; Barthes, "Myth Today," 112–13. See Arthur Asa Berger, *Signs in Contemporary Culture: An Introduction to Semiotics* (New York: Longman, 1984), 9–13 for a discussion of the arbitrary relationship between the signifier and signified.

17. Antonio Sant' Elia, "Manifesto of Futurist Architecture 1914," in Apollonio, 170; also qtd. in Charles Jencks, *The Language of Post-Modern Architecture* (New York: Rizzoli, 1977).

18. Qtd. in Frederick L. Gwynn and Joseph L. Blotner, eds., *Faulkner in the University* (New York: Vintage, 1965), 36; Faulkner, *Pylon*, 118.

19. Important electric sign references in *Pylon* can be found on 15, 53, 80, 81, 83, 272, 280, 283–84. Examples of Faulkner's use of Shakespeare's phrase "Tomorrow and tomorrow and tomorrow" can be found in *The Wild Palms* (New York: Random House, Vintage Books, 1966), 18, 19; *Pylon*, 284 and chapter titles "Tomorrow" and "And Tomorrow"; *Requiem for a Nun*, 206, 210, 275, 283, 284; *Absalom, Absalom!* (New York: Random House, Vintage Books, 1972), 290.

20. Faulkner's comment is quoted in Gwynn, 178.

21. Faulkner, *The Wild Palms*, 96; hereafter cited parenthetically in the text.

22. Lewis Mumford, "The City," in Harold E. Stearns, ed., *Civilization in the United States: An Inquiry by Thirty Americans* (New York: Harcourt, Brace and Co., 1922), 11.

23. Stephen Graham, *New York Nights* (New York: George H. Doran, 1927), 17, 22.

24. William Faulkner, *Intruder in the Dust* (New York: Random House, 1948), 33; hereafter cited parenthetically in the text.

25. Ave Pildas, *Movie Palaces* (New York: Clarkson N. Potter, 1980), 19; qtd. in Michael Webb, *The Magic of Neon* (Salt Lake City: Gibbs M. Smith, 1983), 42.

26. See Faulkner, "Golden Land," in *Collected Stories of William Faulkner* (New York: Vintage, 1977), 711.

27. Stern, 27, 36, 106, 110, 121, 125; David Gebhard and Harriette Van Breton, *L.A. in the Thirties: 1931–1941* (N.p.: Peregrine Smith, 1975), 5–6, 44; Martin Grief, *Depression Modern: The Thirties Style in America* (New York: Universe Books, 1975), 83; Webb, vii, 34–36, 48, 50, 54; Wirz, 25; see also Liebs.

28. William Faulkner, "The Tall Men," in *Collected Stories of William Faulkner*, 57–58; see Faulkner, *Sanctuary* (New York: Random House, Vintage Books, 1987), 158, 160–61, 203 for descriptions of rooms illuminated by street signs or lights; hereafter cited parenthetically in the text.

29. William Faulkner, "On Privacy," in Meriwether, 71.

30. F. Scott Fitzgerald, *The Great Gatsby* (New York: Scribner's, 1925), 99; Theodore Dreiser, "The Color of Today," *Harper's Weekly*, 55 (14 December 1901), 1272–73; F. Scott Fitzgerald, "My Lost City," in Edmund Wilson, ed., *The Crack-Up* (New York: New Directions, 1956), 31; Vladimir Nabokov, *Lolita* (New York: Berkley, 1955), 202.

31. William Faulkner, "Delta Autumn," in *Go Down, Moses* (New York: Modern

Library, 1955), 340–41; hereafter cited parenthetically in the text.

32. Cleanth Brooks writes: "For Faulkner's Uncle Ike the wilderness has been violated, the dark rich land has been looted. In place of its power and mystery there is now simply the meaningless litter of civilization: neon signs and shining this-year's automobiles and broad plumb-ruled highways and buildings constructed of sheet iron (*William Faulkner: The Yoknapatawpha Country* [New Haven: Yale University Press, 1963], 31).

33. "Neon wilderness" is Nelson Algren's phrase; Algren, *The Neon Wilderness* (New York: Hill and Wang, 1960); Henry David Thoreau, *Walden* (Boston: Houghton Mifflin, Riverside, 1957), 116–17.

34. William Faulkner, *As I Lay Dying* (New York: Random House, 1930), 165.

35. William Faulkner to Editor, *Oxford Eagle*, 13 March 1947, in Meriwether, 202–3.

36. Faulkner, *Requiem for a Nun*, 242; hereafter cited parenthetically in the text. Edmond Volpe observes: "The town develops, suffers the ravages of the Civil War, becomes modernized and neonized" (*A Reader's Guide to William Faulkner* [New York: Farrar, Straus and Giroux, 1964], 269).

37. See Stern 28, 118; Jill Stone, *Times Square: A Pictoral History* (New York: Macmillan, 1982), 129–30; Webb, vii. In the 1950s Times Square began to decline, its neon sign "spectaculars" the victim of corporate reluctance to invest in an image whose connotations were changing, its neonized movie palaces the victim of television and of the middle-class exodus to the suburbs, its image of the Great White Way giving way to a new image of honky-tonk.

38. Peter Blake, *God's Own Junkyard: The Planned Deterioration of America's Landscape* (New York: Holt, Rinehart and Winston, 1964); Lady Bird Johnson's plea is qtd. in Liebs, 65. Although commercial neon had sharply declined in the 1960s, "pop art rescued it from the junkpile" (Webb, 60). Beginning in the sixties, artists began to use neon in sculpture and to call their creations art. (See Stern, 88–105 and Webb, 60–80 on neon art.) Chroniclers and champions of pop sensibility such as Tom Wolfe also began to hail the old neon craftsmen as genuine artists and to applaud their "Electrographic Architecture." See Wolfe, "Electrographic Architecture," *Architectural Design*, 39.2 (July 1969), 380–82. In this essay, Wolfe asserted that since Bauhaus-influenced "serious" artists viewed exterior ornament such as neon with suspicion, "it was left to commercial artists . . . to create something wild enough and baroque enough to express the new age of motion and mass wealth" (381). Architect Robert Venturi's *Learning from Las Vegas* (Cambridge, Mass.: The MIT Press, 1977) influenced a spate of books that continue to this day which treat American vernacular roadside architecture quite seriously.

39. William Faulkner, *The Mansion* (New York: Random House, Vintage Books, 1965), 285, 283.

40. J. E. Cirlot, *A Dictionary of Symbols* (New York: Philosophical Library, 1962), 351–52; hereafter cited parenthetically in the text.

41. William Faulkner, *The Town* (New York: Random House, Vintage Books, 1961), 316; hereafter cited parenthetically in the text.

42. William Faulkner, *The Hamlet* (New York: Random House, 1931), 183; hereafter cited parenthetically in the text.

43. The wheel-figure passage in *The Mansion* in which Mink "became aware of a convergence like the spokes of a gigantic dark wheel lying on its hub" is on 283.

44. For a passage linking light and nature's cycle see Faulkner, "The Bear," in *Go Down, Moses*, 328–29.

45. In *Absalom, Absalom!* Faulkner links creation and the biblical "Let there be light" when he writes: "creating the Sutpen's Hundred, the *Be Sutpen's Hundred* like the oldtime *Be Light.*" Faulkner, *Absalom, Absalom!* (New York: Random House, Vintage Books, 1972), 9. In *Mosquitoes* Faulkner links sunrise to the biblical "Let there be light": In the morning mist "might be heard yet the voices of the Far Gods on the first morning saying, It is well; let there be light" (133).

46. F. T. Marinetti, "The Variety Theatre," in Apollonio, 131.

47. Qtd. in Gwynn, 199. Faulkner does, in fact, associate his return to Mississippi with natural light. In his essay "Mississippi," Faulkner writes: "The next summer he returned . . . remembering: the pre-dawn, to be broken presently by the violent near-subtropical yellow-and-crimson day almost like an audible explosion" ("Mississippi," in Meriwether, 29). It is perhaps relevant to note that currently in Oxford, Mississippi, there are no signs, neon or otherwise, directing tourists to Faulkner's home, Rowan Oak. The curator of Rowan Oak, Howard Bahr, is quoted as saying: "People are accustomed to being lured. . . . They cannot accept a historical site that does not proclaim itself with signs and advertising" (qtd. in Robin Street, "Bahr of Rowan Oak," Oxford Times [22 July 1986], 2B).

The High Sheriff of Yoknapatawpha County: A Study in the Genius of Place

Louis D. Rubin, Jr.

Critics of literature have never been especially comfortable with the term "genius"—and for good reason. Too often it is used as a substitute for the kind of rigorous reading of works of fiction and poetry that can enable us to recognize and understand the dynamics of those works. There is the tendency, when a literary artist is described as having "genius," to stop right there and simply marvel at what has been written, as if all bets were thereby cancelled and any effort at intelligent examination of what is actually going on in a story or poem would be irrelevant.

Yet what other term can better describe the literary phenomenon that was William Faulkner?

From his early years onward, William Faulkner was convinced that his was not merely talent but genius. He happened to be quite right, but many years were to pass before anybody else, except perhaps his friend Phil Stone, was ready to concede that he was what he purported to be. Thus in order to enforce upon his family and fellow townsfolk the notion that he was unique and special—and perhaps to reassure himself as well—he adopted a variety of disguises and poses, some of which later became a source of embarrassment to him. As is well known, the citizenry of Oxford took to calling him "Count No-Count" because of what they considered his uppity ways and his affectation of being superior to the ordinary customs and pursuits of his community, with so little in the way of worldly achievement to justify it. When fiction began appearing under his name in the *Saturday Evening Post*, which was the nation's most prestigious mass-circulation magazine, those Oxfordians who did much reading at last saw evidence that something might be said for William Faulkner's lofty estimate of himself after all. But my guess is that it was not until the movie of *Intruder in the Dust* actually began to be filmed in Oxford by MGM, and Hollywood actors, cameramen, and technicians showed up on the Square, that it finally became evident to the rank and file of his fellow citizenry that, as they would probably have put it, Bill Faulkner had a right to think he was something special.

My dictionary—the Merriam-Webster *New International*, Second Edition, 1952—offers several definitions for "genius." The word is derived from the Latin, "tutular deity or genius of a person or place, taste, talent, genius," from *"genere, gignare*, to beget, bring forth." In Roman religious usage, a genius was the "attendant godling or spirit of a person or place; tutular deity. Primarily, the genius is the protecting companion, almost the fortune, of the man with whom it is born and dies." Another definition of the word is "extraordinary mental superiority; esp. unusual power of invention or origination of any kind; as, a man of *genius.*" This latter usage is illustrated with a quotation from James Russell Lowell: "Talent is that power which is in a man's power; *genius* is that in whose power a man is." The description of this particular way of defining the word concludes, "Also, a man endowed with transcendent ability; as, Milton was a rare *genius.*"

It is obvious, from such description, that there is an association of the word with the supernatural, which by definition would make it beyond human explanation and understanding. Lowell's distinction between genius and talent, with the suggestion that a man's genius controls him, whereas a man's talent is under his control, verges on this notion, for a power that can dictate the behavior of someone beyond his capacity to do anything whatever about it must surely come from outside—though whether from above or below is another matter. Another way to put it might be to say that a man possesses talent, but is possessed by genius, in the same way that we used to believe that people could be possessed by demons, spirits, and the like.

Presumably this notion is related to the Greek myth of the nine Muses, originally nymphs or mountain goddesses fathered by Zeus, and later domesticated on Mount Helicon, where they presided over the fine arts. The Christian writer Boethius denounced them as lascivious and immoral creatures who took possession of men's souls and diverted them from the exercise of reason. Moreover, the idea that a genius is "endowed with transcendent ability" suggests a quality of an extrahuman kind, or as Immanuel Kant would have it, something that is *a priori*, beyond the limits of human experience, so therefore beyond knowledge. In theology, God is prior to and above the universe, existing apart from what is mortal and material.

Nowadays we are not so ready to view such problems theologically. We tend to regard someone not as possessed, but as driven—by unconscious compulsions that are seemingly irrational. The kind of power that Lowell described as possessing a man is seen as the result of psychological forces, and behavior that is uncontrollable is believed to be the product of mental illness—insanity, psychosis, madness. Such compulsion is no longer thought of as lunacy—that is, affected by the baleful influence of the moon—but as caused either by one's own psychological endowment or else by external, environmental factors: family, community, occupation, politics, and so on. And from Plato onward, there is a formidable tradition of viewing literary creativity as a species of insanity, whether temporary or permanent. "The lunatic, the lover, and the poet," Shakespeare deposed, thereby grouping three examples of persons whose behavior defied rational explanation.

In Faulkner's later years, when his literary performance had fallen off somewhat—though second-rate Faulkner was still better fiction than most writers' best—he must have looked back to the period from 1929 through the late 1930s, when he was writing most of his finest work, with a feeling almost of awe. Indeed he said as much to a young friend, Joan Williams, in 1953: "And now I realize for the first time what an amazing gift I had: uneducated in every formal sense, without even very literate, let alone literary, companions, yet to have made the thing I made. I dont know where it came from. I dont know why God or gods or whoever it was, selected me to be the vessel. Believe me, this is not humility, false modesty: it is simply amazement. I wonder if you have ever had that thought about the work and the country man whom you know as Bill Faulkner—what little connection there seems to be between them."[1]

I find the terms Faulkner used fascinating: "why God or gods or whoever it was, selected me to be the vessel." He makes an almost total separation between his everyday self and the person who wrote the books. It is as if he subscribed to the "tutulary deity" notions of the Romans, and believed that the literary creativity that had brought the novels into existence had been the work of a kind of separate being that had taken possession of him and had guided his imagination. This is what the Greeks meant in their notion of a "muse"—an inspiring goddess of art. There is also the image of being selected to bear the sacred message as if it were wine in a goblet, as when in Acts 9:15 God informs Ananias that the hitherto-hostile Saul of Tarsus is His chosen vessel for promulgating His doctrines.

It was at about this time, too, in 1953, that Faulkner wrote the piece about his friendship with Sherwood Anderson back in the mid-1920s, with its striking conclusion. Meeting Anderson in New York after several years' estrangement, he said, "again was that moment when he appeared taller, bigger than anything he ever wrote. Then I remembered *Winesburg, Ohio* and *The Triumph of the Egg* and some of the pieces in *Horses and Men*, and I knew that I had seen, was looking at, a giant in an earth populated to a great—too great—extent by pygmies, even if he did make but the two or perhaps three gestures commensurate with giant-hood."[2]

The implication is that even though Anderson produced comparatively little work that was of major stature, what distinguished him from the rank and file of journeymen writers was the presence within Anderson of the same kind of "amazing gift" that he himself possessed, and that made both of them, because of the nature of their imaginations, giants among ordinary mortals in their ability to create works of art out of language.

Faulkner also declared that as an artist Anderson had neither the "power and rush" of Melville, nor the "lusty humor for living" of Mark Twain. Nor did he exhibit "that heavy-handed disregard for nuances" of Theodore Dreiser. What Anderson had was "that fumbling for exactitude, the exact word and phrase within the limited scope of a vocabulary controlled and even repressed by what was in him almost a fetish of simplicity, to milk them both dry, to seek always to penetrate to thought's uttermost end."[3] Disregarding for now the suggestions there for what Faulkner thought about the nature of his own particular artistic gift, we might note that what is implied is that Anderson's genius compelled him to strive for a clarity and simplicity of utterance beyond that of popular discourse. Anderson came to his art, Faulkner said, with a "humility and an almost religious, almost abject faith and patience and willingness to surrender, relinquish himself to and into it."[4] Here again is the notion that true genius takes possession of its bearer, causing him to give his life over to his art with a dedication, a consecration even, beyond that of normal human experience. Just as Faulkner spoke of himself as having been "selected" to be the "vessel" whereby his stories were created, so Sherwood Anderson is one "whom the vocation of art elected and chose to be faithful to it."[5] It is something like the youthful narrator of James Joyce's story "Araby," who sees himself as bearing his chalice safely through a swarm of foes,[6] even though at that juncture he is not yet the "priest of eternal imagination" that he will later proclaim himself in *A Portrait of the Artist as a Young Man* after rejecting the Jesuit ministry for the vocation of artist.[7]

2

When Faulkner, writing to Joan Williams, distinguished between "the country man whom you know as Bill Faulkner" and the author who had created his novels, he implied that he did not understand the source of the "amazing gift" that made the fiction possible. He stressed the fact that the milieu in which he had grown up had not been "literary," and that his formal schooling had not been of a kind that is customarily undergone by literary people. Yet he was careful to make such reference only to his *formal* education—for he grew up in a Southern university town and his acquaintance included persons of considerable learning, notably Phil Stone, who came back home from Yale to practice law in Oxford, Mississippi, loaded with books of poetry and filled with enthusiasm for what was being written and talked about in contemporary literary circles. His friendship with Stone, which the latter described accurately as a tutelage, as well as with the author and dramatic critic Stark Young were scarcely the customary intellectual fare for a small Southern community.

Such involvement with contemporary literature and ideas certainly had the effect of helping to confirm the young Faulkner's distance from the everyday concerns of his family and community. But before writing off Faulkner's artistic inclinations as alien to the everyday life of early modern Mississippi, it is well to keep in mind that the literary history of the twentieth-century South is made up to an inordinate degree of writers who likewise grew to maturity in Faulkner's own native state before, during, and after his time—including not only Stark Young but William Alexander Percy, Maxwell Bodenheim, James Street, Eudora Welty, Hubert Creekmore, Tennessee Williams, Richard Wright, Elizabeth Spencer, Shelby Foote, Walker Percy, Ellen Douglas, and so on into our own day. Moreover, Faulkner was not without an example of the literary life to emulate in his own family—his great-grandfather William C. Falkner, who between railroad building, politicking, war, and several blood-feuds wrote and published books of fiction and nonfiction, including at least one novel, *The White Rose of Memphis*, that was widely popular in its day.

It will be recalled that the classical origins of the word "genius" involved a close association with a particular locale; the tutulary deity might inhabit either a person or a place. The literary imagination of William Faulkner was deeply anchored in what he liked to call his little postage-stamp's-worth of Mississippi soil. His fellow Mississippian Eudora Welty has written eloquently about the essential role of place in fiction—one of the lesser deities, she calls it, that preside over literary creativity. And surely, observing that distinguished array of Mississippi authors, anyone would have to conclude that the locale must have been involved in the literary situation that evoked the writings of Faulkner, Welty, and the others.

The similarity between the Southern circumstance in the early decades of this century and that of Ireland toward the close of the previous century has been remarked by Cleanth Brooks, who in comparing Faulkner and William Butler Yeats notes the importance, in the social and political background of both writers, of a provincial society, a strong folk element, a powerful religious presence, a rural and small town environment with a certain level of violence and a stress upon manners, a heritage of defeat in war, economic stagnation, a colonial economy, a pantheon of heroes and a palpable mythology, and in both writers and their cultures the confrontation of all these elements with the oncoming modern urban, industrial juggernaut of nineteenth- and twentieth-century Western society.[8]

In an often-cited comment from an introduction prepared for a hoped-for reissue of *The Sound and the Fury* in 1933 but not published during his lifetime, Faulkner had some pronouncements to make about the artist in the South. Unlike the situation in New York or Chicago, he declared, there was no place for art in Southern life. In the sense of being any kind of live, imaginative entity, the South, he said, died with the Civil War; what has been happening in the region since then is the work of outsiders trying to remake it in the image of the Midwest. The would-be Southern writer must choose between being an artist and being a man— between, that is, either living through and in his art, or else functioning as part of the community; and if he chooses art, which has no existence in Southern life, he must give it existence within himself: "It is his breath, blood, flesh, all."[9] Thus the Southern writer is writing about himself, "not about his environment: who has, figuratively speaking, taken the artist in him with one hand his milieu in the other and thrust the one into the other like a clawing and spitting cat into a croker sack. And he writes" (412).

Faulkner sees the Southern writer as electing either of two alternatives. One is to write "a savage indictment of the contemporary scene"—I assume he had in mind Thomas Wolfe, T. S. Stribling, or Erskine Caldwell, all three of whom were widely read just then. The other is to withdraw "into a makebelieve region of swords and magnolias and mockingbirds which perhaps never existed anywhere" (412)—along the lines, perhaps, of Stark Young (who wrote a very popular novel entitled *Swords and Roses*) or any of a number of lesser chroniclers of plantation glories before the War.

Both courses of action, Faulkner declared, were sentimental, and were manifestations "of violent partizanship, in which the writer unconsciously writes into every line and phrase his violent despairs and rages and frustrations or his violent prophesies of still more violent hopes." Neither alternative is the product of detachment and calm objectivity: "I do not believe there lives the Southern writer who can say without lying that writing is any fun to him. Perhaps we do not want it to be" (412).

As Faulkner saw it, then, the Southern writer may use his art in order to attack his community, or else as a means of escaping from it. Both responses appear to involve the element of compulsion;

the fiction is written in response to the felt presence of the community. To write is to enter into a kind of dialectical relationship, in which the writer's status as a member of the Southern community forces him into violent struggle with his status as artist. In his Nobel Prize address Faulkner used almost the same image to describe what writers do; he referred to "the problems of the human heart in conflict with itself which alone can make good writing because only that is worth writing about, worth the agony and the sweat."[10]

So the force of the "tutelary deity" that possessed Faulkner and made him its chosen vessel for creating fiction would appear to have taken the form of a quality inherent in his community situation, and that propelled him into conflict with that aspect of his own identity involving his role as a citizen of his community. "I dont hate it!," as Quentin Compson furiously insists to himself at the close of *Absalom, Absalom!*[11] And the Faulkner who wrote an essay on the State of Mississippi for *Holiday* magazine some years after composing that novel spoke of himself as "loving all of it while he had to hate some of it because he knows now that you dont love because: you love despite; not for the virtues, but despite the faults."[12] To be a Southern writer, therefore, is to be caught up in a love-hate relationship with the Southern community of which the writer is a citizen, and be driven to create works of literary art in response to the ways of that community.

Most people who inhabit a community, of course, do not write novels about it. And just as obviously, most of those who *do* write novels can scarcely be described as being possessed by anything having to do with genius, whether tutelary or otherwise. The genius would seem to manifest itself in the *quality* of the response. At first glance Faulkner might seem to be suggesting, in his comments on the Southern writer's relationship to the Southern community, that it is the intensity of the quarrel that accounts for the success of the art, or lack of it. If so, that formulation can hardly stand up to much examination, for surely the degree of violence characterizing any such love-hate relationship that an individual might have with the community cannot of itself ensure artistic achievement, even if the individual happens to be a writer. Clearly it is not the intensity of the conflict itself, but the intensity with which the conflict is recreated through being given shape in language, that accounts for the literary achievement. The ability to make the "sound and fury" signify something, one might say, the degree to which the writer can give form and meaning "in every line and phrase" to "his violent despairs and rages and frustrations or his violent prophesies of still more violent hopes," is what matters from an artistic standpoint. It is there, we may say, that the "genius" comes in: in the ability to make sense of the intense literary response to the time and place, as these interact with and against the personality of the writer.

But let us make it clear what is involved, or rather what is *not* involved, when we talk about a novelist making "sense" of his experience. It used to be that we looked principally to philosophers and clergymen for such things as "sense" and "meaning"; nowadays we look to physical scientists and occasionally to social scientists. To the extent that one can predict the mutations of the stock market, analyze and enunciate the causes of physical or mental distress, diagnose and repair an automobile engine, prescribe the proper course of action to be followed during a football game or a military campaign, or fathom and make use of the needs of the electorate, one is said to possess knowledge, and to be wise, within one's own area of expertise at least. Plato's ideal was the philosopher-king, who governed because he was wisest as well as kingliest. We equate "sense" and "meaning" with abstract truth; the wise person is one who can discern and enunciate the universal principles, whether of matter or of the mind, that lie behind the surface particulars and individual instances.

Now what room is there for a novelist or a poet in that concept of what wisdom is? As noted earlier, there is a long tradition, extending at least as far back as Plato, of the poet being thought mad, and his art as the product of inspired raving. (There were no novelists around at the time, but I believe that Plato would gladly have included them in his indictment if he had only known about them.) Of course we have all heard the equivalent of Emily Dickinson's "much madness is divinest sense." Is this how we should consider an author like Faulkner as being involved in the wisdom business? Do we assume that the truths of "the human heart in conflict with itself" came to him through a kind of godlike frenzy?

On the relatively few occasions when Faulkner indulged himself in any kind of commentary on current events, he did not demonstrate extraordinary insight or startling sagacity. His public statements are not exceptional either in their content or their phraseology. They are for the most part sensible, appropriate, but not in their own right unusual or compelling. Nor was he what is called a "philosophical novelist," which is to say, a novelist such as Proust or Conrad or Walker Percy, the documentation of whose fictional world, as Robert Penn Warren (no slouch with an idea himself) wrote of Conrad, strives constantly to rise to the status of commentary on that world, and "for whom images always fall into a dialectical configuration, for whom the urgency of experience, no matter how vividly and strongly experience may enchant, is the urgency to know the meaning of experience."[13]

The ideas implicit in Faulkner's fiction can be gotten at through a process of induction, but there is almost never the sense that the fiction has been shaped importantly to assert or even to illustrate the ideas. Moreover, if we do isolate and identify such ideas, they will tend to seem fairly elemental and even obvious, in the line of truisms about human nature. In his Nobel Prize acceptance speech Faulkner spoke of the need for the novelist to allow "no room in his workshop for anything but the old verities and truths of the heart, the old universal truths lacking which any story is ephemeral and doomed—love and honor and pity and pride and compassion and sacrifice."[14] That is not exactly a call for the novelist to become involved in the intricacies and subtleties of philosophical inquiry.

Faulkner considered himself to be, first and last, a storyteller, a maker of tales. He did not even like to think of himself as an intellectual, and was notably uncomfortable in the company of other writers. His comment about the French as being too prone to allow ideas to take precedence over life itself is indicative of his attitude toward excessive intellectual formulation. To an extent this stance represented a kind of defensive posture, of course; *he* wasn't an intellectual, but a countryman, a farmer—just a plain old Mississippi boy who happened to write *The Sound and the Fury.* The reasons for this stance have been discussed elsewhere, and have to do with precisely that Southern community identity that he said he found so antithetical to the role of artist, so that being a Southern writer figuratively involved the equivalent of thrusting a snarling cat into a croker sack. Suffice it to say that it was important to the way that Faulkner thought about himself that he not appear to be cut off from the everyday customs and attitudes of the people of Oxford, Mississippi.

He was a writer of fiction who thought about his craft in terms of plots, dialogue, scenes. He published numerous stories in that quintessentially middle-class popular magazine of his day, the *Saturday Evening Post.* He enjoyed reading detective stories, and wrote some of his own in order to make money. For some years he supported himself and his family by working on movie scripts in Hollywood; the noted director Howard Hawks said that he was especially good as a troubleshooter who could take a key scene that wasn't working and make it work.[15] He was apparently a much better screenwriter than someone like Scott Fitzgerald—in large part, one assumes, because he approached the writing of film scripts solely as a skilled craftsman plying a trade. Where Fitzgerald was obsessed with achieving success and artistic renown in Hollywood, Faulkner was putting in time in order to earn enough money to go home to Mississippi and write fiction. That he made some use of certain cinematic devices in writing his novels, particularly for purposes of comedy, is quite obvious; but it is also obvious that he placed very little stock in the cinema as an art form. There is no indication whatever that when writing for the movies Faulkner was ever caught in the kind of struggle between the demands of the Southern milieu and those of art that he described as the habitual condition of the Southern writer. If any "agony and sweat" were involved, any "violent despairs and rages and frustrations," there is no record of it. Such conflict took place within him only during the writing of his prose fiction.

3

In his never-used introduction to *The Sound and the Fury*, he said an odd thing. Having declared, as we have seen, that the Southern writer's response to his milieu is either a savage indictment or an escape into a make-believe romantic region, he went on to comment that he himself had tried both approaches, and that when he read *The Sound and the Fury* again, five years after he had written it in 1919, he began to see that in writing that novel "I seem to have tried both of the courses. I have tried to escape and I have tried to indict." Writing that novel "was the turning point: in this book I did both at one time" (412).

We cannot be sure exactly what he meant by this, and he offered no real explanation. We can readily identify the presence within the book of an indictment of the contemporary scene: the decline of the once-proud Compson family; the ineffectuality of the alcoholic father and the vanity and selfishness of the neurasthenic mother; the debased evil of Jason, the "first sane Compson since before Culloden" as Faulkner ironically described him in the 1940s;[16] and above all else, the weakness of Quentin. There is no place in twentieth-century Yoknapatawpha County for anyone of Quentin's sensibility; and the qualities that might in an earlier and less decadent day have been allied with a determined fortitude and the ability to act effectively and decisively upon his beliefs and ideals, have in Quentin's time become hypersensitivity, an overdelicate fastidiousness, and despair. In the helpless vulnerability of the idiot-victim Benjy, the degradation of the Compsons is exemplified.

Where, however, is the other kind of response to the contemporary scene, the escape from it into a romantic South that never was? He goes on in the unpublished preface to say that in creating Candace Compson he was, without realizing it, "trying to manufacture the sister which I did not have and the daughter which I was to lose" (414). In the love that Caddy gave to her brothers and the integrity with which she confronted her family situation, presumably she represented what was lacking in the author's life.

Yet if that is what Faulkner meant by the statement that in writing *The Sound and the Fury* he had "tried to escape" from what actually was, it is a curious business, because in the novel itself Caddy can hardly be said to have provided Quentin with very much sisterly solace. The story centers on the *loss* of Caddy and what she meant for Quentin and Benjy, in what Faulkner went on to refer to as "the dark, harsh flowing of time sweeping her to where she could not return to comfort [Quentin]," and that must "sweep her into dishonor and shame too" (413).

Did Faulkner mean, therefore, that in getting into the writing of *The Sound and the Fury* both the indictment of the contemporary Southern scene and the escape from it, he had enabled himself to move *beyond* the need to do either, so that in that novel and henceforth he would no longer be dominated by the compulsion to respond to his milieu in the way that he said the Southern writer always had to do? And that writing *The Sound and the Fury* constituted the "turning point" in his career because from that time onward he could at last write his fiction in terms of making it artistically satisfying, shaping and developing it as a master craftsman does, rather than merely using it as a means of expressing his personal despair, anger, and frustration or his wish to escape?

If that *is* what he had in mind, as seems likely, then it might be well to ask this question: what does *The Sound and the Fury* offer that none of the first three novels—not even that *Flags in the Dust* in which he discovered his fictional country of Yoknapatawpha County—provides? What was it about *The Sound and the Fury* that makes it the first novel in which William Faulkner's tutelary genius of place or whatever manifests itself so strikingly?

Faulkner spoke of the writing of his fourth completed novel as a time of delight. Composing the Benjy section, he declared, provided "that ecstasy, that eager and joyous faith and anticipation of surprise which the yet unmarred sheets beneath my hand held inviolate and unfailing" (414). Clearly the remark directly contradicts the statement, made several pages earlier in the same never-published introduction, that "I do not believe there lives the Southern writer who can say without lying that writing is any fun to him." He began writing *The Sound and the Fury*, he says, after he had gone several years without finding a publisher for *Flags in the Dust*, and after his published novels had failed to earn him much in the way of royalties: "one day it suddenly seemed to me as if a door had clapped silently and forever to [*sic*] between me and all publishers' addresses and booklists and I said to myself, Now I can write. Now I can just write" (412–13).

Whether this was literally true or not—like more than one person of great literary talent, Faulkner did not always confine his imaginative writing to his novels and stories—there is undoubtedly an appropriateness to the statement, in that with this novel the author's way of writing fiction underwent a decisive change. *Flags in the Dust* had been turned down by the publisher of his first two novels, and eleven other houses were to reject it before it was finally accepted by Harcourt, Brace and Company. Whatever was going on in Faulkner's mind at the time—and apparently it was a period of considerable emotional upheaval—he seems to have decided to write his new book without any heed to the practical concerns of the literary marketplace. For whatever reason, he said goodbye for the time being to the conventional ways of telling a story and let his imagination run free.

In choosing to tell his story through the eyes of an idiot, Faulkner did something new for him: he took for his storytelling method the flow of consciousness itself. He had read *Ulysses*, of

course, and admired it greatly, and it seems likely that without
Joyce's novel there might never have been *The Sound and the
Fury.* Yet neither the Benjy nor the Quentin section that followed
it is stream-of-consciousness as Joyce wrote it: Faulkner was not so
much interested in portraying the *act* of consciousness, as in *using*
its representation as a way to tell a story. What Joyce helped him to
see was that it was possible to tell a story from inside the character's mind, not just from the outside and above, summarizing the
activity of that mind. And for what Faulkner wanted to do, this
was a crucial discovery. For it enabled him to portray the impact of
experience, and especially of the past upon the present, in the
way that such experience is encountered: *as it impinges upon the
process of consciousness.* What he did was to divest himself of the
customary authorial strategy of interpreting cause and effect for
the reader, so that he could describe the mind in the act of
receiving the experience that caused the effect.

Why did he want to show that? Because, I believe, what
fascinated him most about human personality was its liability and
vulnerability to received experience, whether in the form of
childhood trauma, historical tradition, family membership, community involvement, or whatever. For Faulkner the individual
does not stand alone and independent, and choose whether to be
involved in life: he (or she) is a complex being whose identity is
made up of a concatenation of forces, and any freedom of action
that the individual achieves in time is in the line of the recognition
of necessity. In *The Sound and the Fury* Quentin Compson envi-
sions the individual as a "gull on an invisible wire attached
through space dragged."[17] He remembers his father giving him a
watch "not that you may remember time, but that you might
forget it now and then for a moment and not spend all your breath
trying to conquer it" (95). His protagonists are all compulsive,
driven persons. Thomas Sutpen in *Absalom, Absalom!* spends his
life ruthlessly seeking the status that as a child he identified as
necessary to his self-esteem. In *As I Lay Dying* the iron will of a
dead woman, herself driven in life by a force that impelled her to

assert her identity, acts beyond the grave to compel her husband and children, each with a different set of motivations, to continue to function as a family until they have taken her to Jefferson to be buried.

Those characters who seek to escape into a place of shelter from the forces that drive them are relentlessly drawn back into the current—as for example Gail Hightower in *Light in August*, Ike McCaslin in "Delta Autumn," Bayard Sartoris in "An Odor of Verbena." Having once acted, they set in motion counterforces that are not to be evaded. In *Light in August* Joe Christmas thinks, "I have never broken out of the ring of what I have already done and cannot ever undo."[18]

In Faulkner's fiction, Time is the shape that necessity takes. The writing of fiction itself is a necessity, not a choice. "[I] wrote a book and discovered that my doom, fate, was to keep on writing books," he declared in his introduction to *The Faulkner Reader*, in 1954. Whether they would be read was unimportant, "[b]ecause one was too busy writing the books during the time while the demon which still drove him still considered him worthy of, deserving of, the anguish of being driven."[19] Only someone like Benjy Compson seems exempt from necessity, and Benjy is an idiot.

So when with *The Sound and the Fury* he moved into the consciousness of his characters, he could display that consciousness as it is impacted upon by the elements that comprise necessity. The result of the discovery was that for the first time he could create characters open to the full flow of language. It was no longer necessary to confine his depiction to the language that the character might speak or even think in, or else stay completely outside the character. He would not have to observe the realistic convention of limiting what his people thought to what was appropriate in vocabulary or syntax to their education or cultural condition, for by showing what their thought meant, rather than how they might phrase it, he could as narrator *translate* that thought into whatever degree of complexity was demanded.

For the first time, therefore, he was able to write about the kind of ordinary, unlettered people who lived in the milieu he knew—in Yoknapatawpha County—and endow them with the complex sensibilities of human beings whose consciousness was restricted by their particular situation. As narrator he could move from telling what they were thinking to characterizing what they were feeling.

Thus he could end the Benjy section of *The Sound and the Fury* this way: "And then I could see the windows, where the trees were buzzing. Then the dark began to go in smooth, bright shapes, like it always does, even when Caddy says that I have been asleep" (94). Surely Benjy knows no such language, and commands no such vocabulary; but by thinking and feeling *for* Benjy, rather than describing Benjy from outside as trying to think, Faulkner can choose the appropriate word to symbolize what Benjy *feels*—the trees are "buzzing," the dark assumes "smooth, bright shapes," and so on.

This is not to say, of course, that Faulkner could not also make full use of the convention of representing vernacular characters with vernacular language when appropriate. The Jason section of *The Sound and the Fury* is a triumph of just that; the youngest Compson brother's vindictiveness and meanness of spirit are convincingly captured in a spoken monologue that is addressed to nobody in particular and the world in general, as if Jason were engaged in a constant self-justification. It is the technique of a writer such as Ring Lardner, brought off with an eye for nuance and an implied but compelling quality of self-incrimination that far surpasses Lardner's bitter sarcasm. The Jason section is a stunning *tour de force*, a virtuoso performance by a maturing artist engaged in using and flaunting the capabilities of an extraordinary talent.

If in the novel immediately preceding this one, *Flags in the Dust*, or *Sartoris* as the truncated version published in 1929 was entitled, there were sections that seem self-consciously "literary" and overly poetic, in *The Sound and the Fury* there are no such awkwardnesses. For in discovering the narrative technique that put him in full command of his prose, Faulkner no longer needed to make an artificial separation between his sensibility as author and that of his characters; he moved *into* his characters' minds, and identified his discourse so convincingly with his characterizations that what he said about them was entirely credible.

In the same way, abandoning the customary conventions of the narrated novel in order to create the sense of reproducing their consciousness had the effect of virtually eliminating from Faulkner's fiction any elements of local color quaintness and folksy caricature that had been present in *Flags in the Dust*. In getting inside the consciousness of his characters he was enabled to view and present them without condescension; the range of his own sympathies was thereby extended and expanded. The distance between the assorted local color blacks in *Flags in the Dust* and the characterization of Dilsey in *The Sound and the Fury* is stunning to contemplate.

The discovery of how to write the new novel was a momentous breakthrough for Faulkner. And it was equally significant for Southern literature as a whole, for what Faulkner's great style offered was a way for the Southern author to apprehend and explore his personal and community experience without either condescension or sentimental idealization. Not many of his contemporaries chose to adopt the rhetorical particularities of the Faulknerian high style, which is a good thing. But what they could and did profit from was the way in which the High Sheriff of Yoknapatawpha County showed them how to move among characters representing all degrees of social and cultural sophistication, economic condition, and other distinctions of rank, class and caste, without ever having to "write down." Faulkner did not have to compose rustic pastorale in order to depict dirt farmers, whether white or black; the annals of the poor are neither short nor simple to him. Neither did he have to adopt the two-dimensional facades of the plantation novel in order to write about the Southern squirearchy. For he had discovered how to get past the facades and surfaces and into the minds and hearts of his people, and the string of great novels that began with *The Sound and the Fury* and did not close out until *Go Down, Moses* fifteen years later demonstrated the richness and the availability of what was there in the Southern community.

He did it through technique, through style. Needing to find a way into his material that would enable him to write what he knew, he discovered the method and the language that could take him there. In a very real sense *his style made him wise.* For like every great literary artist, he learned what he thought and felt by writing it down. He did not come to the creation of fiction with an already-developed set of insights and characters and situations, and proceed to write these down. Rather, it was *in writing about them that he learned about them.*

4

Earlier I noted that on the few occasions when he made public statements, wrote essays, articles, or letters, or otherwise commented on public events, Faulkner did not come across as being notably sagacious or impressive. I also asked, rhetorically, whether the artistry of Faulkner should be described as the product of a kind of "divine raving," the putative madness of the poet that, whether through the intervention of his "tutelary genius" or his muse, as the ancients would put it, or the neurotic compulsions of a driven and frustrated psyche as we might describe the process today, was made to speak "divinest sense." How, in short, did the "chosen vessel" get chosen, and the genius manifest itself?

I hope it is obvious that the literary breakthrough that I have described, which enabled the author of several interesting but not terribly impressive novels to become the author of *The Sound and the Fury,* was no blundering happenstance, but an act of the highest intelligence, an artistic achievement embodying, in its depiction of the nature of human experience, a genuine wisdom.

Faulkner's brand of wisdom was not that of the philosopher or journalist or man of science; it was not abstract, logical, paraphrasable, or even in any direct way usable. Because he was a literary artist William Faulkner's intelligence manifested itself through and as the technique of storytelling, and his wisdom in the form of works of fiction entitled *The Sound and the Fury, As I Lay Dying, Light in August, Absalom, Absalom!,* and so on.

It is not that these novels "mean" this or that about life, or that they "teach" us this moral or that, or even that they allegorize or demonstrate the "truths" of religion, or history, or psychology, or what have you. They may very well do all those things and more, yet they are not "about" knowledge; rather, they *are* knowledge. The difficulty is that we have been so trained to think of knowledge as being something abstract or usable, or more often both, that we fail to remember that a work of art can be equally something that we "know," and that the knowledge it has to tell us is concrete and particular, not abstract and general.

When Faulkner referred in his Nobel Prize speech to the "old verities and truths of the heart—love and honor and pity and pride and compassion and sacrifice," he wasn't discoursing on the moral lessons afforded us by great works of literature. What he was doing was saying what great literature *was*—not what it signified, or counselled, or meant, but *was*. The good novel helps us to recognize our own experience by giving form and shape and order—beginning, middle, end: causality—to an imagined experience created in language. When we read Faulkner's first major work of fiction, what we know is *The Sound and the Fury.* And clearly only a very formidably intelligent and wise person could be capable of providing us with *that* knowledge.

So to return to the matter of William Faulkner's "genius," we might recall that one of the several dictionary definitions of genius that were cited was "extraordinary mental superiority; esp. unusual power of invention or origination of any kind; as, a man of *genius.*" The sole owner and proprietor of Yoknapatawpha County was clearly such a person. One can account for what he wrote only through recognizing that he must have been, *had* to be a person of tremendous intelligence, and that the intelligence took the form of writing stories for us to read.

Unlike the abstractable and extractable, "usable" knowledge of science or philosophy or the like, each of Faulkner's works of knowledge unites thought *and* emotion, and expresses these in the form of characters and scenes and actions. In so doing it is unique. This is what "genius" means, for a writer. Science, theology, history, philosophy can tell us *about* emotion, can analyze its causes and its effects. But the work of art can *be* emotion for us to know. The paradox of the work of literature is that the more truly particular and unique it is, the more universal and general is its knowledge, the more profound its wisdom. It is not only about us, it is *for* us.

Yoknapatawpha County is Everyman's home country. The High Sheriff intended it that way.

NOTES

1. Letter to Joan Williams, prob. 29 April 1953, quoted in Joseph Blotner, *Faulkner: A Biography*, 2 vols. (New York: Random House, 1974), 2:1457.

2. William Faulkner, "A Note on Sherwood Anderson," *Essays, Speeches, and Public Letters*, ed. James B. Meriwether (New York: Random House, 1965), 10.

3. Ibid., 5.

4. Ibid., 7.

5. Ibid., 9.

6. James Joyce, "Araby," *Dubliners* (New York: Modern Library, n.d.), 6.

7. James Joyce, *A Portrait of the Artist as a Young Man: Text, Criticism, and Notes*, ed. Chester G. Anderson (New York: The Viking Press, 1968), 221.

8. See Cleanth Brooks, "Faulkner and W. B. Yeats," *William Faulkner: Toward Yoknapatawpha and Beyond* (New Haven: Yale University Press, 1978), 329–44.

9. William Faulkner, "An Introduction to *The Sound and the Fury*," [ed. James B. Meriwether], *Mississippi Quarterly*, 26 (Summer 1973), 411. Further quotations from this work will be cited parenthetically.

10. "Address on Receiving the Nobel Prize for Literature," in *Essays, Speeches, and Public Letters*, 119.

11. William Faulkner, *Absalom, Absalom!* (New York: Random House, 1936), 378.

12. William Faulkner, "Mississippi," *Essays, Speeches, and Public Letters*, 42–43.

13. Robert Penn Warren, " 'The Great Mirage': Conrad and *Nostromo*," *Selected Essays* (New York: Random House, 1958), 58.

14. "Address on Receiving the Nobel Prize for Literature," 120.

15. Blotner, *Faulkner: A Biography*, 2:1125.

16. William Faulkner, "Appendix: Compson," *The Sound and the Fury & As I Lay Dying* (New York: Modern Library, *n.d.*), 16.

17. *The Sound and the Fury & As I Lay Dying*, 123. Further quotations from this work will be cited parenthetically.

18. William Faulkner, *Light in August* (New York: Modern Library, 1950), 296.

19. William Faulkner, "Foreword," *The Faulkner Reader* (New York: Random House, 1954), x.

Contributors

Joseph Blotner, professor of English at the University of Michigan, has lectured extensively in the United States and Europe on American literature and particularly on the work of William Faulkner. Among his many publications are *Faulkner in the University*, edited with Frederick L. Gwynn; *William Faulkner's Library: A Catalogue; Faulkner: A Biography*, published in two volumes in 1974 and in a revised, one-volume edition in 1984; *Selected Letters of William Faulkner*; and *Uncollected Stories of William Faulkner*. Professor Blotner serves on the editorial board of *The Faulkner Journal* and has edited Faulkner works for Random House, Garland Publishers, and the Library of America.

William Brevda has taught in Illinois and Mississippi and is currently an assistant professor of English at Central Michigan University. Among his publications are *Harry Kemp: The Last Bohemian*, a critical biography, and articles in *The Markham Review, Bulletin of Bibliography*, and *North Dakata Quarterly*. He is currently working on a book-length study entitled "The Neon Rainbow: Electric Signs in American Literature."

Louis J. Budd is James B. Duke Professor of English at Duke University and the editor of *American Literature*. He is the author of *Our Mark Twain: The Making of a Public Personality*, editor of three collections of critical essays on Mark Twain, and coeditor of *Toward a New American Literary History; Essays in Honor of Arlin Turner*.

Tom Dardis is professor of English at John Jay College of the City University of New York. From 1952 to 1972 he worked as an editor, first for Avon Books and then as editor-in-chief for Berkley Books. He is the author of *Some Time in the Sun: The Hollywood Years of Fitzgerald, Faulkner, West, Huxley, and Agee* and *The*

Thirsty Muse. His articles have appeared in *American Film, Journal of Popular Film and Television, Resources for American Literary Study, Western World, Chicago Sun-Times,* and the *Los Angeles Times.*

Susan V. Donaldson has published articles and presented papers on several literary and visual artists from the South and is working on a book-length study entitled "Reluctant Visionaries: Audience and Artistic Vocation in Modern Southern Literature and Painting." Among her publications are two articles on William Faulkner, "Subverting History: Women, Narrative, and Patriarchy in *Absalom, Absalom!*" and "Isaac McCaslin and the Possibilities of Vision." She teaches at the College of William and Mary.

Leslie Fiedler is Samual Clemens Professor of English at the State University of New York at Buffalo. Among his more than thirty books are *An End to Innocence: Essays on Culture and Politics, Love and Death in the American Novel, No! in Thunder: Essays on Myth and Literature, The Inadverent Epic,* and *What Was Literature: Class, Culture, and Society.* His works of fiction include *The Second Stone: A Love Story* and *Nude Croquet and Other Stories.* A past vice president of the Popular Culture Association, Professor Fiedler has also been an associate editor of several journals, including *Quarterly Review of Film Studies* and *Studies in Black Literature.*

Leon Forrest is chair and professor of African-American Studies at Northwestern University, where he also holds a joint appointment in the English Department. Before joining the faculty at Northwestern in 1973, he edited Chicago community weeklies. He is the author of three novels, *There Is a Tree More Ancient Than Eden, The Bloodworth Orphans,* and *Two Wings to Veil My Face,* and has published fiction and essays in *Iowa Review, Carlton Miscellany, Callaloo, Chant of Saints,* and other journals and collections. He also wrote the libretto for the opera *Soldier Boy, Soldier.*

George Garrett is writer-in-residence at the University of Virginia. Author of seven volumes of poetry, seven books of stories, six novels, and two plays, he has also worked on screenplays for Hollywood films and written literary criticism, including an important early study of Faulkner's poetry. Professor Garrett has served on the editorial staffs of *Transatlantic Review, Hollins Critic, Contempora,* and *The Film Journal* and is the editor of fifteen collections of stories, poems, essays, and film scripts.

M. Thomas Inge is Blackwell Professor of the Humanities at Randolph-Macon College. Author or editor of more than two dozen books on American literature, he has written extensively on Faulkner and on popular culture. His studies of Faulkner include *Essays on "Light in August,"* a casebook on "A Rose for Emily," and a lengthy entry for the American Humorists volume in the *Dictionary of Literary Biography.* Professor Inge edited the three-volume *Handbook of American Popular Culture* and is general editor of the new series on popular culture published by the University Press of Mississippi.

Anne Goodwyn Jones is associate professor of English at the University of Florida. She won the Jules F. Landry Award for *Tomorrow Is Another Day: The Woman Writer in the South, 1859-1936,* a book that combines biography, social history, feminist criticism, and textual analysis. Coeditor of *The Marjorie Kinnan Rawlings Journal,* she is currently working on "Faulkner's Daughters," a study of women writers of the Southern Renaissance.

Bruce Kawin is professor of English and film at the University of Colorado, Boulder. A poet as well as a specialist in film history and contemporary British and American fiction, he is the author of *Telling It Again and Again: Repetition in Literature and Film, Faulkner and Film,* and *The Mind of the Novel: Reflexive Fiction and the Ineffable.* He has also written a film textbook and edited *To Have and Have Not* and *Faulkner's MGM Screenplays.*

David Madden is writer-in-residence at Louisiana State University. His many publications include the novels *Cassandra Singing, Bijou, The Suicide's Wife, Pleasure-Dome,* and *On the*

Big Wind; The Poetic Image in Six Genres, a collection of essays on writing; *The New Orleans of Possibilities*, a collection of stories; and scores of critical essays and reviews.

Louis D. Rubin, Jr., is University Distinguished Professor of English at the University of North Carolina and founder and president of Algonquin Books of Chapel Hill. Among his many publications are *The Faraway Country: Writers of the Modern South*, *The Curious Death of the Novel: Essays in American Literature*, *The Writer in the South: Studies in a Literary Community*, *William Elliott Shoots a Bear: Essays in the Southern Literary Imagination*, and *A Gallery of Southerners*. He is also the author of two novels, *The Golden Weather* and *Surfaces of a Diamond*, and has edited numerous works, including *The American South: Portrait of a Culture*, *A Bibliographical Guide to the Study of Southern Literature*, and *The History of Southern Literature*.

Judith L. Sensibar is associate professor of English at Arizona State University. Her publications on Faulkner include essays in *Mississippi Quarterly, William Faulkner: Modern Critical Views*, and *Psychoanalytic Studies of Biography;* an introduction to *Vision in Spring*, which she edited; *The Origins of Faulkner's Art;* and *Faulkner's Poetry: A Bibliographical Guide to Texts and Criticism*. Professor Sensibar is an AAUW fellow and the recipient of two ACLS grants, the most recent (1988–89) for research on her critical biography of Faulkner. -

Index